MANAGING NEGOTIATIONS

Managing Negotiations is a collection of seven global, real-life case studies on prominent negotiations in the realm of international business and politics.

The book combines the rigorously researched frameworks of academia with the real-world challenges of negotiations. The cases combine scientific negotiation management practices as well as theories with real-world examples that demonstrate how to conduct successful negotiations and which prominent pitfalls to avoid. The topics discussed reach from mergers & acquisitions, collective bargaining, international diplomatic treaties to international free trade agreements. Each case study starts with an overview comprising three key objectives and ends with the key learnings as well as reflective questions for class discussion.

This casebook can be used as recommended reading on Negotiation and Strategic Management courses at postgraduate, MBA and Executive Education level and serves as a guide for practitioners responsible for contract management, negotiation and procurement.

Thorsten Reiter is a lecturer at the University of St. Gallen and a Corporate Strategist specialized in Strategic Innovation located in Zurich, Switzerland. In his work, Reiter focuses on how a robust innovation capability can successfully be established as the most important part of an organization's strategy.

MANAGING NEGOTIATIONS

A Casebook

Thorsten Reiter

LONDON AND NEW YORK

Cover image: © Getty Images

First published 2022
by Routledge
4 Park Square, Milton Park, Abingdon, Oxon OX14 4RN

and by Routledge
605 Third Avenue, New York, NY 10158

Routledge is an imprint of the Taylor & Francis Group, an informa business

© 2022 selection and editorial matter, Thorsten Reiter; individual chapters, the contributors

The right of Thorsten Reiter to be identified as the author of the editorial material, and of the authors for their individual chapters, has been asserted in accordance with sections 77 and 78 of the Copyright, Designs and Patents Act 1988

All rights reserved. No part of this book may be reprinted or reproduced or utilised in any form or by any electronic, mechanical, or other means, now known or hereafter invented, including photocopying and recording, or in any information storage or retrieval system, without permission in writing from the publishers.

Trademark notice: Product or corporate names may be trademarks or registered trademarks, and are used only for identification and explanation without intent to infringe.

British Library Cataloguing-in-Publication Data
A catalogue record for this book is available from the British Library

Library of Congress Cataloguing-in-Publication Data
Names: Reiter, Thorsten, author.
Title: Managing negotiations : a casebook / Thorsten Reiter.
Description: Milton Park, Abingdon, Oxon ; New York : Routledge, 2022. | Includes bibliographical references and index.
Identifiers: LCCN 2021036907 (print) | LCCN 2021036908 (ebook) | ISBN 9780367615345 (hardback) | ISBN 9780367615352 (paperback) | ISBN 9781003105428 (ebook)
Subjects: LCSH: Negotiation in business--Case studies. | Negotiation--Political aspects--Case studies. | Consolidation and merger of corporations--Case studies.
Classification: LCC HD58.6.T55 2022 (print) | LCC HD58.6 (ebook) | DDC 658.4/052--dc23
LC record available at https://lccn.loc.gov/2021036907
LC ebook record available at https://lccn.loc.gov/2021036908

ISBN: 978-0-367-61534-5 (hbk)
ISBN: 978-0-367-61535-2 (pbk)
ISBN: 978-1-003-10542-8 (ebk)

DOI: 10.4324/9781003105428

Typeset in Bembo
by MPS Limited, Dehradun

CONTENTS

1 Introduction to the casebook   1
   Thorsten Reiter

2 The acquisition of Whole Foods Inc. by Amazon   3
   *Charles-Armand Roger Sollberger Solari, Piotr Wojtaszewski,
   and Sandra Frei*

3 Negotiation of the Iran nuclear deal   27
   Irena Marina, Julien Petat, and Adrian Budac

4 The Air France strikes   50
   Niklas Harder and Adriano Käppeli

5 Walt Disney's acquisition of 21st Century Fox   70
   *Valentin Steinhauser, Georgia Sofia Botsis, and
   Robin-Resham Singh*

6 The Lufthansa strikes   92
   Max-Philip Dirk, Leon Guckelberger, and Patrick Eschler

7 Bayer vs. Monsanto   121
   Luca Franziscus, Julia Reis Coury, and Luca Loris Gerini

8 The Trans-Pacific Partnership agreement   145
   Amanda Wegener and Michele Floridia

| 9 | Closing remarks on the casebook
Thorsten Reiter | 160 |

Index 161

1
INTRODUCTION TO THE CASEBOOK

Negotiations are an integral part of every professional's daily tasks and not seldom essential to their overall success both in their careers as well as their work's objectives. This applies to managers, politician lawyers, economists as well as almost any profession that involves the interaction with other people. It is therefore worrisome to find that a structural education in negotiation management cannot be seen widely spread in the syllabi of Universities and higher education programs around the world – even more so, when we look at the European academic landscape. If at all negotiation management is seen as a subset of marketing and sales or provided in complimentary classes by external coaches, who try to generalize from their individual experience as an FBI negotiator or car salesman. However, if Universities want their students to leave with a full tool kit on what it takes to have a successful career, they must adopt a more structured or – even better – managed approach to negotiations.

A negotiation management approach has multiple benefits – especially when compared to the briefly mentioned generalizations from individual experiences as it is a grounded empirical research and therefore applicable to many different contexts and negotiations across professional fields. One can only try to guess what a management professional is supposed to take away from the stories of a successful hostage negotiation. Furthermore, when understanding how negotiations are structured, students of negotiation management can acquire a sharper conceptualization and also of global negotiations, which they encounter in the daily news outlets, which in turn enables them to come to more accurate conclusions on the parties involved, their motives and the strategies they employ. Most importantly, however, negotiation management improves the negotiation skills of anyone, independently from any predisposition toward specific "favorable" behavior. Most nonmanagement-related approaches to negotiations tend to focus on "how to behave to be a successful negotiator." Amongst those traits are often "assertiveness" or general mantras

DOI: 10.4324/9781003105428-1

such as "never to give in." Empirical research, however, shows, that again these prescriptions cannot be generalized to any negotiator or any given negotiation. Therefore, by understanding the higher concept behind negotiations, understanding who is involved and how to structure negotiations, any negotiator can use this knowledge to improve her negotiation outcome or still better improve the outcome for all parties involved in the negotiation.

This touches upon another important aspect of negotiation management, which takes into account that most negotiations are not one-shot negotiations, where the winner takes it all and never has to interact with the opposing party again. Relationship building is an important part in any professional's life and cannot be put aside, when negotiating with her stakeholders. Therefore negotiation management puts a high emphasis on "integrativity" or "win-win" outcomes, also by understanding the opposing party's position and finding ways of how both parties can leave the people better off than when they sat down. This is a skill specifically trained by a management approach to negotiations and which generally cannot be found in generic prescriptions.

Besides literature on negotiation management itself, we can also see a lack of real-world cases, which apply those highly useful constructs to real-world and well-known negotiations. This is important to show students of negotiation management that these constructs are in fact widely applicable and train them in their ability to recognize them as well as support them to familiarize themselves with this conceptual thinking when facing real-world negotiations.

These objectives are precisely what "Managing Negotiations – A Case Book" wants to achieve. By seeing the constructs of negotiation management literature applied on world famous negotiations from the past 10 years, students learn how to structure negotiations along important phases, actors, motives and strategies, in order to become better negotiators themselves. The best way to apply this case book in a class or course is to hand out local newspaper articles on the discussed negotiations beforehand. This way students can see the negotiation – or parts thereof – as they would usually perceive them: fragmented, unstructured and without a clearly identifiable construct beneath. After having discussed what they believe to be the different parties involved, their objectives and discussions about the potential benefit or detriment to the relationships of the parties involved, they will have the opportunity to view the negotiation again through a negotiation management lens. This way, they familiarize themselves with the most important concepts needed to improve their own negotiation skills by witnessing them on real-world examples. Most of the cases also specifically discuss the element of "integrativity" mentioned before. Since it is such an important element in an increasingly complex and interdependent world, it will be beneficial to their own advancement in this global environment.

2
THE ACQUISITION OF WHOLE FOODS INC. BY AMAZON

Charles-Armand Roger Sollberger Solari, Piotr Wojtaszewski, and Sandra Frei

> *The key objectives of this case study for the student is to get a clear picture of the negotiation in the form of negotiation controlling. After reading this case, students should be able to give insights into the following aspects of the negotiation:*
>
> 1. *Identification of the items on the negotiation agenda*
> 2. *Analysis of the negotiation tactics used*
> 3. *Evaluation of the integrative potential realized in the negotiation*
> 4. *Evaluation of the negotiation outcome for the parties involved*

Introduction

A negotiation is the process of agreeing on one or more objects of exchange between parties with at least partially different preferences, in the course of which the parties try to influence the generally possible solution in their favor (Voeth & Herbst, 2015, p. 5). We are always dealing with negotiations in our daily lives – for example, when planning a trip with someone. These negotiations arise spontaneously most of the time, and we face them without any kind of preparation or action plan because the result is not of big importance to us. But what about the big negotiations where the outcome significantly impacts those involved? Can they be handled in the same easy way? The answer is no.

An example of a negotiation with significant impact is the recent Amazon Whole Foods merger in which Amazon paid an amount of $13.7 billion for Whole Foods. Given the nature and monetary size of the agreement, we can say without any doubt that these negotiations were of vital importance to both companies and therefore the two parties will do everything possible to obtain the best result with respect to their interests. This means that they will plan, organize and lead the negotiations very carefully.

The careful planning, organization and lead of negotiations are considered as negotiation management. It is crucial for every party involved in the negotiation. To emphasize negotiation management's importance, this chapter analyzes the Amazon Whole Foods merger from a negotiation management perspective. In order to do this, background information will be provided in a first step that will allow a better understanding of the case. In a second step, key negotiation events in which negotiation management played an important role will be analyzed. In the end, a brief summary with the most important results will be given.

Grocery industry

According to Nielsen TDLinx and Progressive Grocer, the U.S. supermarket industry generated approximately $649 billion in sales by 2015, which was an increase of 2% over the previous year (Whole Foods Market, Inc., 2016, p. 2). This represents about 5.6% of the total disposable income of Americans (Basker, 2016, p. 368). With 77,978 operating establishments, this industry also provides 2.4 million employments all over the country (Barnes Reports, 2017, p. 7).

In the recent decades, this mega-industry has become increasingly consolidated. In 1997, the four largest supermarket chains held 21% of the market. Today, they have a market share of 44%. In just 22 years, they doubled their market share to almost 50%. Only Walmart, the biggest player, controls 25% of the market (Kelloway & Miller, 2019, p. 9). Although the structure–conduct–behavior paradigm of the standard industrial organization theory would indicate that this market concentration would lead to less competition and a high profit, it has been empirically demonstrated that this is not the case for the grocery industry (Corstjens & Vanderheyden, 2010, pp. 1, 20). Therefore, the companies holding big market shares are constantly in competition and have to differentiate themselves in order to make a profit.

Another trend in the industry that is increasingly worrying different supermarket chains is the increasing saturation in the grocery industry. "Saturation" in retailing means that a maximum number of profitable stores in a consumer market might exist, which then means that in order for a new store to achieve financial viability, an existing store is forced to close down.

In grocery retailing, the overall expenditure by consumers on food and related products has risen only very slowly over time, when monetary inflation is taken into account. This means that in order to grow, firms have had to attempt to increase their market share (Guy, 1994, p. 1).

Another characteristic of the industry is the importance of technology and innovation. For over a century, the grocery industry has led technological advances and has been the source of the most important innovations in retailing. First were the chain stores, the self-service model and the Bic Box format (Basker, 2016, p. 389). Then, along with the computerization came the first barcode scanners that allows to collect data for the management. After that, loyalty programs were introduced that allow to collect more precise data by connecting each shopper with a loyalty card account. Finally, with the advent of the Internet, came e-commerce shaking up traditional retailing (Lauren, 2016, pp. 5, 6).

History shows that the grocery industry has been reformed several times. With the advent of digitalization and the increasing importance of smartphones, further reforms are certain. Changes are going to happen very quickly, and to survive, retailers are going to have to adapt at an increasingly rapid pace (Lauren, 2016, p. 1). Identifying new trends and adopting new technologies could be key differentiators for the success of retailers' future growth strategies (p. 45).

One of the latest trends in the market is the increase in demand for natural products. According to Natural Foods Merchandiser, in 2015, sales of natural products were $109.7 billions, corresponding to approximately 16.6% of total sales in the grocery industry. Sales of this type of product increased by 7%, compared to 2% for all sales (Whole Foods Market, Inc., 2016, p. 2). This has led to a rising number of companies offering natural products, increasing competition in this field. In addition to competing for consumers, there is also competition for suppliers who are becoming increasingly scarce.

In conclusion, the U.S. food industry, despite being well consolidated, is highly competitive. The strategy of growing with new establishments is no longer sufficient. In order to grow, companies have to increase their market share by differentiating themselves from their competitors. Innovation and technology will be crucial to lead the industry, as well as quickly identifying new trends in consumption.

Whole Foods

The Whole Foods Market, Inc. is an American public multinational supermarket chain founded in 1978 and based in Austin, Texas. Based on 2015 sales ranking from Progressive Grocer, it is the largest natural and organic foods supermarket in the United States, the fifth largest public food retailer and the tenth larger food retailer overall. By 2016, they operated 456 stores across the United States, Canada and the United Kingdom, visited by eight million customers each week (Whole Foods Market, Inc., 2016, p. 1).

The year 2013 represented a turning point for the company. At the end of the year, their shares reached their historical maximum value with a price of $65 per share. In the last 7 years, the company doubled its revenue and tripled its profits. Whole Foods was planning to expand the number of stores from about 400 to 1,200. It seemed to be at its peak. However, the situation took a turn of 180 degrees. The share price began to decline gradually to half its value, and it has hovered around $30 between 2015 and 2017. In addition, in 2017, the company reported six successive quarters of declining same-store sales and a 3% decline in store traffic, equivalent to 14 million fewer customer visits (Foster, 2017). In February 2017, the company announced the closing of nine stores, representing the first downsize since 2008 (Helmore, 2017). Whole Foods also abandoned its plan to open 1,200 new stores (Daniels, 2017). In just a few years, the future of whole became very uncertain.

There are many reasons that may explain the company's downfall, but undoubtedly one of the most important factors was the increased competition. As mentioned before, despite being a consolidated industry, there is a high level of competition. In such a situation, it is possible for not-market-leading companies to obtain high profits – even higher than the leaders' profits: in case of the industry being highly segmented and then achieving high-product differentiation by specializing in a particular niche (Corstjens & Vanderheyden, 2010, p. 3). This was the case with Whole Foods. The company was a pioneer in the segment of natural and organic food and one of the main drivers of this trend, which at the time of its first store opening, was still very unknown. The company became highly specialized in this niche and started manufacturing its own exclusive brands. However, with this trend emerging, big competitors, who had not been involved in this niche so far, began to enter aggressively and with lower prices. Sprouts Farmers Market, Whole Foods' most direct rival, was found to be on average 19% cheaper than Whole Foods and by 2016, Kroger, the largest mainstream supermarket chain in the United States, passed Whole Foods in annual sales of natural and organic products (Foster, 2017; Helmore, 2017).

Due to the saturation of the niche, it is crucial to review Whole Foods' growth strategy. Its strategy is described as follows in its 2016 annual report: "Our growth strategy is to expand primarily through news store openings (...)" (p. 5). As mentioned, this strategy becomes much less effective in a saturated market, because in order to install a profitable store, you have to force another to close. This complicates things for Whole Foods, especially because the company is not characterized by having the lowest prices, being even nicknamed "Whole Paycheck" (Maverick, 2019). Now that more and more companies are getting into the natural and organic products cart, Whole Foods has less and less competitive advantages.

This complex scenario, which Whole Foods' management faced along with pressure particularly from JANA Partners, was what led to the consideration of selling the company. In search of finding a suitable buyer, tech giant Amazon appeared who is a world leader in innovation, technology and digital services – qualities crucial to succeed in the grocery industry. With these capacities, Amazon could revitalize Whole Foods' business model. An example of Amazon applying its capabilities in the grocery industry can be seen in the recent opening of its first Amazon Go store, which through the use of cameras and sensors allows shoppers to buy without checkouts – but instead through an app (McFarland, 2018).

Amazon

Amazon.com, Inc., is an American multinational technology company that focuses on e-commerce, cloud computing, digital streaming and artificial intelligence founded by Jeff Bezos in July 1994 in the state of Washington (Amazon.com, 2018). According to Forbes, it is the 2018 largest company in the world. In the same year, it also became the second company to reach $1 trillion of market capitalization (DePillis & Sherman, 2018).

With the purpose of being the "everything store" and with the goal of entering the $600 billions grocery market, Amazon entered the grocery industry even before acquiring Whole Foods – with their online shop Amazon Fresh (Cusumano, 2017, pp. 25–26). Amazon knows how to dominate online sales, but these do not constitute a substantial percentage of all sales in the grocery industry, being only 1% of total worldwide sales (Lauren, 2016, p. 6). In order to have a larger market share, Amazon needs to have a physical presence. Whole Foods with more than 400 shops distributed in the whole country can provide Amazon that. The physical presence can also contribute to the online sales by being closer to the customers, which is crucial when delivering fresh food.

Another possible reason for buying Whole Foods is to expand the database and improve customer profiling. Whole Foods data is a treasure trove of customers' buying preferences and habits. We are talking about the data from wealthy Whole Foods' customers, with an average disposable income of more than $1,000 per month, who can turn out to be profitable for Amazon as there is lot of scope for high-margin upsell opportunities. This huge amount of data can ultimately help Amazon to tailor-make the shopping experience for its customer and increase upselling (Nadar, 2018, p. 37).

A synergy can be established with Amazon Prime. According to a Morgan Stanley report, approximately 80% of Amazon Prime members in the United States (some 38 million people) are not customers of Whole Foods. At the same time, around 38% of Whole Foods shoppers (some 5 million U.S. households) are not subscribers to Amazon Prime services. By offering special tariffs to prime subscribers at Whole Foods shops, the two companies can cross-sell. Amazon Prime subscribers will have an incentive to shop at Whole Foods shops, and Whole Foods customers will have an incentive to subscribe to Amazon Prime. As large parts of both groups belong to high socio-economic segments, Amazon can greatly benefit from increased sales. Furthermore, with this strategy Amazon can increase convenience for customers and consequently increase the loyal customer base (Nadar, 2018, p. 38).

In addition to the mentioned ones, there are many further synergies that may arise from this agreement. Such as home delivery, vertical integration, reduced prices and risk diversification (Nadar, 2018, pp. 37–39). This not only encourages negotiations but also gives room for a win-win outcome.

Negotiation management

Negotiation management can be defined as the process of planning, organizing, leading and controlling the efforts of organizational members and the use of other organizational resources in order to achieve stated organizational goals (Stoner, 1989, p. 3). Negotiation management as pointed out in the introduction should focus on those negotiations that are of particular importance to the company and in which the expenses associated with negotiation management can therefore be represented (Voeth & Herbst, 2015, p. 53).

The process of negotiation management can be divided into six subtasks: negotiation analysis, negotiation organization, negotiation preparation, conduct of negotiation and negotiation controlling. The importance and the efforts destined in each of these tasks depend on the situation and the company's preferences.

In a first step, the negotiation analysis is done. It consists of analyzing the negotiation and estimates its importance. This process is important to determine how intensively a party is going to implement negotiation management or to determine if a certain party even wants to start a negotiation at all. In addition to this, other subjects of the negotiation such as compatibility, integrity, side dealing and exclusion may be analyzed. What is to be analyzed, how and with which parameters depend on each involved party's needs.

The negotiation organization is in charge of managing all the aspects related to the negotiation itself, focusing on how to optimize them. This task covers everything related to the team staffing, the division of the tasks and the management of the negotiation teams, how to influence the other team, as well as the place and the procedures of the hearings. In order to optimize the negotiation, many factors have to be taken into account, which is why a good analysis of the negotiation is very important for this part.

The negotiation preparation is one of the most important and decisive steps in negotiation management. Only if the negotiation has been prepared comprehensively and in detail beforehand, the prerequisites for a successful conclusion are fulfilled. As its name implies, this task consists of preparing the negotiations – meaning the planning of the negotiation behavior and the definition of the objective, motives and strategies. An important part of this task is to establish a good BATNA (best alternative to a negotiated agreement). This not only ensures a second option in case the first negotiation fails, it also increases bargaining power, which is a great advantage when it comes to negotiating.

By conducting negotiations, we can divide the task into three categories: Economic conduct of negotiations, behavioral negotiation management and process-related negotiation management. The first category focuses on the different economic behaviors of negotiating. The second focuses on other aspects that may affect negotiation behavior such as the culture, style and emotionality of the negotiation or the tactics used. The last category focuses on the different phases of the negotiation process.

Last but not least, there is the task of negotiation controlling. The performance of the negotiation is measured that allows to gain knowledge to improve the negotiation management for future negotiations.

Time line

Most negotiations in our lives are two-sided affairs. A child bidding for some money for ice cream isn't free to choose whose parents he asks; he must ask his own. Likewise, two States in a border dispute don't get to choose their neighbors.

Merger and acquisition negotiations are more complex in this regard, as companies are free to choose whom they negotiate with. For this reason, a company looking to be acquired can begin to analyze and prepare for the negotiations before the official process even starts. In their vastness of possibilities, Mergers and Acquisitions negotiations don't have a clear beginning.

In the case of the Whole Foods acquisition by Amazon, Whole Foods was working on its negotiating position long before they even contacted Amazon about a potential deal (Whole Foods Market, Inc., 2017). For this reason, Whole Foods' actions in the months preceding the negotiations with Amazon can also be analyzed through the lenses of negotiation management. During this time, it is useful to think of Whole Foods as if they were negotiating with a potential, rather than specific bidder. The events preceding the official negotiations with Amazon had an enormous impact later on and thus must also be analyzed. To get a clear picture of how the negotiations played out, we must start at the beginning, in the late 2016.

Need for change

Throughout the late 2016 and early 2017, it became clear that Whole Foods needed to change in order to survive. In recent years, the grocery industry has been becoming increasingly competitive (Foster, 2017). Following the public's increased interest in sustainable food in recent years, new companies started to compete in this area (Ciment, 2019). Whole Foods' competitive advantage was shrinking. John Mackey, the CEO of Whole Foods, described the challenges the company was facing;

> ... competition is a wake-up call. We are under extreme external pressure. It happens in any kind of evolution. If you think about species that go under extreme environmental pressure, they either evolve or they go extinct. Whole Foods Market is faced with evolving right now—or possibly going extinct. (Foster, 2017)

More concrete indicators for a need for change have also been difficult to ignore. After reaching a peak of $65 in 2013, the Whole Foods share price dropped to $30 by 2015 and hasn't changed much since (Foster, 2017). In addition, Whole Foods "reported six successive quartersof declining same-store sales... and a 3 percent decline in store traffic in the same period ..." (Foster, 2017). Declining same store sales and store traffic are signs that the company's customers are switching to other stores. This is a symptom of losing much of the competitive advantage that differentiated Whole Foods from other grocery stores. With every other main grocer selling bio Avocados, Whole Foods has become just another supermarket.

As a response, Whole Foods announced major changes. The co-chief executive structure was replaced by the more traditional single CEO structure (Whole Foods Market, Inc., 2017). The company hired a new marketing director and renewed efforts to refresh its Board of Directors. This new leadership was trusted to stir things up internally and disrupt the industry once again. Furthermore, the company formed a special Ad Hoc committee that consisted of the CEO, BoD Chair, and heads of all other committees at the company (Whole Foods Market, Inc., 2017). The Ad Hoc committee would later take the lead in the negotiations about the sale of the company. Finally, Whole Foods hired Wachtell Lipton as legal counsel to the company. Wachtell Lipton is among the most prestigious law firms in the entire United States and specializes in business law. It is known for "regularly handling the most complex and demanding transactions" (Chambers). This hiring could be taken as a sign that management was strongly considering the sale of the company as a potential option.

Here the cross-negotiation analysis concept for negotiation management can be applied. Negotiation management is especially important when the particular deal is extremely significant for the company and when the level of difficulty of the negotiation is high. In the case of the sale of the entire company, there could be no expenses spared. The level of difficulty of the negotiating process was likely to be medium to high, due to the nature of such a complicated deal and Whole Foods' recent weak performance. The management considered negotiation management to be of extreme significance and appropriately hired by many considered the best M&A law firm.

JANA acquisition

On April 10, JANA Partners, an investment firm known for its shareholder activism, disclosed that it acquired 8.8% of Whole Foods' outstanding common stock (Whole Foods Market, Inc., 2017). The purpose of the transaction was to "address the Issuer's chronic underperformance for shareholders," as well as "changing the Issuer's board and senior management composition" (Jana Partners LLC, 2017). In addition, JANA partners wanted to put pressure on the management to improve the use of technology in Whole Foods' stores (Jana Partners LLC, 2017).

This news came as a surprise to the Whole Foods' management. Built by John Mackey, who deeply believes in conscious capitalism, Whole Foods has always prioritized long-term sustainability and stakeholder value (Green, 2019). From Mackey's point of view, the JANA Partners' investment stood for the exact opposite. According to Mackey, the timing on the acquisition by JANA Partners was planned deliberately to coincide with the start of his book tour. In an interview with the *Texas Monthly*, he stated:

> The timing was intentional. They hijacked my book tour. It's not that I think that they were trying to harm the book tour. It's just like, "Okay, the CEO is going to be distracted. He's not going to be able to give full attention to this." (Foster, 2017)

JANA Partners wanted to quickly raise the price of the stock through forcing the management to make changes that favored short-term profitability over long-term sustainability (Foster, 2017). Then, once the price of the stock increased, JANA Partners would sell and profit like they had done many times before. For Mackey, it was a threat toward the socially conscious legacy of the company that he built from scratch.

Here it is important to consider the organization of the negotiations. With the presence of JANA Partners, Whole Foods itself seemingly split into two parties. One which fought for long-term sustainability and image of the business, the other for shareholder value. The negotiation began to take a multilateral form. The management knew that the JANA acquisition increased the likelihood of Whole Foods being sold. They needed to find the right buyer to protect the Whole Foods' legacy, rather than taking apart the company for profit. The difficulty of the negotiation increased substantially because of the JANA acquisition. First, JANA Partners themselves have become another negotiating party. Their different corporate culture and goals meant that the expectations from shareholders were being redefined. Another reason for the increased difficulty of the negotiations were the circumstances. The changes to the board of directors pushed by JANA Partners substantially increased uncertainty at Whole Foods.

Evercore

Anticipating that the nature of the negotiations over the future of the company will revolve primarily around financial matters, the management hired Evercore as a financial advisor to the company (Whole Foods Market, Inc., 2017). Evercore is a global investment banking advisory firm with a focus on mergers and acquisitions. With this move, Whole Foods was beginning to staff its negotiation team. Evercore brought immense experience in the area of mergers and acquisitions. The company has advised on more than $2 trillion of announced M&A transactions since 1995 (Evercore). While Whole Foods' management had competencies in the areas of long-term business development, they decided to bring in M&A specialists with specific negotiation experience and financial analysis skills. In addition, through partially outsourcing the negotiations, they could rely on a more rational and cynical negotiation team, which has been proven to positively influence the negotiation result.

Various offers

In light of JANA Partners' acquisition, other investors also started considering Whole Foods as a possible investment opportunity. On April 18, the Whole Foods' management team received a letter from a mysterious "Company X." It was later revealed that Company X stood for Albertsons, another grocer in the United States. In the letter, Albertsons expressed its interest in pursuing a potential strategic partnership with Whole Foods (Fontanella-Khan, 2017). In the period from April 20 and May 4, Whole Foods received four additional letters of interest from various other private equity firms. These letters were only meant to begin the negotiation process and weren't proposals by themselves.

However, the Whole Foods' management was worried that this is the wrong kind of crowd to be attracting. Private equity companies by their nature want to maximize the economic gain from any deal. This perspective contradicts the principle that Whole Foods was built on: the idea that long-term sustainable growth is preferential to simple economic gain. This difference in preferences meant that Whole Foods and private equity firms had little integrative potential.

Furthermore, the general company culture of private equity companies is vastly different from Whole Foods. Throughout his time at Whole Foods, John Mackey has always promoted the relationship oriented, win-win style of company culture. For example, when Whole Foods was struggling because of high prices, he wouldn't use leverage he had on his suppliers because he feared how this move would negatively impact the reputation and "local feel" of the company (Foster, 2017). Given the incredibly different cultures between the firms, Whole Foods and private equity firms simply weren't a good match. Because of this, and the lack of integrative potential, the management wanted to avoid a situation where the only viable path forward for Whole Foods would be to engage in distributive negotiations with the private equity firms.

Although not a private equity firm, Albertsons also didn't have much integrative potential with Whole Foods. As two large grocers, they were similar in preferences, risk appetites and assessment of the future. The only true source of integrative potential between them was differing resources and skills. Whole Foods was much more experienced in the sale of organic and natural food at scale. Meanwhile, through its many brands, Albertsons was altogether generally invested in all aspects of the grocery industry. In the end, the integrative potential between the two companies was not nothing, but not as high as Whole Foods would like it to have been.

Looking for Mr. Right

With no clear future direction and certain turbulent times ahead, the sale of the company to a candidate who could preserve its legacy was slowly becoming the dominant strategy in the minds of Whole Foods' managers. During the week of April 17, 2017, an exciting new possibility emerged. While on the search for a possible candidate, the management stumbled onto a "recent media report which said that Amazon.com may have previously considered acquiring the Company as part of its internal business development process" (Whole Foods Market, Inc., 2017). For the management, this was an opportunity to negotiate sale in an integrative manner.

The negotiation analysis of integrative potential with Amazon showed huge promise. The two companies generate integrative potential from every possible source. First, Amazon's technological skills and resources could go a long way toward modernizing Whole Foods. One of the main reasons for the acquisition and pressure from JANA Partners was the lack of effective use of technology in Whole Foods stores (Jana Partners LLC, 2017). Furthermore, Amazon had the risk appetite and resources to enact changes that could redirect Whole Foods' recently lost competitive advantage. Specifically, they could combine their own delivery competencies with Whole Foods' natural and sustainable suppliers to reignite the Amazon Fresh initiative (Girotra, 2017).

Most importantly, however, the assessments future states of the world were widely different for each of the two companies. Amazon is a corporation that made to thrive in the era of the internet, and it has a business model to match. In comparison, the core of the Whole Foods' business model has not changed at all from their foundation years. To put it simply, Amazon was considered by many to be "the company of the future," while Whole Foods was one of the companies that Amazon will be put out of business. Another important factor that made Amazon an attractive negotiating partner is that by integrating Whole Foods into its own business; the Whole Foods brand and legacy could continue to thrive. As a result of this negotiation analysis, Whole Foods made a call to the senior vice president of corporate affairs at Amazon, Jay Carney. Amazon shows interest on April 24. Amazon's vice president of worldwide corporate development, Peter Krawiec, indicates that Amazon would be interested in an "exploratory meeting between the parties" (Whole Foods Market, Inc., 2017).

The demands of JANA Partners

On April 26, the top executives from Whole Foods and JANA Partners met in person to discuss perspectives on the company and possible changes to the board of directors. Being the second largest shareholder, JANA Partners had a significant amount of influence. The two parties agreed that the JANA-sponsored candidates to the BoD would be interviewed alongside other contenders (Whole Foods Market, Inc., 2017). Here the Whole Foods' management makes a small concession as part of a bigger strategy. They used a negotiation tactic to postpone the consequences of the JANA Partners' acquisition. Specifically, distribute the negotiation time to lengthen it. This way they can continue to focus on the Amazon negotiations without large disturbances from JANA Partners.

Start of the Amazon negotiations

On April 27, a non-disclosure agreement between Amazon and Whole Foods was signed (Whole Foods Market, Inc., 2017). Naturally, to make an offer, the acquirer must be able to properly value the company. The process of reducing the information asymmetry to the desired level began with the NDA. As a result, the companies could now share important and sensitive information with each other, which would then allow an offer to be made. This is the first step that shows real commitment to being sold from the side of Whole Foods.

The next day, the Whole Foods' board of directors met alongside consultants from Evercore and Wachtell Lipton. They discussed several topics such as JANA Partners' demands, the offer from Company X and the Amazon negotiations. Given the recent developments in the Amazon negotiations and their immense integrative potential with Whole Foods, it is fair to assume that one of the main objectives of the meeting was to form a battle plan for those negotiations.

Furthermore, the interest that Albertsons was showing in Whole Foods could be used to its advantage. During negotiations with Amazon, a BATNA would have been a great tool for the Whole Foods' negotiators. If Whole Foods had a credible BATNA, they could use negotiation tactics such as bluffing and threatening to walk away. If used gracefully, these tactics could increase the value of Amazon's offer.

On April 30, John Mackey met Jeff Bezos in the headquarters of Amazon in Seattle. The main purpose of this meeting was to clarify the reasons for the bilateral interest in the deal. The two CEOs discussed the "potential strategic opportunities between the two companies and areas of complementary capabilities" (Whole Foods Market, Inc., 2017). Through this meeting, the two sides of the negotiations would understand each others' most important motivations and goals for the negotiation and future.

As is often the case, the most important people on both sides met at the beginning to give the negotiations a general purpose and stamp of authority. Once the negotiations have validity for the highest level, the details can be worked out by consultants and lawyers. The involvement of the CEOs would then diminish, before rising again at the end of the deal, or when a complete stalemate is reached. The graph in Figure 2.1 shows the involvement of the most important people in the negotiations throughout their different phases.

Preparation period

During the period of May 1 to May 8, Whole Foods was in full negotiation preparation mode. First, in an effort to secure a great BATNA, an in-person meeting with a representative from Albertsons was scheduled. Second, the Ad Hoc committee developed the battle plan of the negotiations with the help of Wachtell Lipton. The battle plan included potential actions by JANA Partners and responses to them, a plan for the negotiations with Albertsons as well as an overarching long-term company plan (tied to the Amazon negotiations) (Whole Foods Market, Inc., 2017). The interviews for the board of directors' refreshment process took place. Their results were discussed on May 7 at a general BoD meeting. Finally, Whole Foods and Amazon.com entered into a supplement to their non-disclosure agreement.

First steps of the battle plan

As a result of the battle plan that was created during Whole Foods' preparation period, Ms. Sulzberger, member of the board, and a representative of Wachtell

The acquisition of Whole Foods Inc. 15

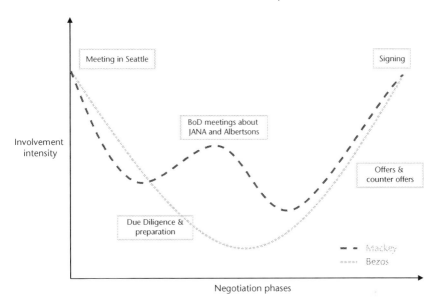

FIGURE 2.1 Involvement intensity over negotiation phases (based on Whole Foods Market, Inc., 2017).

Lipton met in-person on May 8, 2017, with senior representatives from JANA Partners. Ms. Sulzberger informed JANA Partners about Whole Foods' imminent board refreshment and other planned initiatives without mentioning the negotiations with Amazon. The proposed solution was the nomination of two of the JANA Partners' sponsored candidates to the board of directors if JANA Partners would agree to a standstill period of about 18 months to provide Whole Foods a time needed to pursue its initiatives (SEC filing). On the same day, the BoD received an email from the Company Y, a second industry participant, whose name is unknown. Company Y inquired whether Whole Foods was interested in having a meeting regarding a potential business relationship between the two (SEC filing).

On May 9, 2017, a senior representative from JANA Partners called up Wachtell Lipton to announce that the company was not interested in the proposed settlement, especially due to the inclusion of the standstill restrictions (SEC filing).

Whole Foods' proposal toward JANA Partners can be interpreted as one last thought on Whole Foods' side to uplift the company out of its own powers by refreshing the board and bringing new skillsets in. Hereby Whole Foods was intending to "make" the company and therefore to invest into internal skills rather than "buy" or in the company's case "sell" to keep up with the rising competition. Another possibility is that Whole Foods was making another concession as part of its overall strategy to keep JANA Partners out of any interference with the on-going negotiations with Amazon. Since JANA Partners was not willing to accept the settlement, Whole Foods must have pursued the ambition to sell the company to the best fitting buyer from this day on – the consequences of JANA Partners' acquisition on the company could no longer be delayed.

Later on May 9, the BoD appointed a new CFO as well as Ms. Sulzberger as the new Chair of the BoD. Further, the BoD executed several appointments and resignations from the board (SEC filing). Whole Foods sacked five people out of its 12-member board of directors, many of whom had been with the company for a long time (Foster, 2017). From this point on, some of the more traditional corporate leaders with fewer ties to Mackey were gone.

Moreover, the new BoD and the Ad Hoc committee had discussions about their next steps of the battle plan. The fact that Whole Foods was not going to be sold to a private equity firm was fixed in this plan. Mackey said in an interview with *Texas Monthly* that "These people, they just want to sell Whole Foods Market and make hundreds of millions of dollars, and they have to know that I'm going to resist that. That's my baby" (Forster, 2017).

Securing a BATNA

On May 18, 2017, Sulzberger, Mackey and a representative from Evercore met with representatives from Albertsons. Albertsons' representatives declared its interest in pursuing a merger-of-equals transaction. They further stated that $35 to $40 per share would be a fair value. Albertsons' representatives neither explain further their vision about a potential transaction structure nor did they elaborate on the rationale for the estimated valuation range they proposed (SEC filing).

On the same day, a conversation took place with representatives from Company Y. They said that they had an interest in exploring a commercial relationship, a supply arrangement between the two firms, yet, no acquisition or merger of the company was proposed.

Earlier in this chapter was mentioned that between Whole Foods and Albertsons, there was little integrative potential identified. Moreover, since the rationale behind the estimated value range Albertsons suggested was not explained, Whole Foods does not know on what the evaluation was based, yet, the company received a reference frame for its market value. Therefore, if the company was sold to a seller with higher integrative potential, the price per stock could be even higher. Another benefit for Whole Foods is that the company has now secured a BATNA

Whole Foods' share closed 2.1% higher after the *Financial Times* reported Albertsons' interest while some analysts said Albertsons' interest in Whole Foods could spark a bidding war if other supermarket chains indicated that they would also like to buy the high-end grocer (Fontanella-Khan, 2017). This gives the company room for better leverage in the preferred deal: The Amazon negotiations.

Following the conversation with Company Y, Amazon might have also analyzed this potential business partner regarding its integrative potential. The potential that a very similar conclusion resulted as with Albertsons is fairly high since the company is an another industry participant. The potential Amazon merger remains the prioritized negotiation.

Amazon's confident offer

On May 23, Whole Foods received a written offer from Amazon to acquire the company for $41 per share of common stock, which was still subject to confirmatory due diligence, satisfactory documentation and final board approval. Further, Amazon wrote that it believes that the offer represented was compelling and of certain value for Whole Foods' shareholders, considered its interest in the company to be highly sensitive, and stated that it reserved the right to terminate discussions if there was any leak of its interest in the acquisition (SEC filing). The letter also contained an indication that Amazon viewed the proposed acquisition as a strategic investment.

This part marks the start of the dialogue phase between Amazon and Whole Foods. Through making an offer to acquire the company for $41 per share of common stock, Amazon showed its definite interest in a deal. From this point on, it is important to analyze the two parties' conduct in the negotiation. Amazon starts the actual negotiation between the two companies with a dominant negotiation style by threatening to end the negotiations in case of any leak or rumor. With this statement as well as by emphasizing that the offer was compelling, Amazon is implying that there is not much room for negotiation around the offer that Amazon had just made.

On May 25, a representative of Goldman Sachs, Amazon's financial advisor, called a representative of Evercore to emphasize that Amazon was extremely sensitive with respect to confidentiality and not willing to engage in a multi-party sale process (SEC filing). Goldman Sachs also emphasized that Amazon believes to have submitted a very strong proposal.

Amazon uses its confidence that it made a very good proposal to pursue a power-based negotiation conduct. The Harvard Law School states that "power is often defined as lack of dependence on others." It further elaborates that "this kind of power in negotiation corresponds to one's BATNA." Therefore, if a party has a strong BATNA going into a negotiation, it is less dependent on the opposing party to reach the own needs than it would be if it had a weak alternative or no alternative at all. Therefore, Amazon either had a very strong BATNA or it was bluffing and threatening Whole Foods in order to leverage negotiation power. Amazon further knew from the media what Whole Foods' BATNA was and that it was a worse alternative. The "rules of the game" were clearly Amazon's. The company demanded a bilateral negotiation that meant a stop to all other negotiations as well as harsh consequences if the company goes against Amazon's rules.

Power-based negotiations

A meeting with the BoD, the management as well as representatives from Wachtell Lipton and Evercore was held on May 30. The company's long-term outlook and business plan, assumptions, timelines and key risks were discussed. Other points discussed were the talks with Amazon including its offer and overtures made by Albertsons, company Y and the four private equity firms. The BoD reaffirmed its previous decision to not solicit proposals from private equity firms that was also strengthened by concerns about leaks causing Amazon to terminate negotiations as well as the view of the management and Evercore that the price suggested by Amazon was likely to exceed the price level that a private equity firm could be expected to pay (SEC filing & Business Insider, 2017). Evercore further reviewed with the board multiple financial analyses and valuation perspectives and discussed Amazon's proposal relative to the alternatives available to Whole Foods (SEC filing).

After having discussed potential responses, the BoD decided that a counter proposal to Amazon at a price of $45 per share was the most effective response. On the same day, representatives from Evercore communicated the counter proposal to representatives from Goldman Sachs that reacted with disappointment at the higher price as they had previously informed that Amazon believed that it had made a very strong proposal (SEC filing).

The meeting's outcome was once again that Amazon due to its huge integrative potential is the best potential buyer regarding fit to Whole Foods' long-term plans. Whole Foods then had to define a negotiation strategy. Whole Foods' BATNA was Albertsons' offer of a merger-of-equals transaction at $35–$40 per share with little integrative potential. Whole Foods' reservation (lower limit) is at $35–$40 per share according to its BATNA. Its aspiration would be at a slightly higher price due to more integrative potential and therefore more synergies. In a next step, Evercore made a counter proposal at $45 per stock that disappointed Goldman Sachs due to the advisor being certain that Amazon's offer was very strong. This reaction implies that Amazon has set a very limited bargaining zone and Whole Foods pursued an either very ambitious or an overly ambitious negotiation objective by proposing a price of $45. While a very ambitious negotiation goal leads to a significant increase in one's own negotiation profit overly ambitious goals often lead to a decline in results (Voeth & Herbst, 2015).

Reaching an agreement

On June 1, representatives from Evercore met with Goldman Sachs' representatives to discuss the spread between Amazon's offer and the counter proposal. The Goldman Sachs' representatives said that Amazon was considering other opportunities instead of the Whole Foods' acquisition and had even been considering to not respond to the counter proposal at all. According to the *Business Insider* (2017), the e-commerce giant came close to walking away from the deal. Goldman Sachs further communicated that as a last stretch Amazon was willing to offer $42 per share and also emphasized that this was Amazon's best and final offer (SEC filing). If this offer were not accepted, Amazon would disengage from its efforts to acquire Whole Foods and pursue other alternatives. Moreover, Amazon expected that no other potential bidders would be approached while the negotiation between the two companies was going on and that Whole Foods promptly gives a yes or no response to the $42 offer. Amazon's willingness to move forward on the acquisition quickly if Whole Foods responded favorably as well as Amazon's wish to discontinue any relationship if the company did not agree to the offer was well signaled by the Goldman Sachs' representatives.

Later this day, the board of directors together with Wachtell Lipton and Evercore discussed the negotiations with Amazon. Following the discussion, the BoD unanimously authorized Evercore to inform Goldman Sachs that Whole Foods was willing to negotiate an acquisition at a $42 per share price (SEC filing).

By offering a transaction of $42 per share, Amazon made a small concession of $1 per share. The dominant power-based style is displayed by Amazon's demand that no other potential bidders would be approached while this negotiation was going on. Moreover, Amazon is pursuing a transaction-related process objective. The company is very determined to either close the deal or terminate the negotiations quickly. To receive an answer promptly, the firm is building up time pressure and to achieve a fast closing, Amazon is threatening to walk away from any other response than a yes. Due to Amazon's proposal being better than Whole Foods' BATNA, the board of directors eventually unanimously gave their agreement to sell the stocks to Amazon.

Finalizing the transaction

Starting from June 2, representatives of Sullivan & Cromwell, Amazon's legal counsel, sent a draft merger agreement to representatives of Wachtell Lipton (SEC filing). Over the next 10 days, Wachtell Lipton and Sullivan & Cromwell negotiated the terms of the merger agreement.

Ten days later, representatives of Wachtell Lipton, the board's chairwoman, Mackey, and another director of the company participated in a call with members of Amazon's senior business and legal team as well as representatives of Sullivan & Cromwell. The goal was to resolve the major open issues on the draft merger agreement (SEC filing). Following the described discussions, executives of both companies had a meeting at the headquarters of Amazon to discuss operational and organizational matters.

Whole Foods and Amazon have reached the solution phase in which the negotiation has become multilateral again – multilateral in the sense of both parties having their boards, management and financial as well as legal advisors involved. To discuss important operational and organizational matters at last, both companies' executives meet. As mentioned before in part, the involvement of the hierarchically most important people from both parties is high at the end of the negotiation to finalize the deal.

On June 15, the BoD, the management and representatives from Evercore and Wachtell Lipton met to review the drafted merger agreement and to consider the suggested transaction. Representatives of Wachtell Lipton reviewed the terms of the drafted merger agreement while representatives from Evercore reviewed the financial analyses of the consideration proposed in the agreement. Evercore then announced that the transaction at $42 per share price was fair from a financial point of view. Eventually, after extensive discussions, the BoD unanimously determined the merger to be fair and in the best interests of Whole Foods, approved the merger agreement and authorized the company to enter into the agreement. On the same evening, the parties executed the merger agreement. The following morning, Whole Foods and Amazon issued a press release announcing the merger (SEC filing).

Amazon and Whole Foods have reached the closing phase. In a multilateral process, Whole Foods' legal advisor, Wachtell Lipton, reviewed the legal terms, its financial advisor reviewed the financial terms while the company's own chair and executives reviewed operational and organizational matters. As a result, the transaction was judged as a fair deal and in the best interest of the company and should therefore be agreed to.

Post-sale

An hour after the press release, Amazon's stock had risen by about 3%, adding $14 billion to its value. According to Meyer (2017), "Amazon basically bought the country's sixth- largest grocery store for free." Nevertheless, Amazon's new full entry into another industry did not quite explain the rise of its value – Amazon paid a premium to buy the grocer. Instead, the boost in share price suggested something more ominous: An enormous amount of economic power was now concentrated in Amazon, and investors believed that it is stifling competition in the retail sector and the broader American economy (Meyer, 2017). Whole Foods' share price traded at $43 – above Amazon's offer price as displayed in Figure 2.2.

Summarized, Amazon's acquisition of Whole Foods allowed the company to grow beyond e-commerce and sell groceries in hundreds of stores while collecting significant shopper data and incorporating Amazon Pickup Lockers into physical stores. Meanwhile, Whole Foods could profit from Amazon integrating supply chain elements and technology into their brick and mortar stores. Whole Foods could further lower its prices and scale up after its recent declines in sales and market share (Gelfand et al., 2018).

A year later, the initial optimism at Whole Foods had shrunk. Amazon and Whole Foods may have seen value in capitalizing on each other's strengths, but the two firms failed to investigate their cultural compatibility beforehand (Gelfand et al., 2018). The companies stood on a fault line where tensions often erupt in mergers – when tight and loose cultures merge. Amazon's culture is tight – characterized by consistency, routine and precision – while Whole Foods' culture is loose – open, creative and more disorganized. According to Gelfand et al. (2018), mergers with more pronounced tight-loose divide the perform worse overall.

It looks like the merger between Amazon and Whole Foods was a win-win situation for both parties regarding integrative potential, but the companies' different corporate cultures were a fact that was neglected. Time will tell whether the

FIGURE 2.2 Whole Foods share price. Source: Factset Data as of December 16, 2019.

two companies will be able to overcome their cultural differences in order to profit even more out of this merger or if this problem cannot be resolved easily.

Summary

This chapter's objective was to emphasize the importance of negotiation management for companies. In order to achieve this, the Amazon and Whole Foods merger case was studied and the main events, previous to, during and post negotiation were analyzed through the lens of negotiation management. In this section, the main findings will be summarized.

The first finding is that Whole Foods had been preparing for potential negotiations even before the first negotiation proposals arrived. An implication for this was the hiring of Wachtell Lipton as the company's legal consultant. Wachtell Lipton is known for successfully handling negotiations with a high level of complexity. Therefore, the firm could help in all legal processes a potential deal might require. However, this measure cannot be interpreted as a definite sign of wanting to sell the company from Whole Foods' side, since the company also showed signs of wanting to continue operating by making several organizational changes, such as distancing itself from the co-chief executive structure.

Following the engagement of Wachtell Lipton, Whole Foods also hired Evercore as its financial consultant, a world-class company specialized in M&A. This reaffirmed the assumption that Whole Foods was preparing for a negotiation regarding the sale of the company. Now that the Whole Foods has expertise in both the legal and financial fields, it is better prepared to pursue a rational negotiation, aiming for a fair deal. Since a significant amount of resources were allocated to hiring the two renowned consultancies, it can be concluded that Whole Foods' management rated the negotiation as very important to the firm.

An important event marked JANA Partners' acquisition of 8.8% of Whole Foods common stock. This not only increased the likelihood that the company would be sold but also had several implications for the organization of subsequent negotiations – JANA had very different interests from Whole Foods and therefore, the company wanted to prevent any influence from JANA Partners' side. JANA wanted to generate short-term profit, while Whole Foods wanted to generate long-term sustainable growth. This conflict of interest would make the negotiations more difficult, since Whole Foods' management would have to negotiate not only with a potential buyer but also with JANA.

From that moment on, different business offers from different companies began to arrive. Besides four offers from private equity firms, the most prominent one was Albertsons', an industry competitor, which expressed its interest in pursuing a potential strategic partnership with Whole Foods. Although these offers should have been good news for the management, they rather raised concerns. Negotiation outcomes depend not only on personal performance but also on the negotiating partner's behavior. In this case, the negotiating partners were private equity companies which by their nature only want to maximize the economic gain from any deal or other grocers that did not have the resources to generate the modernization that Whole Foods needed. In addition, the interested companies did not have much synergy potential, making it difficult to generate value in a deal. However, these negotiations, as will be explained later, will be of strategic value in the negotiation with Amazon.

Eventually, Amazon joined the race to acquire Whole Foods. It immediately positioned itself as the best option. This was due to the high potential for synergy, which would give Whole Foods greater value and therefore allow it to reach a better deal. Whole Foods therefore showed a high level of commitment toward Amazon from the beginning, signing a non-disclosure agreement to share sensitive information and reduce information asymmetry.

Even though Amazon was clearly the best option, Whole Foods continued to hold discussions with the other companies. The cause behind this might have been the building of a best possible BATNA, which would allow the company to have a good second option in case the negotiations with Amazon failed – it can be interpreted as Whole Foods' strategy to improve its negotiating position.

Even though Whole Foods had a BATNA, Amazon still entered the negotiations in a high-power position due to it being a much better option. Amazon made use of this power by launching a strong first offer that could hardly be beaten by someone else and by being emphasizing how strong the offer was. Amazon also threatened to stop the negotiations if they were made public. These actions show that Amazon pursued a dominant negotiation style.

After Amazon's first offer ($41 per share), Whole Foods launched a counter-offer of $45, which almost triggered Amazon to stop the negotiations. This shows that Amazon had a very limited bargaining zone. In contrast, Whole Foods had a very ambitious or even an over-ambitious negotiation objective. Despite this,

Amazon decides to announce its final offer of $42 per share, which Whole Foods eventually accepted.

In conclusion, both, Whole Foods and Amazon, made use of negotiation management. Both companies analyzed the negotiation in depth and developed an action plan according to their interests in the negotiation. Whole Foods improved its BATNA and highlighted the integrative value of the agreement, which helped to improve its bargaining power. Amazon for its part, aware of its strong position, led the negotiation in a dominant manner, showing its inflexibility.

Whole Foods' negotiation management can be declared as successful because the grocer achieved to close a fair deal with the preferred buyer. While Whole Foods profits from modernization through Amazon's technological resources, Amazon benefits from Whole Foods' infrastructure, knowledge of the grocery market and shopper data, making the merger a win-win for both involved parties. In the medium-term, there is a clash of different corporate cultures, numbing the enthusiasm for the merger of the two firms. Eventually, the long-term conclusion of the deal is still in the open.

Lessons learned by negotiation controlling
- **Items on the agenda**

Whole Foods' objective was to find the best buyer with the biggest integrative potential for the company – a buyer with the resources to modernize the grocer's business regarding the use of technology. Amazon fulfills this criteria and promotes and advances Whole Foods' long-term interests. The company also takes over all the employees including the CEO, Mackey. A long- term analysis will show whether the long-term sustainability, which was important to Whole Foods, can be further maintained by Amazon.

- **Negotiation strategies and tactics**

Whole Foods successfully pursued its objective to either uplift the company through building up on new skillsets or to sell the firm to a buyer that values long-term sustainability even though its second largest shareholder, JANA Partners, was making this process harder due to its different interests. Once Whole Foods' definitely decided to sell the company, it staffed the negotiation team with a legal and a financial advisor, making the sales process more rational. Since the sales process was executed in a rational and effective way, Whole Foods' process objective goal was successfully reached.

Throughout the negotiation, Amazon pursued a power-based, dominating negotiation style while Whole Foods was the weaker party. The negotiation was led according to Amazon's rules of the game. The firm was demanding a bilateral negotiation, a stop to all other negotiations and was very serious about confidentiality. Amazon further utilized tactics such as time pressure and threats. Last but not least, the technology giant knew Whole Foods' BATNA from the news and knew its own offer was better that led to enormous leverage. Summarized, Whole Foods was clearly the weaker party in the negotiations with Amazon, and the company was clearly more depending on Amazon than the other way around. Nevertheless, Whole Foods resulted in closing a deal with a company offering the best price and the biggest integrative potential.

- *Integrative potential realized*

Whole Foods evaluated each interested buyers' integrative potential and eventually successfully sold the company to the buyer with the biggest integrative potential – Amazon. Whole Foods would have solely been an add-on to the two grocers' businesses and a traditional acquisition for the four private equity firms rather than a transformative transaction like the merger was for Amazon's grocery business.

- *Negotiation outcome*

Amazon compared to Whole Foods started into the negotiations with a stronger position. The tech company is considered as the company of the future while the grocer was struggling with decreasing stock prices and rising competition in the market, which created an imbalance in the negotiation. Through the involvement of Whole Foods' executives, management, Ad Hoc committee and especially through outsourcing the legal and financial aspects of the negotiation to a legal as well as a financial advisor, Whole Foods managed to negotiate a fair deal from all different perspectives involved.

References

Amazon.com, Inc. (2018). Annual report 2018. Retrieved from https://ir.aboutamazon.com/static-files/0f9e36b1-7e1e-4b52-be17-145dc9d8b5ec

Barnes Reports. (2017). *2018 U.S. Industry & Market Outlook [Report]*. Martinsville, VA: Barnes & Co.

Business Insider. (2017). Retrieved from https://www.businessinsider.com/breaking-it-down-amazon-tough-negotiations-how-the-whole-foods-deal-went-down-2017-12?r=US&IR=T. Accessed December 14, 2019.

Chambers. (n.d.). Wachtell, Lipton, Rosen & Katz. Retrieved from https://chambers.com/law-firm/wachtell-lipton-rosen-katz-usa-5:4210. Accessed December 19, 2019.

Ciment, S. (2019, August 13). We shopped at both Whole Foods and Trader Joe's, and the Amazon-owned chain was disappointing in comparison. Retrieved from https://www.businessinsider.com/whole-foods-or-trader-joes-best-healthy-grocery-store-2019-8?r=US&IR=T. Accessed December 19, 2019.

Corstjens, M., & Vanderheyden, L. (2010). Competition, risk and return in the US grocery industry. *Review of Marketing Science*. doi: 10.2202/1546-5616.1095

Cusumano, M. A. (2017). Amazon and Whole Foods: Follow the strategy (and the money) checking out the recent Amazon acquisition of Whole Foods. *Communications of the ACM*, 60(10), 24–26. doi: 10.1145/3132722

Daniels, J. (2017, February 8). Whole Foods makes 'difficult but prudent' call to close 9 stores, moderate growth. Retrieved from https://www.cnbc.com/2017/02/08/whole-foods-closing-9-stores-moderating-store-growth-strategy.html. Accessed December 20, 2019.

DePillis, L., & Sherman, I. (2018, October 4). Amazon's extraordinary 25-year evolution. Retrieved from https://edition.cnn.com/interactive/2018/10/business/amazon-history-timeline/index.html. Accessed December 20, 2019.

Ellickson, P. B. (2016). The evolution of the supermarket industry: From A&P to Walmart. In E. Basker (Ed.), *Handbook on the economics of retailing and distribution* (pp. 368–391). Cheltenham, UK: Edward Elgar Publishing.

Evercore. (n.d.). Who we are. Retrieved from https://www.evercore.com/who-we-are/where-we-are. Accessed December 19, 2019.

Fontanella-Khan, J. (2017). Albertsons explores bid for high-end grocer Whole Foods. Retrieved from *Financial Times*: https://www.ft.com/content/045caddc-290d-11e7-9ec8-168383da43b7. Accessed 14 December 2019.

Foster, T. (2017). The shelf life of John Mackey. Interview in *Texas Monthly*: https://features.texasmonthly.com/editorial/shelf-life-john-mackey/. Accessed 14 December 2019.

Gelfand, M., Gordon, S., Li, C., Choi, V., & Prokopowicz, P. (2018). One reason Mergers fail: The two cultures aren't compatible. Retrieved from *Harvard Business Review*: https://hbr.org/2018/10/one-reason-mergers-fail-the-two-cultures-arent-compatible. Accessed 16 December 2019.

Girotra, K. (2017, July 7). Unpacking the Amazon-Whole Foods deal. Retrieved from https://knowledge.insead.edu/operations/unpacking-the-amazon-whole-foods-deal-6586. Accessed December 19, 2019.

Green, D. (2019, May 2). How Whole Foods went from a hippie natural foods store to Amazon's $13.7 billion grocery weapon. Retrieved from https://www.businessinsider.com/whole-foods-timeline-from-start-to-amazon-2017-9?r=US&IR=T#in-2017-an-activist-hedge-fund-jana-partners-purchased-a-stake-in-the- chain-shuffled-the-board-and-pushed-it-to-lower-prices-to-better-compete-with- more-mainstream-chains-17. Accessed December 19, 2019.

Guy, C. (1994). Grocery store saturation: Has it arrived yet?. *International Journal of Retail & Distribution Management*. doi: 10.1108/09590559410051359

Helmore, E. (2017, April 29). Hard times for Whole Foods: "People say it's for pretentious people. I can see why." Retrieved from https://www.theguardian.com/business/2017/apr/29/whole-foods-hard-times-retail. Accessed December 20, 2019.

Jana Partners LLC. (2017, March 29). Form schedule 13D. Retrieved from https://www.sec.gov/Archives/edgar/

Kelloway, C., & Miller, S. (2019). Food and power: Addressing monopolization in America's food system. Retrieved from https://openmarketsinstitute.org/wp-content/uploads/2019/05/190322_MonopolyFoodReport-v7.pdf

Lauren, D. (2016). How technology is transforming physical retail: Current shopping behavior and future trends in grocery stores (Bachelor Thesis, Universität St. Gallen). Retrieved from https://eds.a.ebscohost.com/eds/detail/detail?vid=4&sid=9faaa9a3-cde5-47e1-9027-c66b50598c79%40sessionmgr4008&bdata=Jmxhbmc9ZGUmc2l0ZT1lZHMtbGl2ZQ%3d%3d#AN=stgal.000881868&db=cat00327a

Maverick, J. B. (2019, October 29). How expensive is Whole Foods, really?. Retrieved from https://www.investopedia.com/articles/markets/100715/how-expensive-whole-foods-really.asp. Accessed December 20, 2019.

McFarland, M. (2018, October 3). I spent 53 minutes in Amazon Go and saw the future of retail. Retrieved from https://edition.cnn.com/2018/10/03/tech/amazon-go/index.html. Accessed December 20, 2019.

Meyer, R. (2017). When does Amazon become a monopoly?. Retrieved from *The Atlantic*: https://www.theatlantic.com/technology/archive/2017/06/when-exactly-does-amazon-become-a-monopoly/530616/. Accessed 14 December 2019.

Nadar, D. S. (2018). Amazon's acquisition of Whole Foods: A case-specific analytical study of the impact of announcement of M&A on share price. *IUP Journal of Business Strategy*, 15(2), 31–45. Retrieved from https://search.ebscohost.com/login.aspx?direct=true&db=bsu&AN=130845868&site=eds-live

Stoner, J. (1989). AF, and Freeman, R. Edward, Management. ISO 690.

Voeth, M., & Herbst, U. (2015). Verhandlungsmanagement – Planung, Steuerung und Analyse, 2. Aufl., Stuttgart 2015.

Whole Foods Market, Inc. (2016). Annual report 2016. Retrieved from http://www.annualreports.co.uk/HostedData/AnnualReportArchive/w/NASDAQ_WFM_2016.pdf

Whole Foods Market, Inc. (2017). Form PRE 14A. Retrieved from https://www.sec.gov/Archives/edgar/

3
NEGOTIATION OF THE IRAN NUCLEAR DEAL

Irena Marina, Julien Petat, and Adrian Budac

KEY OBJECTIVES OF THE CASE STUDY

The key objectives of this case study for the student are to understand the context of the negotiation, by conceptualizing the following aspects:

1. Understand the historical foundation on which the Comprehensive Plan of Action is based.
2. Identify the underlying red thread between Iran and the global community
3. Identify one main reason for the chronically damaged US–Iran relationship
4. Identify the negotiation party with the biggest incentive to disrupt the negotiations
5. Identify the negotiation party that gained in negotiation power and relevance by curbing the disruptions of the negotiations

---

Introduction

"If it were ever possible to control at will the rate of disintegration of the radio elements, an enormous amount of energy could be obtained from a small amount of matter" Ernest Rutherford (1904).

The quest for gaining energy through the physical process of nuclear fission exists since the beginning of the 20th century. Ancient Greeks had called the tiniest elements on earth the atoms, as atoms means indivisible in Greek. Since then, many physicians have brought the science forward. In the beginning of the 20th century, scientist knew atoms are still divisible and contain large amount of energy that can be released, thanks to the process of fission. This occurs when isotopes like Uranium-235 absorb loose neurons, become instable and split into two atoms and some free neurons while releasing energy under the form of heat. A chain reaction happens when the released free neurons become absorbed by further isotopes. Under the right conditions, it becomes a self-sustaining chain reaction that, when controlled by humans, can be used to produce energy and electricity. In 1905, Albert Einstein developed his famous theory of the relationship between mass and energy: $E = mc^2$. His theory was confirmed in 1939, and on December 2, 1942, the first ever self-sustained nuclear reactor was brought to life under the name of Chicago Pile-1. Since this happened to be during World War II, physician focused their efforts on developing a nuclear weapon that could be used to gain advantage over the allied enemies. On July 6, 1945, the world's first nuclear bomb is tested in Mexico under the name Manhattan project. On August 6 and 9, 1945, two atomic bombs, respectively, called Little Boy and Fat Man are dropped over Hiroshima and Nagasaki in Japan. Following the damages made by the bombs, Japan surrenders on August 15, and the world realized the power of the new weapon. During the decade of 1950, researches focused on the peaceful and economical use of nuclear fission to insure a reliable energy source. On October 1, 1957, "the United Nations creates the International Atomic Energy Agency (IAEA) in Vienna, Austria, to promote the peaceful use of nuclear energy and prevent the spread of nuclear weapons around the world" (U.S. Department of Energy). During the following years, the use of nuclear powerplant continuously grew around the world. Also, some further four countries became nuclear weapon powers up until 1964. Afterwards, on July 1, 1968, 190 nations ratify the Treaty for Non-Proliferation of Nuclear Weapons. By signing, Iran as a nonnuclear-weapon power state agreed not to acquire any technology leading to the possession of nuclear weapons. But as Iran secretly launched its own program before 2003, a diplomatic tension raised between Iran and the United Kingdom, France, Germany, China, Russia and the United States. After several years of threatening and negotiation under high pressure, the members finally agreed on a long-lasting solution called the Joint Comprehensive Plan of Action (JCPOA) in 2015. The following text analyzes the background that led to the signing of the deal and discusses whether the long-term solution will pass the test of time or more precisely why we, in December 2019, know it didn't (U.S. Department of Energy).

Negotiation analysis

History and context

The negotiation leading to the JCPOA in July 2014 has a strong historical background considering that Iran's first treaty to regulate its nuclear activities dates back to 1968. Since then, several concerns have been expressed over the decades regarding Iran's noncompliance with the clauses of that agreement. Those concerns were not based on the nature of the nuclear activities, which were not illegal according to the treaty, but on the fact that Iran tried to conceal them, thus raising suspicions about its nuclear arsenal intentions (House of Commons, 2007). Iran seems to have continued its nuclear weapons program until 2003 (Kerr, 2019). As a result of these events, several sanctions have been imposed by the United Nations Security Council, the United States and the European Union over the years, but despite these "Iran continued to enrich uranium, install additional centrifuges, and conduct research on new types of centrifuges" (Kerr, 2019).

The different deals and negotiations leading to the final agreement are briefly presented below.

Non-Proliferation Treaty

The Non-Proliferation Treaty (NPT) was the first international agreement addressing the issues of nuclear capabilities, which aims "to prevent the spread of nuclear weapons and weapons technology, to promote cooperation in the peaceful uses of nuclear energy and to further the goal of achieving nuclear disarmament and general and complete disarmament" (United Nations). It was opened for signatures in July 1968 and entered into force in March 1970 with a total of 191 States that joined it since then (UNODA). As agreed in the original treaty, a conference took place 25 years later, in May 1995, and the treaty was extended indefinitely.

By ratifying the treaty, the signing parties have agreed, among other things, to respect the following main points specified in the final document: Each nuclear-weapon State Party agreed not to transfer any nuclear weapon or technology enabling the acquisition of such a device; each nonnuclear-weapon State Party agreed to decline the transfer of any nuclear weapon or technology enabling the acquisition of such a device as well as to accept the safeguards system (Treaty on the Non-Proliferation of Nuclear Weapons, 1970) implemented under the supervision of the International Atomic Energy Agency (IAEA) and undergo inspections conducted by the Agency to ensure compliance with the Treaty (United Nations). The NPT members have also been granted "the inalienable right to develop and use nuclear energy, and to benefit from the obligation by all parties 'to facilitate' the 'fullest possible exchange' of nuclear technology" (Gilinsky, 2014, p. 122).

Joint Plan of Action

Also known as the interim agreement, the Joint Plan of Action (JPOA) issued in Geneva on November 24, 2013, was a first six-months accord reached between the Islamic Republic of Iran and the world powers, which made it possible to reach an acceptable compromise for both parties (BBC, 2013). The treaty aimed to find a "mutually-agreed long-term comprehensive solution that would ensure Iran's nuclear program will be exclusively peaceful" (FARS, 2013) and was implemented on January 20, 2014, for a period of six months. The negotiations were established in good faith since Iran's right to develop peaceful nuclear technology had been recognized, and the world powers were receiving crucial information about Iran's nuclear agenda (FARS, 2013). The deal was therefore considered as the first step in the negotiation toward the more conclusive JCPOA.

Iran agreed among other things to provide more transparency into its nuclear program by giving detailed information about its facilities, to grant greater access to its sites for IAEA inspectors (Office of the Press Secretary, 2014) as well as to "stop enriching uranium beyond 5%, and 'neutralize' its stockpile of uranium enriched beyond this point" (BBC, 2013) that can easily be further enriched to a weapon-grade level. In return, some of the economic sanctions imposed by the United States and the European Union would be lifted progressively over the six months, and Tehran would receive sanction relief amounting a total of $6 bn to $7 bn on different sectors if it implements its commitments (Office of the Press Secretary, 2014).

Prelim/framework agreement

On March 26, 2015, the diplomatic corps representing the eight negotiating parties met in Lausanne for eight days of negotiations leading to the Iran nuclear deal framework that essentially outlined the terms of the final deal. Some of these outlines were derived from the previous agreement of 2013 and could therefore be relatively effortlessly negotiated. The details, however, were way more difficult to settle as the parties had several differences regarding numbers, measures, etc. (Labott, Castillo, & Shoichet, 2015).

Although some points were not fully discussed at that time and there was still some ground to cover, a significant progress was acknowledged (BBC, 2013). The key points agreed during the discussion were Iran's accord to scale down its stockpile of low-enriched uranium, to reduce the number of its operating centrifuges by two-third, to modify certain of its existing facilities and not to build any new site during the following 15 years (Office of the Press Secretary, 2015). On the other side, the world powers and the European Union committed to lift sanctions progressively, thus allowing Iran to regain economic stability (BBC, 2013).

The parties were seeking to stablish a final treaty within the next few months with a deadline of June 30.

Object of negotiation

The concrete object of the negotiation has not changed over the years, as the original intention of the NPT in 1968 was already to prevent the spreading of nuclear weapons in order to guarantee the maintenance of world peace. In consequence of Iran's noncompliance with the safeguards system implemented by the International Atomic Energy Agency under the accord and its persistent noncooperation with the inspectors of the IAEA, the country has found itself in the slider of the world powers as it was suspected of "secretly aiming at developing a nuclear bomb" (BBC, 2013). Iran's lack of transparency toward the IAEA was the principal source of concern that led to various suspicions, although the nation has always denied those claims. The objective of the E3/EU + 3 was to ensure the exclusively peaceful purpose of the Iranian nuclear program, but as the diplomacy failed in 2005, the United Nation Security Council, the European Union and the United States decided to put pressure on the country in order to make it surrender and meet the demands of the international community by imposing heavy sanctions.

When negotiations resumed in 2013, the Islamic Republic of Iran was asked to undertake measures, such as reducing its uranium enrichment capacity, as well as enabling monitoring and verification of its compliance with the terms of the treaty, in order to ensure that it would not develop nuclear weapons. In exchange, the world powers would lift the sanctions imposed on Iran allowing the country to recover economically and its right to develop atomic energy for civilian purposes would be asserted.

The intention of the JCPOA was to ensure the continuity of the measures implemented two years earlier, as the JPOA was signed. As a framework had already been set and the broad outlines discussed, the major difficulty of the negotiation was in the details that had to be agreed upon by the eight parties. The deal aimed to put an end to a situation threatening world peace and security, and the parties were aware that the negotiations presented an opportunity to improve diplomatic relations with Iran (Borger & Lewis, 2015) by establishing an environment of confidence and mutual respect (United Nations – Security Council, 2006).

Negotiation parties

From the beginning, the negotiation was bilateral since the Islamic Republic of Iran was opposed to the world powers and their claims. However, the eight different parties have to be presented since their positions are, although converging toward the same objective, somewhat different and their negotiation tactics and styles can be influenced by their own geopolitical factors and interests.

P5+1 is referring to the five permanent members of the U.N. Security Council, the United States, Russia, the United Kingdom, France and China, which are acknowledged within the NPT as nuclear powers (Traynor, 2009), plus Germany (Vaez, 2013, p. 8). In the context of the negotiations about the Iran nuclear deal, these nations are also referred to as the E3/EU + 3, a term that therefore includes the three members of the European Union – the United Kingdom, France and Germany – the European Union itself, as well as the three other parties – the United States, Russia and China.

Iran

Iran's objective in the negotiation has always been to assert his inalienable right, as a signer of the NPT, to develop and use nuclear energy for civilian purposes, as well as to lift the economic sanctions imposed by the U.N. Security Council, the United States and the European Union. The nation has always denied the accusations about its intention to develop nuclear weapons (Borger & Lewis, 2015). It found itself in a weak position during the negotiation as the only nation standing against the major world powers and being oppressed by the various economic sanctions for over a decade.

Since the early 2000s, the Islamic Republic of Iran has expressed on several occasion its position on the atomic bomb: "in accordance with our religious principles, pursuit of nuclear weapons is prohibited" (CNN, 2005) and felt therefore they were deprived of their rights and on energy independence.

United States

On July 16, 1945, the United States of America became the first nation to possess the nuclear bomb (U.S. Department of Energy, p. 13). The negotiation was taken extremely seriously under the Obama administration that wanted to ensure that no other nation would develop the nuclear weapon. The relationship with Iran were complicated, as the countries had not talked to each other since Iran's 1979 revolution (Charbonneau & Nebehay, 2015) and the United States were putting pressure on Iran since the Bush administration in the early 2000s (Linzer, 2005).

Russia

Four years after the United States, on August 29, 1949, the Russian Federation became the world's second nuclear-weapon state (NTI, 2018). Regarding the negotiation, the country was really looking forward an agreement, which in their opinion would "have a positive impact on the security situation in the Middle East, with Iran be able to take more active part in solving problems and conflicts" (Charbonneau & Nebehay, 2015). Today Russia still stands by Iran on other bilateral cooperation, manifesting a more or less consolidated opposition to the United States. While Moscow shows pessimism about the nuclear deal's viability, it supports Iran's decision to stop complying with some JCPOA restrictions, with a view toward saving the deal rather than undermining it. In early December, foreign minister called on the remaining parties to the deal not to launch dispute resolution mechanisms (Sveshnikova, 2019).

United Kingdom

The United Kingdom became a nuclear power on October 3, 1952 (Chadwick, Oliphant, Fuchs, & Penney, 2017). Britain agreed that the nuclear deal that U.S. President Donald Trump has threatened to scrap remains the best way of stopping Tehran from getting a nuclear arsenal, British Prime Minister's office said.

France

The French Republic tested its first atomic bomb on February 13, 1960 (NTI, 2018). France's foreign minister suggested that Paris was seriously considering triggering a mechanism within the Iran nuclear deal that could lead to U.N. sanctions, given Tehran's repeated breach of parts of the 2015 accord with world powers. But the three European powers have failed to make good on the trade and investment dividends promised to Iran under the deal as they have been unable to shield Tehran from renewed U.S. sanctions that have strangled its vital oil trade.

China

The Popular Republic of China was the last nation that it has been identified that reaching a nuclear capability and testing its bomb in 1964 (NTI, 2019). The nation wanted to be less confrontational. China and the three European signatories to the 2015 nuclear deal have agreed to enhance cooperation to ensure the implementation of the fraying agreement, according to a top Chinese diplomat.

Political directors from France, Germany and Britain visited China and met their Chinese counterpart to exchange views on the Iranian nuclear issue.

Germany

Although the Federal Republic of Germany is not a nuclear power, it plays an important role in the international stage and therefore took part in the negotiations as a major European economic power. The mechanism involves a party referring a dispute to a Joint Commission comprising Iran, Russia, China, the three European powers and the European Union and then on to the U.N. Security Council if that commission cannot resolve it.

The European Union

Federica Mogherini was the European Union foreign policy chief and played a coordinator role in the negotiation of the JCPOA (Charbonneau & Nebehay, 2015).

Negotiation Preparation

This Part will look more closely at likely preparations by the different parties in order to achieve their respective negotiation goals. We will commence with a BATNA analysis for each negotiation party. After that there will be an overview of followed strategies by the parties. To conclude this examination of preparatory measures token, we will take a closer look at the concession management.

Best Alternative to a Negotiation Agreement (BATNA)

BATNA is an abbreviation for Best Alternative to Negotiated Agreement and means precisely this; it defines which the preferred course of action for a respective party would be in case that a satisfactory deal cannot be concluded, implying that BATNA should lead to an worse outcome in relation to previous set goals than the of the current or future negotiation. The formulation of a BATNA contributes to the designing of reservation and aspiration ends to objectives, with the BATNA itself ideally bordering the reservation end (Voeth & Herbst, 2015, p. 162). Knowing one's own BATNA can make or break effective preparations and it therefore plays a crucial part in successful negotiation management. As or perhaps even more advantageous would be also to assume the BATNA of the opposite side. One's negotiation partner's BATNA should likewise correspond with their reservation end, which in turn could be used as one's own realistically achievable aspiration end. (pp. 162–164)

In order to determine each sides BATNA in practice, negotiation management offers BATNA analysis as a tool, which will be used to determine the BATNAs of Iran and its counterparts. BATNA analysis usually consists of twelve questions but in order to accommodate this praxis- oriented tool to a corresponding research situation with a bird's-eye view on all involved parties we will instead use a redacted and customized set of three questions:

- "What does the respective party assume about its counterpart's motives?"
- "What feasible alternative options to the treaty do exist?"
- "How do those options compare to the previous set goals?"

Each country will be examined through a domestic lens, in the sense that only respective available knowledge and self-made assumptions will be used. Through this method the respective BATNA could be determined hypothetically in the same way it originally was by the different parties.

Iran

Since the ascendance of the United States as the sole global superpower and its profound interest in the Near East Region, it can be argued that the US is Iran primary antagonist in this negotiation. As was publicly stated by government representatives, Washington condemns any measures taken toward weaponization by Iran's nuclear program, because it is seen as the most disruptive influence on the stability of the Near East and on world peace at large (Waltz, 2012, p. 3). Prior it was shown that Iran's leadership claims its primary objective is to develop a civil nuclear industry, because it has a sovereign right to do so and to lift existing economic sanctions (Kaussler, 2013, p. 3). This domestic view will also be used by this analysis as Iran's true intentions are still a source of debate. Keeping that in mind, what alternative actions besides concluding a deal could Teheran take?

The first possibility would be to keep the status quo, which consists of continuing with the unrestricted development of the nuclear program. Because of the possible dual usage of a nuclear industry and the profound US assumptions, that Iran will indeed pursue both civil and military applications of its nuclear program, the most probable action of the US would be to hold on to the status quo and keep imposing sanctions, assuming that further no proof of potential military application is found.

Without further proof the US would not have a legitimate reason to intervene militarily. With North Korea as a leading example, Teheran has a reason to believe, that even if it plans to advance the program militarily, the US would not necessarily attack, if all the other powers keep imposing sanctions (Waltz, 2012, p. 2). Nevertheless, by following this path, Iran would be able to achieve only one of its core goals. A second course of action would be all out renounce the idea of a nuclear program, civil or military. In time, global sanctions would potentially be lifted or at least sized down, which were originally imposed to this outcome in mind. An abbreviation of this would be self- imposed restrictions on the nuclear program of similar dimensions to those imposed by the final JCPOA. Both of those alternatives would demand a revaluation by Teheran of its main goals, because it would mean a change in the stance that Iran is acting rightfully. Foreign powers could perceive such action as a sign of weakness and internally the government could lose its face (Maloney, 2012, paragraph 39 or Jessen, 2017, p. 8), as backing down from a sovereign right without resistance can be interpreted as bowing to foreign powers by the populace, resulting in domestic unrest (Richter, 2012).

All of the alternatives and their respective outcomes would in fact lack the accomplishment of at least one goal, while a successfully negotiated agreement would not. Therefore, pursuing the diplomatic route would indeed be most favorable for Teheran. Through the lens given above, domestic unrest would pose a more realistic threat to the power of the ruling government than an attack by the United States, thus being Teheran's BATNA.

United States and European Union

The United States continuously reasserts its belief that Iran's ultimate goal is to weaponize enriched Uranium. Acting under those assumptions, the United States primarily wants to prevent the development of nuclear weapons as a means to prevent decreasing stability in the region. There is also support from some political groups in Washington to topple the government of Iran and install a new regime with a western outlook (see Maloney, 2012).

As it is the case for Iran, the United States simply could retain the status quo, trying to submiss the Iranian government with economic sanctions. Similarly, if one takes North Korea as an example for the potential effectiveness of this policy in regard to stop the production of nuclear weapons into account, it may not achieve its intentions, rendering the status quo as undesirable for Washington.

A second option for the United States could be to unilaterally lift the economic sanctions imposed on Iran. There is some scholarly support for this course of action, as it could be potentially more stabilizing, if there is a balance in nuclear power in the Near east (currently only Israel possesses a nuclear arsenal in the region) (see Waltz, 2012). However, this view contradicts the U.S. government assumptions that a nuclear Iran poses the biggest threat to peace and stability and thus can be ruled out.

Finally, the United States could execute aerial strikes over nuclear plants or wage a full out war against Iran. Supporters of this option claimed that military action would be much more effective than economic sanctions to reduce nuclear capacities in the long term. A military option could also be used to advance a regime change. In addition, it would be more realistic than to negotiate a satisfactory treaty, given the various stances of the parties and reciprocal lack of trust (quote?). Obama considered himself that the most likely alternative to successful negotiations would be an act of war (Gärtner & Akbulut, 2017, S. 177).

As a result, and because of Washington's openly voiced opinion, a military option would be the most viable alternative.

The member states of the European Union and more specifically the EU3 (France, Germany and the United Kingdom) have a similar outlook on their own goals and Iran's motives. Main objective of the Europeans was to have proof of the peaceful nature of Iran's nuclear programme (Jessen, 2017, p. 12). The key difference lies in the European aversion to armed conflict and therefore the European Union would not see a military solution as the best alternative (p. 3).

China and Russia

As for the non-western powers, Russia and China both have considerable interests and therefore high stakes at play.

According to an unofficial source, China shares the U.S. view on the potential weaponization of Iran's nuclear program and is concerned about it (Fiore, 2011, paragraph 1). That said, China's considerable economic interests play a major role in detecting viable alternatives to a treaty. Because of those interests, it can be implied that China's primary objective is a stable Near East and growing its own influence over Iran and the region as a whole (paragraph 5). Thus, a military conflict would be of benefit to China. Likewise, unilateral actions such as lifting sanctions could have the same effect, since Beijing expects a U.S. military intervention in that scenario (Almond, 2016, paragraph 13). If the United States takes aggressive action against Iran, existing trade routes would be put at risk, as would be Chinese influence. At the same time, China would suffer from potential diplomatic repercussions such as sanctions imposed by Washington (paragraph 13). As a result, Beijing's practical options are severely limited and completely dependent on Washington's actions, leading us to the conclusion that no real BATNA exists.

Moskow states as well, that it has no interest in a nuclear Iran, suggesting Russian leaderships belief in such a possibility (Borshchevskaya, 2016, paragraph 3). Russian actions until then were indicating heavy interests in substantially growing economic ties as well as moves toward a strategic alliance with Iran (paragraph 4). A Russian-backed military intervention could thus be ruled out. In addition, Moskow's goal, to act as a counterweight to the western powers, leads to its main objective: to decrease western influence while increasing its own (paragraph 9–10). On the surface, Russian's interests are aligned with Washington while beneath Russia sees the United States as its main adversary. For unilateral measures, the same argument as in China's case could be pointed out. Clearly, a successful negotiated treaty would be the best option by large margin, with a potential BATNA in unilateral measures, since Russia is not dependent on energy imports like China and current economic ties are still not as significant as in future plans.

In conclusion, only the United States has a strong enough BATNA that depending on changes in Washington's stance on the Iranian question could even surpass the reservation end for negotiated treaty. Consequently, the United States is the most likely party to abandon the diplomatic route; a hypothesis that was proven to be true by the Trump administration's announced retreat from the JCPOA on May 8, 2018.

Strategies in negotiation

The next part assesses the underlying strategies employed by the different parties during the negotiations. Voeth and Herbst (2015) outline five basic strategies:

- competition strategy (win–lose)
- adjustment strategy (lose–win)
- cooperation strategy (win–win)
- avoidance strategy (lose–lose)
- compromise strategy (p. 176).

The competition strategy is primarily concerned with putting emphasis on pursuing one's self-interest, taking the negotiation partner's positions very little in account. Long-term implications of this strategy on future negotiations are equally often ignored. The competition strategy is as a consequence not suitable if one expects to be involved in a long-term relationship with one's negotiation partner. Conversely, if one can expect the negotiation partner to apply this strategy, it could be useful to reciprocate it (pp. 176–177).

The adjustment strategy serves the exact opposite purpose, since it implies to give priority toward the negotiation partner's objectives. The relationship plays a more important part than the outcome of one sole negotiation. This could in turn lead to an advantageous position in future negotiations with the same party (p. 177).

Cooperation as a strategy can work in favor of everyone if both parties identify integrative potential, which could be used to respect the positions for every party involved equally. If one party makes visible or concealed use of the competition strategy, cooperation is prone to failure in advancing one own's positions (pp. 177–178).

The avoidance strategy makes use of destructive behavior in order to disrupt the negotiation process. Such behavior is viable if the negotiation in question is of little interest and importance for the party employing it, or if it is obvious that there is no bargaining zone (p. 178).

All the mentioned strategies can be combined into the compromise strategy. For some objectives, priority is given to achieving one's own goals, while for other objectives, the negotiation partner's positions are standing in the spotlight. Blatantly existing integrative potential is being used to resolve potentially disruptive conflict. While not granting the same outcome benefits as would, for example, employing a competition strategy, compromises are beneficial if a balance of power between the parties involved exists (p. 179).

P5+1

Before formal negotiations for the JCPOA or even the JPA began, the strategy of the P5+1 toward formal negotiations mainly consisted of "Great Power diplomacy, aiming to check Iranian capabilities rather than pursuing a security and political partnership based on justice and trust" (Kaussler, 2013, p. 2). Because of this focus on achieving their own agenda with no regards to Iran's interests, it can be concluded that the P5+1 nations were using a competition strategy. However, since the ascendance of Obama into the White House, his stance on Iran was that there is always an open (diplomatic) hand to reach in hindsight, but in the early years of the Obama administration, this stance did not translate into actual negotiations (Maloney, 2012). On the contrary, Washington imposed even higher economic sanctions upon Iran, followed by similar actions from the other P5+1 nations (Jessen, 2017, p. 24). Yet in March 2013, the first of five secret meetings between Iran and United States officials took place and, together with informal bilateral meetings going back from 2008 during the Bush administration, lay the groundwork for renewed official multilateral negotiations (Jessen, 2017). Obama has proven with his proactive stance that Washington is taking a diplomatic option seriously. Iranian officials were at first pessimistic about any real common ground but were convinced otherwise after the conclusion of the first secret meeting. Coupled with the economic leverage, Obama's actions and show of genuine interest in negotiations were creating a base of trust, which in turn lead to the opening to formal negotiations for the JPA. It was also possible because then new elected Iranian president Rohani showed similar interest in achieving a successful treaty. Moreover, Obama also shifted "the red line" of the Bush administration away from zero nuclear enrichment, adjusting Washington's reservation limit of the bargaining zone. Altogether, those changes are indicating that the United States moved away from a strong competition strategy toward compromise.

In stark contrast to the United States, the EU3 did not show a bellicose stance toward Iran, never having threatened it with military action (Kaussler, 2013, p. 1). Their policy prior to the renewed negotiations was nevertheless characterized by the same power politics Washington was using. During the advanced negotiations of the JCPOA, the EU3 assumed a role of a peaceful negotiator and compromise proposer, indicating their shift toward a compromise strategy as well (Jessen, 2017).

In addition, Russia delivered a proposal that was fundamental to the settlement of the JCPOA, while diplomats attending the formal negotiations pointing out a "remarkable display of unity" between the P5+1 nations (Jessen, 2017). The latter two facts are implying that Moscow and Beijing are also a transition from a competition toward a compromise strategy.

Iran

As was the case with the P5+1 nations, Iran was employing power politics as "seen by its leaders as the vanguard of the Muslim World itself, the Iranian government framed the conflict within a right-based context and therefore gave itself little room for meaningful concessions at the negotiation table" (Kaussler, 2013, p. 3). Therefore, Iran was equally following a competition strategy. This changed gradually after first diplomatic breakthroughs at the secret bilateral meetings with the United States and the election of Rohan as president. Since then, Iran diverged from its initial position, showing the will for compromise.

Concession management

Since it is very unlikely to achieve the aspiration outcome for every negotiated objective, concessions are bound to be necessary in order to settle a satisfactory deal. The management of concessions can largely be divided into three different parts:

- "Planification of the first offer"
- "Planification of the first concessions and setting the agenda for negotiation objectives"
- "Course of Concessions" (Voeth & Herbst, 2015, pp. 180–181)

The first offer becomes a cognitive anchor, which will serve as an orientation point for the future negotiation process. It is therefore advantageous for one's party to put the first offer on the table. In order to lessen the effect of a cognitive anchor, the receiving party should immediately give a counter response (pp. 181–182).

Likewise, the party who makes the first concession gains more psychological leverage over its counterpart. This effect adds up, if the same party also made the first offer. An agenda for negotiation objectives should be created to determine that concessions are to be made first. The order of concessions should start with the least important objective to one's own party and moving up on the degree of importance. The other side's assumed order of objective importance should also be taken into consideration, as one's agenda for negotiation objectives is to be settled based on both parties' likely preferences (p. 184).

The course of concessions should be determined for one's own party and the negotiation partner. To respond to concessions made by the other party, one could follow two main strategies: the reciprocity strategy and aspiration level strategy. Employing the reciprocity strategy, one would match concessions made by the other side with concessions of a similar magnitude, at the same time and at the same frequency. The aspiration level strategy dictates that the response to a concession made by the other side should consist of only comparatively small concession or even none at all (pp. 185–189).

In general, if very few concessions are made in the early phase, a given negotiation could unnecessarily be made arduous and would drag out.

Concessions made

Because of its long and profound historic background, there is no traditional first offer that could function as a cognitive anchor for the JCPOA. Many of the final proposals were already discussed in the past and dismissed in between. Owing to the plethora of discussed proposals, every party based their expectations on those past actions.

During the formal negotiations, it was becoming clear that there was ample room for concessions to be made on each side (Jessen, 2017, p. 34). Whenever one side made a concession, it was met reciprocally from the other. It can be therefore assumed that both sides were making use of a reciprocity strategy to manage their course of concessions. This may be not very surprising because a government can lose its face and credibility if it makes concessions without getting something of equal value and interest back.

Conduct of negotiation

As mentioned previously, the JCPOA has a long historical background and the diplomatic conflict went through many various phases. During the last years before finding an agreement, the phases going from 2012 to 2015 seems to be the decisive one. This time-lapse is seen as the one in which negotiation could properly occur, thanks to intensified talks and effectiveness.

Because of the sanctions previously set by the United States and the European Union, Iran faced a serious economical low with Inflation raising from 32% to 45% during summer 2013 and oil exports dropping 40% in comparison to the previous year (Jessen, 2017). As elections had to be hold in Iran, reformists used the economic situation as their main argument for reopening nuclear negotiations. This occurred in Iran's former lead negotiator Hassan Rouhani to gain victory over its rivals, as Barack Obama did too and started his second term. "Moreover, he [Hassan Rouhani] transferred the responsibility of the negotiations from the conservative National Security Council and back to the MFA and appointed moderate allies to administrative key positions" (Jessen, 2017). Also, he made the strategic move of being first to show interest in bringing the nuclear negotiations forward.

As it was later revealed, secret bilateral meetings in Oman between the United States and Iran had created a phase where some fundamental assumptions and frameworks for the further negotiations have been discussed from 2011 to 2013. For instance, those meetings led the United States to move away from their will of a zero-enrichment policy. As the negotiations were deadlocked, it is a game changer that the U.S. administration agreed to negotiate toward a controlled transparent enrichment. It has to be mentioned that Iran had made this proposal years before in 2005 (Gärtner & Akbulut, 2017; Jessen, 2017).

During further negotiations, France took in the role of the "hard guy" aiming stricter regulations then the other parties. While the French Foreign Minister argued that the targets were legitimated by national pride and France's relations with other countries from the Middle East (Jessen, 2017), the authors are raising the questions whether this was a role play. By targeting more difficult agreements, France offers the United States the possibility to make concessions so they can increase their diplomatic relations with Iran.

As there wasn't already much trade between the United States and Iran, it was the sanctions set by European countries that gave leverage to parties opposing Iran. During the phase, Russia presented a new framework regarding further negotiations. While two unsuccessful meeting took place in Kazakhstan, the election of Hassan Rouhani unlocked the diplomatic situation (Jessen, 2017).

With the help of the secret meetings, the changed mindset of the U.S. administration led by a president starting its second term, Iran and the opposing countries found an agreement during their talks in Geneva. On November 24, 2013, the interim JPOA was implemented. It contained two separate steps. The first one applied immediately for six months and was renewable. Iran would stop building and enriching activities and cooperate with the IAEA, while the opponents waived sanctions. In that time started the new negotiation phase of the timelapse. The second step contained the implementation of the long-term agreements that would have been reached during the first step (Jessen, 2017).

The most intense period of diplomatic engagement went from the implementation of the JPOA up until the implementation of the JCPOA. Diplomats met in different bilateral, trilateral formats or with the whole group of parties. Also, specific roles were assigned, namely the responsible of Foreign Ministers, the responsible for discussions with field specific experts or the responsible of political directors. Everything was put together to one concrete plan of action by the European Union (Jessen, 2017). In this phase, negotiations kept moving forward with a total of more than a meeting every three day over the year in 2015. Also, confidentiality was built up, thanks to small and stable composed teams.

Furthermore, Catherine Ashton from the European Union was praised as the most skillful diplomat for this specific case. But as an Iranian official said: "there is no genuine political power behind her" (Jessen, 2017). Therefore, she acted as an agent, consultant and mediator but not as an arbitrator as she hasn't got the power of taking decisions. It must be noticed that the success of this phase is highly due to the positive personal relations negotiating partners cared with each other.

Also, she benefited from the European Union never having threatened Iran with military power in opposition to the United States (Jessen, 2017). Like President Obama said, engaging military power to interfere into Iran owning a nuclear weapon has always been an option, the last option. He stated that the

United States would not hesitate if Iran builds a nuclear bomb or blocks the Hormuz channel. By setting these rules, the United States gave a bargaining zone that could be used before starting a physical opposition. But should Iran have crossed the line, then the United States would have had to intervene as they would lose their credibility if they did not. Regarding this threat, the U.S. administration is profiting from its well-known diplomatic, economic and military power. On the opposite side, Iran lacks a credibility as they didn't close the Hormuz channel despite having announced they would if the United States applies sanctions, which they did (Gärtner & Akbulut, 2017). This clearly shows that the United Sates had more leverage during this part of the negotiation process.

Also, the different parties didn't claim the same interests when finding agreements during the second phase. On the one hand side, this made the discussion more complex (Jessen, 2017); on the other side, it also gave potential room for concessions. This intensive phase lead to reaching the JCPOA. With its implementation day started, a new phase in which better diplomatic relations might lead to long-term agreements on other excluded tension fields, for instance, the ballistic missile program (Gärtner & Akbulut, 2017).

Barack Obama himself stated during his speech at the American University regarding the JCPOA that it is only focusing onto Iran's nuclear program. It is not an All-In Pact. The JCPOA has great potential to set the fundamentals of better long termed relations between his country and Iran. It is a great step forward, and agreements have been found despite cultural differences and tensions in other fields that have been excluded. In this particular case, Iran had made clear in 2013 that it wouldn't negotiate its ballistic missile program by any means. Iran was hoping that the United Nations Security Council would waive their sanctions in new resolutions. In mid-2014, 28 senators reached out to Obama stating that he shall not exclude the ballistic missile intrigue under any circumstances. As a response to it, the ancient resolution 1929 (2010) got included again as resolution 2231 (2015). But while "Iran shall not undertake any activity related to ballistic missiles" in 2010, "Iran is called upon not to undertake any activity related to ballistic missiles" in 2015. During the new phase following the implementation of the JCPOA, Iran tested new missile in 2015. Unilateral measures were taken by the United States following the request of some senators, but it raises the question whether you can violate a call? The United States stated that Iran's action is not a violation of the JCPOA but rather a provocation and a violation of the UNSC resolutions. Also, why did the word use change? Was it a concession made by the United States to find an agreement? An answer to this question cannot be found, but the problematic gives an insight into the difficulties of the phase that follows the JCPOA up until today, which is discussed in the sixth part of this case study.

Negotiation tactics

The negotiation leading to the final agreement, the JCPOA, took place between top diplomats representing the eight parties on July 14, 2015, in Vienna, Austria.

After almost two years of negotiations and particularly thanks to the framework established in Lausanne a few months before, the foreign ministers were able to reach an accord that was acceptable to all. But before reaching this final stage, however, the parties have come a long and thorny way.

In 2005, at the beginning of the discussions regarding the Iranian nuclear program, the European Union offered a set of economic and technological incentives on condition that Iran agrees to abandon some of its nuclear activities (Aljazeera, 2005). It can be argued that, by this approach, the European Union did not seek discussion but rather wanted to impose its offer in a relatively passive aggressive manner. The Iranian responded defensively, feeling that their inalienable right to develop a peaceful nuclear program was threatened and refusing to collaborate (CNN, 2005). The situation became confrontational and threats began to emerge from both sides.

In 2006, the Security Council threatened Iran with various economic and diplomatic sanctions if the nation refused to suspend its uranium enrichment, because after several years of negotiations, the Iranian still hadn't agreed to comply with the measures imposed by the NPT (United Nations – Security Council, 2006).

Aggressive and confrontational tactics were not fruitful for either side and on the contrary led to hostilities. Diplomacy failed again, as the countries were unable to talk to each other.

A change of tactics and more precisely of attitude was noticed on the Iranian side following the election of their new president Hassan Rouhani in 2013 (Labott, Castillo, & Shoichet, 2015), who was willing to reopen the negotiations. The Iranian population seemed to be ready to make compromises as well in order to lift the sanctions oppressing the country for about a decade (2012).

The United States and Iran had not talk to each other officially and directly in 35 years, since Iran's 1979 revolution and those previous historical events marked the nation.

United States and Iran had a cold attitude in the negotiation and mistrusted each other because of previous historical events and influenced by their culture: "mutual mistrust had been a serious problem in the talks" (Labott, Castillo, & Shoichet, 2015).

During the negotiation of the Iran nuclear deal framework, the Iranian negotiator seemed to be "under tremendous pressure as the Leader's deadlines were not negotiable" (Charbonneau & Nebehay, 2015).

The Americans were adamant that if Tehran fails to abide by the terms of the contract, the sanctions will be reinstated straight away (Charbonneau & Nebehay, 2015) and even threatening to worsen sanctions (BBC, 2013) a difficult to get them to reconsider their demands. Iran has promised to make drastic cuts to its nuclear program in return for the gradual lifting of sanctions as part of a historic breakthrough in Lausanne that could end a 13-year nuclear standoff.

In a joint statement, the European Union's foreign policy chief, Federica Mogherini, and the Iranian foreign minister, Mohammad Javad Zarif, hailed what they called a "decisive step" after more than a decade of work. The deal reached

Tehran, people took to the streets to celebrate, looking forward to the prospect of life without sanctions. In his remarks in Lausanne, Kerry mentioned "Throughout history, diplomacy has been necessary to prevent wars and to define international boundaries, to design institutions, and to develop global norms."

Negotiation controlling

As mentioned before, the JCPOA regulates many aspects of Iran's nuclear program. It aims to stop Iran from developing and therefore possessing a nuclear weapon. A failure to agree would lead to countries like Saudi Arabia to find themselves enclaved between two countries possessing nuclear weapons, namely Israel and Iran. This would lead to an escalation and an arms race in this geopolitical tense region (GlobalSecurity.org). Therefore, some points of the deal include the following restrictions. Over the next 15 years, enrichment of uranium will only be allowed within the Natanz region. The production, acquisition and transfer of uranium concentrate will be monitored in conversion facilities over the next 25 years. Also, the IAEA will take a close look onto the storage of superfluous centrifuges, as well as their different components. For instance, only centrifuges of IR-1 types can be used, and the site in Fordow is limited to 1,044 pieces. Also, Fordow does not have the right to enrich uranium, and Iran is not allowed to reprocess its combustion waste by any means, nor to build such facilities or even conduct research (Gärtner & Akbulut, 2017). To implement and to daily monitor every aspect of the deal, the IAEA is given the right of transparency of every step. Iran showed itself as cooperative by granting visas to the chosen experts and "has continued to permit the Agency to use on-line enrichment monitors and electronic seals which communicate their status within nuclear sites to Agency inspectors, and to facilitate the automated collection of Agency measurement recordings registered by installed measurement devices" (International Atomic Energy Agency [IAEA], 2019, p. 6). According to its latest report, on October 28, 2019, the IAEA verified that the Heavy Water Production Plan was in action and that Iran's stock was within the limit of 130 metric tons. On July 1 and 8, 2019, the IAEA verified Iran's stockpile of enriched uranium, as well as on November 3, 2019. Also, on November 6, 2019, the IAEA kept an eye on the centrifuge facilities and the implementation of a natural UF6 cylinder. Like every report since the implementation of the JCPOA up until July 2019, the IAEA declared Iran's conduct to be in conformity with the agreements (International Atomic Energy Agency [IAEA], 2019).

On January 16, 2016, when the international nuclear watchdog reported for the first time that Iran had complied with all the requirements, the United States of America and the European Union lifted their sanctions. To help implement the JCPOA, the United States bought 32 tons of heavy waters from Iran on April 22, 2016, and Iran sold low-enriched uranium to Russia (GlobalSecurity.org).

Despite the overall positive results of the JCPOA and Iran maintaining its promises, the deal has not been supported by everyone. The United States concluded the agreements under Barack Obamas presidency, but disagreements have been expressed from the beginning on by presidential candidate Donald Trump. From his point of view, the JCPOA is "the worst deal ever negotiated" (*The Times Editorial Board*, 2018). At a time were the United States had the most leverage, this outrageous deal has been signed although "a constructive deal could easily have been struck at the time" (*The New York Times*, 2018).

In Trump's opinion, the deal gave new economic power to Iran by suspending sanctions although Iran hadn't planned to abandon its nuclear program. He made his statement clear during the presidential elections of 2016. Especially, he was upset that the ballistic missile program had been excluded from the Vienna negotiations. Trump aimed to renegotiate the JCPOA. As president in office, he threatened the other members of withdrawing from the JCPOA unless renegotiations were considered (Davenport, 2018). As the countries adhere to the requirements for six months, president Trump waived his sanctions on January 12, 2018, in order "to keep the United States in compliance with the deal, but he coupled that action with an ultimatum by saying he would not reissue the waivers again unless the deal is fixed [by the 12 May 2019]" (Davenport, 2018). As he had promised in earlier stages of his campaign, he wanted to renegotiate four critical points, of which three are related to the nuclear deal. First, there must be a regulation regarding the ballistic missile program. Second, he aspired to extend the time limits that are set to expire as mentioned before. Then, he wanted to ensure that Iran will never get close to possessing a nuclear weapon. And finally, he targeted to extend the access permissions of international inspectors onto the sites (Davenport, 2018). While the European countries considered renegotiating the ballistic missile program, they clearly declined renegotiating the nuclear deal. In this deadlock situation, France president Emmanuel Macron tried to act as an arbitrator to prevent Trump from withdrawing (Carrel, 2018).

Regarding the negotiation conduct, Trump had made promises during his campaign and had set a deadline for a new deal if the other parties wanted the United States to continue fulfilling the requirements. As those conditions were not met, he had to withdraw from the JCPOA. By not doing so, he would have lost his credibility regarding the power of the United States in international diplomatic and geopolitical affairs. During his announcement on May 12, 2018, he said: "Today's action sends a critical message. The United States no longer makes empty threats. When I make promises, I keep them" (*The New York Times*, 2018).

It must be added that Israel largely influenced president Trump's decision. On Monday, April 30, 2019, Israeli Prime Minister Benjamin Netanyahu unveiled 55,000 pages and a wall of CD that he said contains the proof, that Iran has had a secret nuclear weapon program from 1999 to 2003. Despite the large amount of material and proofs, Netanyahu's presentation didn't change the opinion of the members of the JCPOA. But it gave Donald Trump a large basis onto which he could rely in order to fund his withdraw decision (Prusher, 2018). On Tuesday, the IAEA stated that they knew about the Iranian efforts prior to 2003. They added that Iran didn't advance on the program up to 2009 and that there is no proved evidence for Iran to have carried out any activities regarding the development of nuclear weapons since then (International Atomic Energy Agency [IAEA], 2018).

> Tamara Cofman-Wittes, a senior fellow in the Center for Middle East Policy at the Brookings Institution in Washington, D.C. says one of the key flaws in Netanyahu's presentation was his failure to offer a better option for containing Iran's nuclear ambitions. (Prusher, 2018)

Therefore, Netanyahu's didn't help the actual negotiation process. But as Israel never supported the JCPOA and has good diplomatic relationship with the United States, his declaration aimed to act like a consultant onto the United States.

Following his decision, Donald Trump raised sanctions on Iran economy and dismantled the financial channel included in the JCPOA since the first step. In consequence, Iran struggles with economical trade difficulties and sees food and medical shortage raising. As a reaction to this, and to gain leverage in further negotiations, Iran is slowly withdrawing from the JCPOA. As implicitly mentioned before, Iran isn't totally fulfilling the requirements since July 2019, when they first announced their stock of enriched uranium exceeds the set limit of 300 kilogram. Later this year in September, Iran announced they will use a larger amount of even more advanced centrifuges than what has been agreed on. On November 5, 2019, Iran announced that they will be injecting uranium gas in Fordow and therefore enrich uranium despite the agreement. As all those initiatives are reversible, Iran threat the remaining countries within the deal on a controlled aggressive way. But nevertheless, it increases the pressure on the European nations that must try to lift of the sanctions the United States applies on Iran if they still want to hinder Iran from accessing the nuclear weapon.

On December 4, 2019, the United Nation released the joint letter reached in by the United Kingdom, Germany and France stating four examples that indicate the presence of nuclear-capable missiles in Iran (George & Feleke, 2019).

When looking at the evolution of the JCPOA from 2015 to the mid December 2019, it is clear that while the deal might have been effective in the beginning, it is shrinking in power and leverage since the United States have withdrawn the agreement and Iran started to do so too.

Just before the end of 2019, a spontaneous meeting between President Hassan Rouhani of Iran and Prime Minister Shinzo Abe of Japan might bring in a new party and therefore a new perspective into the diplomatic tension. Japan has great interest in stabilizing the geopolitical and economic situation in the middle east. Because of the good relationship that President Abe maintains with both the Iranian and the U.S. government, he could play a major role in the peaceful negotiation between the two parties (Dooley & Fassihi, 2019). In this case, Japan would act as an arbitrator between Iran and the United States.

Top lessons learned

- *The JCPOA must be understood with respect to its rich historical foundation, which had an enormous impact on the circumstances and context that lead the creation of the treaty as it is.*
- *The underlying red thread is the conflict between Iran and the global community, discussing almost the same objective – nonproliferation of the Iran nuclear program – for now more than 40 years.*
- *The effect of 35 years of diplomatic standstill between Teheran and Washington has left its visible mark to this day on the chronically damaged US–Iran relationship.*
- *The party with the biggest incentive to cancel further diplomatic options was and is the United States, demonstrated by its president Donald Trump in 2018. However, it was also shown that conciliatory measures are indeed applicable to overcome a diplomatic standstill.*
- *The new rising tensions between United States and Iran after both retreated from their respective obligations written down in the JCPOA have led a new power in the form of Japan to the negotiation table, hoping that the current situation will not escalate any further and bringing both parties thus again to the table to talk things out rather than thinking about the alternatives.*

References

Aljazeera. (2005). Iran rejects "unacceptable" EU nuclear proposals. Aljazeera. BBC. (2005, September 18). Iranian president's UN speech. BBC News.

Almond. (2016). Online Source: https://thediplomat.com/2016/03/china-and-the-iran-nuclear-deal/

BBC. (2013, November 24). Iran agrees to curb nuclear activity at Geneva talks. BBC News. BBC. (2015, April 3). Iran nuclear talks: "Framework" deal agreed. BBC News.

Borshchevskaya, A. (2016). Russia in the Middle East: Motives, consequences, prospects.

Borger, J., & Lewis, P. (2015, April 3). Iran nuclear deal: Negotiators announce "framework" agreement. *The Guardian*.

Carrel. (2018). Online Source: https://www.reuters.com/article/us-germany-usa-iran-idUSKBN1HX153

CNN. (2005). CNN Report on UN Speech. https://edition.cnn.com/2005/WORLD/meast/09/17/iran.president/index.html

Chadwick, J., Oliphant, M., Fuchs, K., & Penney, W. (2017, March 16). British Nuclear Program. Retrieved from Atomic Heritage Foundation: https://www.atomicheritage.org/history/british-nuclear-program

Charbonneau, L., & Nebehay, S. (2015, April 2). Iran, world powers reach initial deal on reining in Tehran's nuclear program. *Reuters*.

Davenport. (2018). Online Source: https://www.nytimes.com/2018/06/09/climate/trump-administration-science.html

Dooley & Fassihi. (2019). Online Source: https://www.arkansasonline.com/news/2019/dec/21/japan-leader-s-visit-to-iran-sparks-hop/

Fiore, M. (2011). *Israel and Iran's Nuclear Weapon Programme: Roll back or containment?* Universitäts-und Landesbibliothek Sachsen-Anhalt.

FARS. (2013, November 26). Iran strongly rejects text of Geneva agreement released by White House. *FARS News Agency*.

Gärtner, H., & Akbulut, H. (2017). Ein diplomatisches Meisterstück: Obama, der Iran und das Nuklearabkommen von Wien. In *Österreichisches Institut für Internationale Politik (OIIP), Internationale Politik*. Wiesbaden: Springer Fachmedien Wiesbaden. doi: 10.1 007/s12399-017-0625-1

George & Feleke. (2019). Online Source: https://edition.cnn.com/2019/12/05/middleeast/iran-nuclear-ballistic-missiles-intl-hnk/index.html

Gilinsky, V. (2014). Nuclear power, nuclear weapons – Clarifying the links. In Henry Sokolski (Ed.), *Moving beyond pretense: Nuclear power and nonproliferation* (pp. 119–147). Carlisle, PA: U.S. Army War College Press.

House of Commons. (2007). *Foreign affairs – Fifth report. Parliament*. London: Foreign Affairs Committee Publications.

Jessen, E. (2017, October 24). *European diplomacy in the Iran nuclear negotiations: What impact did it have?* (B. P. Papers, Ed.). Bruges Political Research Papers. Retrieved from https://www.coleurope.eu/research-paper/european-diplomacy-iran-nuclear-negotiations-what-impact-did-it-have. Accessed December 20, 2019.

Katzman, K. (2019). *Iran: Internal politics and U.S. policy and options*. Washington, DC: Congressional Research Service.

Kaussler, B. (2013). *Iran's Nuclear Diplomacy: Power politics and conflict resolution*. Routledge.

Kerr, P. K. (2019). *Iran's nuclear program: Status*. Washington, DC: Congressional Research Service.

Labott, E., Castillo, M., & Shoichet, C. E. (2015, April 3). *Optimism as Iran nuclear deal framework announced; more work ahead*. CNN World.

Linzer, D. (2005, August 2). Iran is judged 10 years from nuclear bomb. *Washington Post*.

NTI. (2016, October). France. Retrieved from NTI – Building a Safer World: https://www.nti.org/learn/countries/france/

Maloney, S. (2012). Obama's counterproductive new Iran sanctions. *Foreign Affairs*.

NTI. (2018, October). Russia. Retrieved from NTI – Building a Safer World: https://www.nti.org/learn/countries/russia/nuclear/

NTI. (2019, May). China. Retrieved from NTI – Building a Safer World: https://www.nti.org/learn/countries/china/

Office of the Press Secretary. (2014, January 16). Summary of technical understandings related to the implementation of the joint plan of action on the Islamic Republic of Iran's nuclear program. Retrieved from The White House – President Barack Obama: https://obamawhitehouse.archives.gov/the-press-office/2014/01/16/summary-technical-understandings-related-implementation-joint-plan-actio

Office of the Press Secretary. (2015, April 2). Parameters for a joint comprehensive plan of action regarding the Islamic Republic of Iran's nuclear program. Retrieved from The White House – President Barack Obama: https://obamawhitehouse.archives.gov/the-press-office/2015/04/02/parameters-joint-comprehensive-plan-action-regarding-islamic-republic-ir

Prusher. (2018). Online Source: https://time.com/5262607/netanyahu-trump-iran-deal-speech/

Richter, S. (2012). Two at one blow? The EU and its quest for security and democracy by political conditionality in the Western Balkans. *Democratization*, *19*(3), 507–534.

Sveshnikova. (2019). Online Source: https://www.al-monitor.com/originals/2019/12/russia-iran-jcpoa-fordow-sanctions.html

The New York Times. (2018). Online Source: https://www.latimes.com/opinion/editorials/la-ed-iran-haley-20170909-story.html

The Times Editorial Board. (2018). Online Source: https://www.latimes.com/opinion/editorials/la-ed-iran-haley-20170909-story.html

Traynor, I. (2009, April 5). Background: The nuclear nations. *The Guardian*.

Treaty on the non-proliferation of nuclear weapons. (1970). International Atomic Energy Agency.

U.S. Department of Energy. (n.d.). *The history of nuclear energy*. Washington, DC: U.S. Department of Energy. Online Source: https://www.energy.gov/sites/prod/files/The%20History%20of%20Nuclear%20Energy_0.pdf

United Nations. (n.d.). Retrieved from Office for Disarmament Affairs: https://www.un.org/disarmament/wmd/nuclear/npt/

United Nations – Security Council. (2006). Resolution 1696.

UNODA. (n.d.). Retrieved from United Nations Office for Disarmament Affairs: http://disarmament.un.org/treaties/t/npt

Vaez, A. (2013, May 1). Iran's nuclear program and the sanctions siege. *Arms Control Today*, *43*(4), 8–14.

Voeth, H., & Herbst, U. (2015). *Verhandlungsmanagement: Planung, Steuerung und Analyse*. Stuttgart: Schäffer-Poeschel Verlag.

Waltz, K. N. (2012). Why Iran should get the bomb: Nuclear balancing would mean stability. *Foreign Affairs*, 2–5.

World Now. (2012, July 4). *Iranians want end to sanctions, short-lived poll finds*. Los Angeles Times.

4
THE AIR FRANCE STRIKES

Niklas Harder and Adriano Käppeli

KEY OBJECTIVES OF THE CASE STUDY

The key objectives of this case study for the student are to understand the details of the cultural context as well as the outcomes of the negotiation. The following questions should be answered:

1. What are the two main factors to set up the context for the negotiation at hand?
2. What was the outcome of the negotiation?
3. What type of outcome has been reached?
4. Which and how high was the biggest cost factor of the negotiation at hand?
5. What can be hypothesized about the outlook on trade union conflicts in France and how can the 2018 outcome be characterized?

Introduction

"The only thing certain about any negotiation is that it will lead to another negotiation." This quote from the famous American sports agent Leigh Steinberg, the inspiration behind Tom Cruise's character in Jerry Maguire, proves to be especially true for pay negotiations and disputes between companies and their respective labor unions. These reoccurring events often involve strikes and demonstrations as a mean of the unions to pressure the other party to giving in their demands. Since enterprises often act reluctant regarding company-wide wage increases, these conflicts have the potential to drag themselves over months. The resulting high financial and reputational stakes of such negotiations and their disruptive nature – especially if a sector of great public importance such as transportation is affected – makes them a top priority for all the parties involved and an interesting case to analyze under the theoretical framework of negotiation management.

In the course of this chapter, we will examine the 2018 salary negotiations between Air France and its respective unions in the format of a case study. The first part will illustrate the situation, the history and the relationship between the parties, giving the reader an overview over a plethora of cultural and economic elements. Subsequently, the next five parts are based on the different phases of negotiation management, namely negotiation analysis, negotiation organization, preparation for negotiations, conducting negotiations and negotiation controlling.

The analysis of negotiation will first investigate the object of negotiation, the negotiation partner, the negotiation history and the negotiation circumstances. The goal of this part is to understand how these aspects are interrelated and what importance negotiation management can assume. Subsequently, the negotiation organization will deal with the different organizational characteristics of both sides. The last ex-ante phase of negotiation management, preparation for negotiations, will try to categorize underlying motives, strategies, objectives and BATNAs of the two parties. The conduction of the negotiation will then give the reader a clear overview of the story, following the 2018 events chronologically. Finally, the last part will try to evaluate both the deal and the whole negotiation process.

Background

The following part aims to provide the reader with a basic overview of the environment, the important protagonists and the history and culture around French organized labor unions and strikes. The part is organized as followed: Section 2.1 will briefly discuss the history and important dynamics of labor unions and the public reception of important strikes and incidents surrounding those unions. Section 2.2 will provide an overview of the airline industry in general and its defining trends and characteristics. The enterprise in focus of this case study – Air France – is presented in Section 2.3, while Section 2.4 will explain the situation of Air France and its employees prior to the events of 2018. All this information serves the purpose of deepening the understanding of the main influencing factors and the environment that led to the 2018 Air France strikes and pay negotiations.

Unionization and strike culture in France

Similar to many European countries, France has a long tradition of organized labor unions and subsequently worker uprisings and organized strikes that helped shaping work conditions and employment laws during the last century. France legalized strikes partially in 1864 following the emancipation of the working class after the first industrial revolution. And while since then the shape and characteristics of strikes have changed dramatically, it remained a common phenomenon until today. E. Shorter and C. Tilly showed in their work "The Shape of Strikes in France, 1839–1960" that the average French strike changed from long-lasting infrequent events that involved few workers due to the fact that the average scale of an enterprise was small and the workers were poorly organized, to shorter, more frequent occasions in 1960, that involved much more workers – averaging close to 2,200 participants (1971, pp. 66, 73). This trend continued culminating in the massive nationwide strikes of 1995 – where starting with the general strikes of civil workers in October and November against a proposed pay freeze and raise of the retirement age, the movement started spreading, resulting in nationwide general strikes and demonstrations spanning a wide range of sectors and demonstrations (Trat, 1996, p. 227). According to Trat (1996), "another particularity of 1995 was that this was the first time that a public transportation strike proceeded with so little opposition on the part of passengers" (p. 228). This solidarization of the public with the workers and their demands as well as the general acceptance of these strikes played an important role in the following negotiations.

This shows that public opinion and the sociopolitical environment are important factors and tools – especially regarding traffic-related strikes that result in strong inconveniences for the public – that must be considered by all parties. This phenomenon of nationwide general strikes and demonstrations as a mean of the public to exercise political power is an important development that positively influences the frequency of such events with the most recent one being the general strike in the early December 2019, with hundreds of thousand workers collaboratively participating in the walkouts to demonstrate against a planned pension reform by the French premiere minister Emmanuel Macron (Amaro, 2019).

The Airline industry

For the longest time, the international aviation industry consisted of national monopolies that were protected by high regulation and the protective policies of its host countries. From an economic point of view, the aviation industry is a very capital-intensive business with relatively low margins, whose cost structure is mainly driven by the high proportion of fixed costs and the dependency on the oil price, which left little room for economics of scale or other efficiency improvements (Denter & Kolmar, 2014, S. 4). As an example of the dependency of outside factors, one can name the strong exposure to the oil price that was demonstrated by the cumulative losses of the airline industry of over $20 billion from 1990 to 1993 after the oil price surged following the Iraqi invasion of Kuwait in August, 1990.

Starting with the deregulation of the American airline industry in 1978 and further accelerated by the step-by-step liberalization of the domestic European aviation market until 1997, the airline industry had to face a series of disruptions and changes in their environment that reshaped the characteristics of their market

(Thompson, 2002, pp. 273–274). According to Denter and Kolmar (2014), it changed from a "system of regionally segmented monopolies" to a market defined by "interregional hyper competition," which lead to a consolidation of the industry and the rise of low-cost carriers, which increased the competition in the industry even further (p. 2). Another disruption of the industry happened following the events of the terror attacks on September 11, 2001, which resulted in a strong decrease in world-wide demand leading to large-scale layoffs, further consolidation and even bankruptcies like the famous Swissair grounding in October 2001.

To address the new competition and to increase profitability, many airlines started to implement "Hub and Spoke" network structures (see Figure 4.1). Instead of providing connections from every airport to every destination, central hubs were defined. This reduction in connections led to cost savings but also to the concentration of European air traffic at a few large airports like Paris or Frankfurt (Bieger & Wittmer, 2011, p. 86; Denter & Kolmar, 2014, p. 17). This makes strikes at these locations even more effective but also a lot more damaging for the airlines because it increases the subsequent loss in revenue by a multiple.

Air France

Air France was founded in 1933 and is with more than 100 million passengers carried in 2018 one of the world's largest air carriers today (Air France, 2019). Similar to the general situation described in Section 2.1, Air France was a government-hold air carrier that used to hold a national monopoly in the strongly regulated French market. After the deregulation of the domestic European Market, Air France struggled like many of its competitors to remain profitable and during the global recession following the 1990 oil price shock nearly went bankrupt. It regained profitability in 1997 but was hit with a massive pilot strike during the 1998 World Cup in France, that cost the company $166 million and

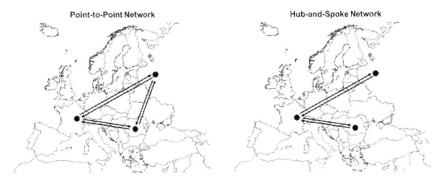

FIGURE 4.1 Difference between P2P and HS Networks (own illustration based on Denter & Kolmar, 2014, p. 15.

almost triggered a Government intervention, following its fear of losing face (Whitney, 1998). In 1999, the company got partially privatized, but the French Government retained their influence as the biggest shareholder of the company. Today it is still holding a 14.29% stake in Air France-KLM – the newly combined company that came to existence after the merger of Air France with the Dutch carrier KLM in 2004 (Clifton, Comin, & Fuentes, 2006, p. 748; van den Berg & Rivet, 2019).

The Air France situation prior to 2018

Following the events described in Sections 2.2 and 2.3, Air France was in a very fragile economic situation, which got even worse after the economic crisis of 2008. In the aftermath of these events, Air France concentrated its strategy on restructuring the business to regain profitability. They froze wages in 2011 next to a series of cost cutting efforts like mass lay-offs in 2012 and 2015, while simultaneously demanding a performance increase of their workers to get back into the black (The Straits Times, 2018). The proposed layoffs of 2015 already triggered a strike by the pilots, but the talks with the union were unsuccessful and 2,900 jobs were cut (BBC, 2015). In 2017, these efforts payed off, when Air France reported an operating profit of €1.49 billion. They planned on reinvesting the money to stay competitive, seeing that their biggest competitors Lufthansa and British Airways performed even better (The Straits Times, 2018) while also arguing that the company was not able to increase salaries without jeopardizing growth. This set the stage for the upcoming strikes and pay negotiations between Air France and its pilots, cabin and ground crew members during the next couple of months.

Important take-aways

The modern aviation industry is characterized by its thin margins, its high exposure to external factors like the oil price and heavy competition, which forced many carriers to address their cost structure. This led to industry wide efforts to reduce costs amongst other things through pay freezes, lay-offs or wage cuts, which increased the dissatisfaction of their workers and their respective trade unions that subsequently increased the frequency of strikes. Air France finds itself in the same situation – struggling with balancing the demands of its stakeholders. On one hand side, they experience the pressure of its shareholders, demanding profits as well as the additional pressure from its main shareholder, the French Government with an interest in maintaining an internationally successful and reputable flag-carrier. On the other hand, they have to address the demands of their employees and the rising risk of strikes that are getting bigger and more expensive, threatening not only the bottom line of the company but also its reputation and with it the reputation of France.

Negotiation management

Negotiation analysis

This section will introduce the negotiation between Air France and its Unions, present the negotiator, the important items on the agenda as well as the motivation of the different parties involved. This part can be seen as a synthesis of part 2 with additional information following some key concepts and frameworks of negotiation analysis that will be provided and explained on the go.

To analyze a negotiation, one can start by looking into a concept called "cross-negotiation analysis" to identify the importance of the negotiation and the potential difficulties that could arise during its course beforehand. Voeth and Herbst list four areas, where such difficulties can arise during the process (2015):

- Object of negotiation
- Negotiation partner
- Negotiation history
- Negotiation circumstances

The object of the negotiation in this case is the demanded salary increase of 6% in 2018 for all staff by the unions after years of accepting a pay freeze, which accounting for inflation and rising prices was equivalent to annual real wage cuts (Air France, 2018c). Since no other topics or side deals are part of this negotiation, it is a classic distributive negotiation. This means that the amount that one side negotiates for itself is directly paid for by the other side. Therefore such negotiations can be described as "zero-sum games" that leave little room for integrative potential (Voeth & Herbst, 2015).

Since the bottom line of Air France is still very fragile – the company was still making a loss in 2017 despite their positive operating profit – a substantial wage increase threatens the competitiveness of the firm. But with the possibility of strikes on the horizon and the knowledge of their incredibly high costs, the financial threat of this negotiation makes it a very high priority for the Air France-KLM leadership.

We established the difficult nature of the object of negotiation that makes it already a potential lose–lose scenario for the company. This difficulty is amplified by their negotiation partner, the unions, that represent the discontent pilots, crew and ground member during these discussions. In the case of the events of 2018, five different unions were involved, representing more than 75% of the employees who voted in the last union election (Air France, 2018i). Representing such a large number of employees means that potential strikes involving all or most of these people could have a massive impact on the airline and European air traffic in general. In addition, the different parties come from different backgrounds that must be taken into consideration during the discussions as well. While the perspective and therefore the arguments of Air France's leadership are largely economical, the union leaders come from a completely different background. Politically more leaning to the left, their main arguments revolve around concepts like fairness and equality.

Even though the unions know how dependent the situation of their employees is on the performance of the company, they proved times and times again that they are willing to enforce their demands with strikes, knowingly and willingly building up financial pressure. This is backed by their negotiation history, where they showed for example during the World Cup in France 1995 – described in Section 2.3 that the reputation and financial stability of Air France is of secondary importance to them. Reputation is important here as well, because it is one of the main reasons that could get the French Government involved in the conflict as a third party, which already has almost happened in 1998. Another important third party in a conflict like this is the public or to put it more abstractly public opinion. While in countries like Germany, strikes in the transportation sector often resonate badly with the public because of the inconveniences that arise for travelers and commuters, we saw before that historically the public solidarized with the workers. But public opinion can change and is also influenced by the portrayal of the media, another important actor in such conflicts.

The last important area of potential difficulties are the negotiation circumstances. During strikes, finances are an important factor that determine how long a side can resist giving in. This is especially important for Air France, where every strike day causes hundreds of cancelled flights translating directly in missed revenue that goes into the millions. With the company just having barely recovered the tough years after the crisis, their cash base is low, and their resilience to strikes is even lower. This increases the pressure on the company dramatically, which is an information known to and counted on by the unions. Both parties are aware that time and financial resources will play a crucial role during the course of the upcoming negotiations.

In summary, it is fair to say that the stakes are high for both parties with lots of difficulties that can and will arise from the history between the protagonists, the nature of distributive negotiations and the time pressure surrounding negotiations accompanied by strikes. Time pressure that translates directly into financial pressure. Win-Win scenarios are difficult to identify, which toughens the negotiation that depend now mainly on the willingness of both parties to make concessions and to compromise and on their resistance to pressure that can come from many directions, mainly the public, the government and the media. In addition, both parties have to keep in mind that the conduct and the outcome of these negotiations have an influence of the future relation between both parties. Especially Air France needs to think long term during the discussion to not just appease the unions for the moment but to reduce the future risk of strikes and maybe even negotiate a framework to ensure that future pay negotiations will be conducted in a less confrontative matter. With the high significance of the outcome of the negotiations for both parties and high level of difficulty, negotiation management has a high significance for these discussions (Voeth & Herbst, 2015, p. 53).

Negotiation organization

The last part established the importance of the upcoming negotiations for both parties and the significant potential for difficulties and conflict that can arise from many areas. Both parties had to keep these factors in mind, when they were stuffing their negotiation teams and laying out their strategies regarding the organization and blueprints of their side of the negotiation. This part will deal with these topics, taking on the perspectives of both sides and with the help from some theoretical concepts and frameworks that can be applied to this scenario.

Negotiation organization unions

Civil aviation workers are not represented by one big union but depending on their role of work have their own representatives. During big pay negotiations, they often unite to increase their collective bargaining power. In France alone, there are seven unions affiliated with the ETF, the European Transport Workers' Federation (CAPA, 2019). In this pay negotiation, there were more than 10 unions involved – representing more than 75% of the employees who voted during the last union election (Air France, 2018i). While this increased their collective bargaining power dramatically, it also toughens the process of the necessary multilateral negotiations beforehand (Voeth & Herbst, 2015). With so many different players involved – all representing different workers with different demands, while also bringing different power positions to the table, it might prove difficult to find common ground and enter the negotiations unified. During the 2018 negotiation, this only succeeded partly, with the SNPC, that represents the majority of Air France Pilots, deviating from the unified approach:

According to the Centre for Aviation (CAPA) "the supply of newly qualified pilots globally has not kept pace with demand growth in recent years (2019)." This increases the negotiation position of the pilots that were historically already in a high-power position. In addition, the SNPC has a history of using his position to exert political influence, for example, by preventing "Air France's aborted new Paris CDG hub subsidiary Joon from adopting a truly low cost structure" (CAPA, 2019). This made them a valuable addition to increase the overall negotiation power but also created the risk that they might abort the collective negotiation to use their power position to negotiate a side deal. This risk proved to be real, when the leader of the SNPC, Phillipe Evan, was demanding a pay increase for his pilots of 10% and thus side-tracking the overall negotiations about an increase of 6% for all staff (Nussbaum, 2018).

Negotiation organization Air France

To address the high importance of the negotiation, the Group CEO of Air France-KLM at this point, Jean-Mark Janaillac got heavily involved in the negotiation. "(He) was appointed CEO in June 2016 after his predecessor failed to reform the airline in the face of union resistance" (Altmeyer, 2018). With Janaillac facing the same resistance, hindering his efforts to keep the company competitive, it is safe to assume that his relationship with the unions weren't at a high point when the pay negotiations of 2018 started. Especially the relationship between Jainaillac and Evain might have been critical for the long duration of these negotiations, with Evain being one of his most vocal critics. According to the French Newspaper, La Figaro Jainaillac later privately blamed him for the failure to win majority support in a staff referendum about his proposition to increase wages by 7% over four years (Habtemariam, 2018).

Negotiation management theory suggests that the negotiation performance decreases after a certain point of involvement (Voeth & Herbst, 2015). This seems to be especially true for higher hierarchy levels (Voeth & Herbst, 2015). Since Jainaillac took responsibility for this failed vote and resigned, one can assume that his personal involvement and his relationship to the unions might have played a factor in the failed proposal and overall negotiations that weren't going well for Air France, with costs already reaching 300 million euros (Altmeyer, 2018). He was replaced in September by Benjamin Smith, formerly a top executive at Air Canada, a controversial choice that was opposed by most of the unions (Corder, 2018). "Nine unions objected to the appointment of a foreigner in the name of 'the defense of our national airline's interests,' in a joint statement," and the Dutch Pilot Union saying its members "will take action ... to change the mind of the KLM" (Corder, 2018). A tough start for Benjamin and a textbook example of one negotiation party trying to influence the staffing of the opposite side.

Preparation for negotiations

Preparation for negotiations represents a crucial phase of negotiation management. Only if a negotiation has been prepared comprehensively and in detail beforehand will the prerequisites for a successful conclusion be met. Of primary importance is especially the expected negotiation behavior of the other side, which should be incorporated into the planning of its strategy. In this regard, a deep understanding of the counterpart is critical for the successful preparation of the oncoming negotiations (Voeth & Herbst, 2015, p. 147).

Motive, objective and strategy

The underlying motives behind the two parties have been already introduced in the previous parts and are quite self-explanatory. We are at the beginning of 2018. Air France, facing increasing global competition, is expected to keep costs under control to maintain profitability and thus positive financial results. At the same time, however, the management is conscious that employee satisfaction is a crucial prerequisite of the overall productivity of its staff and also that their extrinsic motivation is strongly influenced by their remuneration. After a positive 2017, Air

France is ready to concede a pay raise of 1–0.6% to be paid on April 1 and 0.4% on October 1, which however is far away from what unions expect (RFI, 2018a).

After years of freezing salaries, employees have seen their real income decreasing due to inflation. Their goal is therefore to obtain a substantial improvement in their remunerations, which unions quantify in a 6% pay increase (RFI, 2018b). In order to put the management under pressure, Air France employees have one powerful and double-edged instrument to use – the strike. Therefore, unions' strategy will take advantage of the company's financial and reputational vulnerability. On the overall duration of the negotiations, Air France staff will be on strike for 15 days. However, unions should be careful, since the abuse of the strike as a way to enforce their bargaining power can decrease the mobilization of workers, especially if this bothers the public opinion. The more cohesive employees are that the better results can be obtained. Hence, unions should pay attention to these dynamics too.

Air France's strategy should instead face two opposite objectives. On the one hand, strikes cause short-term losses, which in case of prolonged conflicts with unions can result in liquidity and solvency problems. The management estimates daily strike costs of 25 million euros (France 24, 2018). In addition to that, strikes compromise the company's reputation, undermining both its client-relationship and the public trust in Air France. On the other hand, salary concessions are considered to be irreversible and increase the firm's expenses in the long run. In other words, the management faces a trade-off between short-term losses and long-term expense increase. A few days of strike can be tolerated if that means lowering long-term salary concessions, but an excessive duration of the negotiations could imply dramatic consequences. Therefore, finding the optimum is anything but simple. Figure 4.2 is a graphical representation of this situation.

Air France's payoff

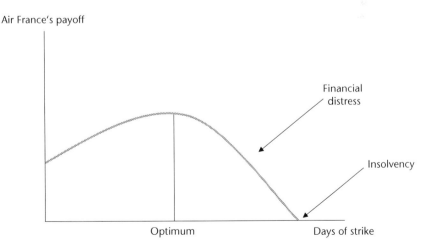

FIGURE 4.2 Air France's payoff related to the duration of the negotiations (own illustration).

BATNA analysis

The best alternatives to a negotiated agreement (BATNA) is the most valuable option one side has if negotiations fail (Voeth & Herbst, 2015, p. 162). In Air France's case, the BATNA analysis is particularly complex, since a plethora of factors are involved, and the resulting scenarios depend on the mutual behavior of the two sides.

First, it is crucial to determine if real BATNAs do exist. The key to answering this fundamental question is understanding if a situation without a deal between the two parts is viable. Regarding unions, their BATNAs depend on their behavior. The status quo can be picked as the best alternative for employees if an agreement with Air France's management would not be possible. However, this option requires a passive attitude from unions, which is a rather unlikely hypothesis, since they are willing to obtain a consistent salary increase even if that means months of unsolved conflicts. In case of prolonged strikes, the situation may potentially end up with solvency problems for Air France. A default can be easily described as the worst alternative to a negotiated agreement (WATNA), which is of course neither in the interest of management nor of unions. Arguably, this option is unlikely to realize. The insolvency of France's flag-carrier would probably be avoided by the French government, which is also one of the major shareholders of the company, as previously highlighted. In this remote scenario, and especially if Air France's crisis would be caused by the strikes, it is easy to imagine French public opinion putting itself firmly against unions' behavior. This would probably lead to the dissatisfaction of employees, bringing them to leave unions and either accept the status quo or a new deal with the management.

As a result of this short logical reasoning, it is possible to conclude that unions do not have a real long-term alternative to a negotiated agreement. Short-term tactics such as leaving the negotiating table and strike are of course more than plausible, but in the long-run, a no-deal situation cannot be seen as a viable option for the employees.

Regarding management, the status quo would be an ideal scenario, which of course is unrealistic for the same reasons discussed before. Unions are expected to increase aggressiveness if Air France firmly refuses to give even small concessions, and hesitant employees are likely to join the mobilization in response to the company's obstructionism. This dynamic would be financially unsustainable and potentially lead to Air France's default, with the difference regarding the previous case that the public opinion would support unions.

A rather extreme option for the management would be the layoff of all the employees involved in the strike. Ronald Reagan adopted this measure in 1981 during a conflict with the Professional Air Traffic Controllers Organization (PATCO), firing 11,345 striking employees (Schalch, 2006). However, this wouldn't be a viable option for Air France, primarily because unions are much stronger than in the United States and employees have more rights. Even if mass layoffs of striking workers were legally acceptable, such a drastic action would be highly unpopular, causing huge damages to the company's credibility, as well as high costs to replace the staff. Put simply, this is not a real BATNA.

To summarize, both parts cannot escape the reach of an agreement, at least in the long term, since none of them have a concrete BATNA. Both have incentives to continue negotiating, without the possibility of leaving the table permanently.

Conducting negotiations

The narration and analysis of the facts will be based on a theoretical framework and will be divided into three different parts, corresponding to the distinctive corporate governance phases. The first one, with Jean-Mark Janaillac as CEO, goes from the beginning of 2018 to his resignation. The second one goes on until the appointment of a new leadership. Finally, the third one analyzes the last stages of the negotiations, in which the new CEO Benjamin Smith concludes an agreement with the unions putting an end to the matter.

Jean-Mark Janaillac's leadership

The starting point is the beginning of 2018. As previously discussed, Air France's initial proposal of a 1% pay increase is far away from unions' expectations, who mainly demand pay raises of 6%, with the major exception of Philippe Evain's SNLP, who targets a 10% increase for the pilots (Habtemariam, 2018). Management's attempt to anchor the pay increase at a low level is thus immediately counterbalanced by unions' ambitious requests. As a result of the distance between the two parties, unions announce their first day of strike action, on February 22, which saw involved the 28% of Air France's staff (Air France, 2018a).

After a month of stalemate, in which the unions complained of a total lack of listening from the management, a new day of strike is announced on March 23 (Le Figaro, 2018a). The management then tries to propose a salary adjustment mechanism to compensate for the effects of the inflation in the previous years, but unions contemptuously reject the offer (Collet, 2018b). Trade union leaders, frustrated by what they judge to be management's inaction, are on the warpath, announcing five new strike days between the end of March and the beginning of April (Alix, 2018).

Only after the intensification of the strikes, the management decides to make a first, important concession, offering a 1% pay increase since April, resulting in a 2% increase for 2018 (Air France, 2018b). Moreover, the company proposes to start a multi-year negotiation, which includes future salary increases over the period 2019–2021. Only three days after the beginning of the new round of negotiations, a press release of Air France (2018c) states that "members of the inter-union association […] refused to enter into these talks on multi-year revaluations, still demanding a 6% pay increase for all staff in 2018." Management's last proposal also included a 3.6% wage growth over the period 2019–2021. On the other hand, unions also make a concession, offering to lower the pay increase to 5.1% for 2018, which management however declined (L'Opinion, 2018).

At this point, the company has already faced seven days of strike, whose costs estimates at 220 million euros, and unions have announced four new days of strike, April 17, 18, 23 and 24. Put under severe pressure, the management decides to opt for a drastic move, proposing what it defines a "final agreement," setting a deadline for Friday, April 20. The offer still includes a 2% increase for 2018, and a 5% wage growth for the period 2019–2021, which corresponds to 1.65% per year (Air France, 2018d). Air France's press release highlights well the drastic nature of the proposal, which the management considers the best and last option they can concede to employees. A few days later the deadline expires, and the agreement does not find the necessary signatures. On April 24, Air France Chairman Jean-Marc Janaillac decides to adopt an even more radical measure, calling employees to vote on its final proposal (Air France, 2018e). With this audacious move, Janaillac put himself in a risky position. His credibility as Air France leadership is strictly linked to the success of the staff consultation. It's an all-in move, which could whether solve the issue in a short timeframe or worsen and prolong the whole situation. However, it should be recognized that this maneuvre has the merit to change the negotiating partner. No longer the trade unions, but directly the workers. It's a paradigm shift, which management hopes to leverage by convincing moderate employees to accept its proposal and end months of conflicts.

The consultation is open from Thursday, 26 April to Friday, 4 May and takes place anonymously. Since February 22, 2018, Air France has faced 11 days of strike action, whose financial impact the company estimates at 300 million euros (Air France, 2018e). Without waiting for the outcome of the consultation, the unions announced four new days of strike, on May 3, 4, 7 and 8. They call on their members to reject the management's proposal. On the other side of the barricade, the French government supports the management of Air France. Prime Minister Édouard Philippe describes Janaillac's choice as a "courageous position." He warns that if the consultation does not produce the desired results, the consequences will not be minimal. The situation is increasingly tense (Collet, 2018c).

May 4 comes and Air France announces the results. With a participation rate of 80.33% in the consultation, 55.44% of employees have rejected the management's proposal. As Jean-Marc Janaillac has announced, he takes his responsibility and submits his resignation (Air France, 2018f).

Looking for a substitute

As the market reacts to Janaillac's decision to quit, Air France's share falls 13.4% (Oliver, 2018). Bruno Le Maire, France's finance minister, appears on television, warning that unions need to show responsibility for "unjustified" salary demands and the French government stake in the company is no guarantee of a public bailout of France's flag carrier. In the meanwhile, the number of strike days comes to 15 and Air France's board is looking for a new leadership that could replace Janaillac, who will stay in charge until May 15 (White & Louet, 2018).

One week later, the board announces a new interim management structure, which will be in place for the period necessary to appoint Janaillac's successor. Former French minister Anne-Marie Couderc is named non-executive chairman, while CFO Frédéric Gagey is appointed interim CEO. (Bayart, 2018). The weeks pass quietly, and the new leadership meets the unions several times. The board of directors announces that until a new CEO is appointed, there will be no mandate for new wage negotiations.

On June 8, unions declare four consecutive days of strike action, from June 23 to 26. Management's reaction comes fast. In a fuming press release, Air France (2018g) states that unions' announcement "is incompatible with the collective interest and with any concern for the company's future." Moreover, the management points out that a meeting with unions is already scheduled for June 14, in which Anne-Marie Couderc plans to illustrate "a series of practical measures and initiatives" (Le Figaro, 2018b).

The meeting takes place. Aiming at avoiding the oncoming strikes, the management announces an exceptional budget for the summer to provide "concrete solutions to problems that affect the daily lives of staff," like for instance an increase in the availability of rest areas for aircrew and the renovation of certain infrastructures (Air France, 2018h). The new measures are successful. The unions cancel the planned strikes, pending the establishment of a new negotiating partner. Interestingly, a few weeks before, during informal meetings, the two parties came very close to concluding an agreement. An offer of a 3% pay increase for 2018, followed by 0.65% at the beginning of 2019, seemed close to being proposed but was blocked at the last moment by Air France's Board of Directors (Le Figaro, 2018c).

Benjamin Smith's leadership

After a quiet summer, on August 16, the Board announces the new CEO of the group. Canadian Benjamin Smith, currently number two at Air Canada, is going to run the company from the end of September. The announcement meets with union discontent, complaining about the first foreign CEO in Air France's history and his retribution (between 3 and 3.25 million euros), considered excessive (Collet, 2018d). Before beginning his mandate, Smith makes a symbolic move, investing 450'000 euros in Air France shares, showing employees his commitment to the future of the company (Collet, 2018e).

The priority of the new CEO is the quick resolution of the negotiations. Therefore, he immediately begins a new round of discussions with unions, who seem to appreciate his direct approach (Le Figaro, 2018d). A week later rumors of a new offer begin to spread, consisting of a 2% pay increase for 2018 (retroactive from January 1) and another 2% raise for January 1, 2019. The proposal is tempting, with Philippe Evain's SNLP as the only critical voice (Collet, 2018f).

On October 19, Air France announces the reach of an agreement with unions, who have accepted management's proposal. All the major unions, representing 76.4% of the employees, have signed the deal, excepting the SNLP. In addition to the 4% pay increase for 2018–2019, the management engages himself in future annual salary negotiations (NAO), which will first take place in October 2019 (Collet, 2018g; Air France, 2018i). The deal, a compromise between the initial 1% offered by the management and the 6% requested by the unions, puts an end to a conflict which cost the company 15 days of strike and 335 million euros.

Negotiation controlling and evaluation

The last phase of negotiation management is negotiation controlling. For organizations can be very important to analyze and evaluate the outcomes of the negotiation process, because only in this way it is possible to enhance future negotiation performances. Without insider information, a negotiation controlling process for Air France's case is nearly impossible to conduct. Anyway, an evaluation of the negotiation will be provided.

Recalling what previously introduced, during the whole negotiation the management has faced a trade-off between short-term losses and long-term expense increase. We now can quantify these two elements. As already mentioned, the costs of the strikes amounted to 335 million euros, to what we must add the reputational damages, which however are quite difficult to estimate. For the calculation of the salary increase, we can take Air France's 2017 wage bill, which was equal to 5.196 billion euros (Air France, 2018l, p. 38). Assuming that the negotiated salary increase has no effect on future pay raises, the difference between a 6% general increase (311.76 million euros) and a 4% increase (207.84 million euros) amounts to 103.92 million euros, which will be saved from the annual expenses of the company for what we can consider an indefinite timeframe. The question is: has it been worthy to accept 15 days of strike and the related losses, reputational damages and the dissatisfaction of the employees to save 100 million euros annually? The answer is complex and depends on several factors, such for instance the discount factor and the time horizon used for the calculations. However, it appears that, especially in such a cheap money environment, in these terms the answer tends to be yes.

Apart from monetary considerations, it is important to notice that the whole negotiation has been highly mediatized. Both parties have tried to exploit public opinion to assert their interests and highlight their claims. The story is full of charismatic figures who have not hesitated to express their opinions in front of a camera. Philipp Evain is probably the most emblematic example in this regard. Moreover, the role played by the French Government should not be underestimated. Especially by intervening in support of the company and stating that there would be no public bailout in the event of financial difficulties, the executive certainly helped to moderate both the demands and the behavior of the trade unions.

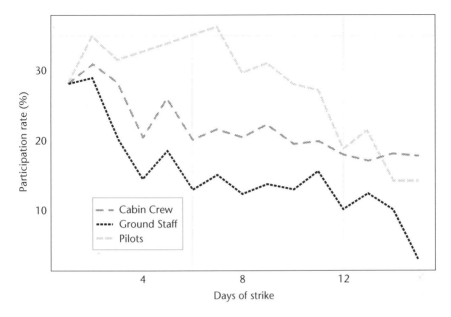

FIGURE 4.3 Participation rate of Air France's employees during the strikes (own illustration).

Finally, the last aspect to mention is the employee mobilization. With the passage of time, and especially with the maintenance of a tough and intransigent position by the trade unions, the rate of participation in strikes by Air France workers has gradually decreased, as shown in Figure 4.3. This has contributed to a softening of union behavior, ensuring above all a period free of strikes after the end of Janaillac's leadership.

To conclude, a clear and univocal evaluation of the negotiation is difficult to formulate. Both parties had legitimate interests, and the agreement reached includes concessions from both sides. Labor negotiations are notoriously tough, and an ex-post judgement is way simpler than the day-to-day conduction of such complex discussions.

Top lessons learned

- *The French strike culture as well as the recent history of Air France until 2017 were the most important factors in setting up the context of the negotiation.*
- *The agreement reached between management and unions encompasses a salary increase of 2% in 2018 and 2% in 2019.*
- *The negotiation outcome represents a compromise between the initial positions of the two negotiation parties.*

- The biggest costs of the negotiation process can be seen in the 335 million euros due to strike losses.
- The trade union conflicts in France are far from over, but at least in the case of Air France in 2018, it has ended favorably.

References

Air France. (2018a, February 21). Strike action Air France traffic forecasts for Thursday 22. Retrieved December 16, 2019, from https://corporate.airfrance.com/en/press-release/strike-action-air-france-traffic-forecasts-thursday-22-february-2018

Air France. (2018b, April 10). Air France Management offers representative unions a multi-year deal on pay negotiations. Retrieved December 16, 2019, from Air France: https://www.airfranceklm.com/en/press-releases/air-france-management-offers-representative-unions-multi-year-deal-pay-negotiations

Air France. (2018c, April 13). Update on the 13 April negotiations. Retrieved December 17, 2019, from Air France: https://corporate.airfrance.com/en/press-release/update-13-april-negotiations

Air France. (2018d, April 16). Pay negotiations: Agreement open for signature until Friday 20 April, 12am. Retrieved December 16, 2019, from Air France: https://prod-corporate.airfrance.com/en/press-release/pay-negotiations-agreement-open-signature-until-friday-20-april-12am

Air France. (2018e, April 24). Air France staff consultation. Retrieved December 18, 2019, from Air France: https://prod-corporate.airfrance.com/en/press-release/air-france-staff-consultation

Air France. (2018f, May 4). A majority of Air France staff have voted "no" in the consultation on the multi-year pay agreement proposed on 16 April. Retrieved December 19, 2019, from Air France: https://www.airfranceklm.com/en/majority-air-france-staff-have-voted-no-consultation-multi-year-pay-agreement-proposed-16-april

Air France. (2018g, June 8). Press release. Retrieved December 17, 2019, from Air France: https://corporate.airfrance.com/en/press-release/press-release-0

Air France. (2018h, June 8). Concrete and immediate measures for all staff. Retrieved December 19, 2019, from Air France: https://corporate.airfrance.com/en/press-release/concrete-and-immediate-measures-all-staff

Air France. (2018i, October 19). Agreement signed between Air France and its representative unions regarding employee compensation. Retrieved from Air France: https://corporate.airfrance.com/en/news/agreement-signed-between-air-france-and-its-representative-unions-regarding-employee?language=fr

Air France. (2018l, February 15). Consolidated financial statements. Retrieved December 19, 2019, from Air France: https://www.airfranceklm.com/sites/default/files/124_afklm_consolidated_financial_statement_2017.pdf

Air France. (2019). The company. Retrieved December 17, 2019, from https://corporate.airfrance.com/en/company

Alix, C. (2018, April 2). Air France: une quatrième grève et un conflit qui s'enlise. Retrieved December 20, 2019 from Liberation: https://www.liberation.fr/france/2018/04/02/air-france-une-quatrieme-greve-et-un-conflit-qui-s-enlise_1640488

Altmeyer, C. (2018, May 4). Air France-KLM CEO to quit after staff reject pay deal. Retrieved from Reuters: https://www.reuters.com/article/us-air-france-klm-ceo/air-france-klm-ceo-to-quit-after-staff-reject-pay-deal-idUSKBN1I5235

Amaro, S. (2019, December 11). France unveils controversial pension reforms, unions say workers' strikes should continue. Retrieved December 18, 2019, from CNBC: https://www.cnbc.com/2019/12/11/france-unveils-pension-reforms-unions-say-strike-should-continue.html

Bayart, B. (2018, May 14). Air France KLM: Anne-Marie Couderc va être nommée présidente intérimaire. Retrieved December 20, 2019 from Le Figaro: https://www.lefigaro.fr/societes/2018/05/14/20005-20180514ARTFIG00197-air-france-anne-marie-couderc-va-etre-nommee-presidente-interimaire.php

BBC. (2015, October 2). Air France to cut 2,900 jobs reports say. Retrieved from BBC: https://www.bbc.com/news/business-34425191

Bieger, T., & Wittmer, A. (2011). Airline strategy: From network management to business models. In A. Wittmer, T. Bieger, & R. Müller (Eds.), *Aviation systems: Management of the integrated aviation value chain* (pp. 77–102). Berlin: Springer Verlag.

CAPA. (2019). European airline labour relations: Multiple unions are a challenge. Aviation leader(50). Retrieved December 19, 2019, from https://centreforaviation.com/analysis/reports/european-airline-labour-relations-multiple-unions-are-a-challenge-481508

Clifton, J., Comin, F., & Fuentes, D.D. (2006). Privatizing public enterprises in the European Union 1960–2002: ideological, pragmatic, inevitable? *Journal of European Public Policy*, 736–756. doi: 10.1080/13501760600808857

Collet, V. (2018a, February 21). Chez Air France, le personnel en grève pour obtenir une augmentation de 6%. Retrieved December 20, 2019 from Le Figaro: https://www.lefigaro.fr/societes/2018/02/21/20005-20180221ARTFIG00374-chez-air-france-le-personnel-en-greve-pour-obtenir-une-augmentation- de8230-6.php

Collet, V. (2018b, March 13). Air France: les syndicats rejettent un "ajustement salarial." Retrieved December 20, 2019 from Le Figaro: https://www.lefigaro.fr/societes/2018/03/13/20005-20180313ARTFIG00328-air-france-les-syndicats-rejettent-un-ajustement-salarial.php

Collet, V. (2018c, April 25). Air France: les personnels votent sur les salaires, les syndicats appellent à la grève début mai. Retrieved December 20, 2019 from Le Figaro: https://www.lefigaro.fr/societes/2018/04/25/20005-20180425ARTFIG00346- les-personnels-d-air-france-votent-sur-les-salaires.php

Collet, V. (2018d, August 16). Le Canadien Benjamin Smith nommé à la tête d'Air France-KLM. Retrieved December 20, 2019 from Le Figaro: https://www.lefigaro.fr/societes/2018/08/16/20005-20180816ARTFIG00265-l-intersyndicale-s-oppose-a-la-nomination-d-un-etranger-a-la-tete-d-air-france- klm.php

Collet, V. (2018e, September 17). Ben Smith investit la moitié de son salaire dans Air France-KLM. Retrieved December 17, 2019 from Le Figaro: https://www.lefigaro.fr/societes/2018/09/17/20005-20180917ARTFIG00297-pour-sa-rentree-a-la-tete-d-air-france-klm-ben-smith-obtient-un-bon-point-en- misant-sur-son-groupe.php

Collet, V. (2018f, October 8). Air France: la direction prête à bouger sur les salaires. Retrieved December 20, 2019 from Le Figaro: https://www.lefigaro.fr/societes/2018/10/08/20005-20181008ARTFIG00299-air-france-la-direction-prete-a-bouger-sur-les-salaires.php

Collet, V. (2018g, October 18). Air France met fin à la crise sur les salaires. Retrieved December 20, 2019 from Le Figaro: https://www.lefigaro.fr/conjoncture/2018/10/18/20002-20181018ARTFIG00373-air-france-les-negociations-sur-les-salaires-avan-cent-a-grand-pas.php

Corder, M. (2018, August 17). Benjamin SMith is new CEO of Air France-KLM, unions worried. Retrieved from AP News: https://apnews.com/da5aaae270b5443782423c79950327bf/Benjamin-Smith-is-new-CEO-of-Air-France-KLM,-unions-worried

Denter, P., & Kolmar, M. (2014). *Grounding Swissair: An elementary economic analysis of some aspects of the European aviation industry.* St. Gallen: FGN- HSG.

France 24. (2019, April 7). Air France cancels 30 percent of flights as pay strike continues. Retrieved from https://www.france24.com/en/20180407-air-france-cancels-30-percent-flights-pay-strike-aviation

Habtemariam, D. (2018, December 12). BTN's 2018 25 Most Influential: Philippe Evain, SNPL union leader. Retrieved from BTN: https://www.businesstravelnews.com/Most-Influential/2018/Philippe-Evain

ITUC. (2019). List of affiliated organisations. Retrieved from International Trade Union Confederation: https://www.ituc-csi.org/IMG/pdf/18_02_02_list_of_affiliates_17th_gc.pdf

Le Figaro (2018a, March 6). Nouvelle grève en prévision chez Air France le 23 mars. Retrieved December 20, 2019 from Le Figaro: https://www.lefigaro.fr/conjoncture/2018/03/06/20002-20180306ARTFIG00172-nouvelle-greve-en-prevision-chez-air-france-le-23-mars.php

Le Figaro (2018b, June 8). Air France: menace de nouvelle grève pour les salaires du 23 au 26 juin. Retrieved December 18, 2019 from Le Figaro: https://www.lefigaro.fr/social/2018/06/08/20011-20180608ARTFIG00385-air-france-menace-de-nouvelle-greve-pour-les-salaires-du-23-au-26-juin.php

Le Figaro (2018c, June 18). Les syndicats d'Air France lèvent leur préavis de grève, sauf les pilotes du Spaf. Retrieved December 20, 2019 from Le Figaro: https://www.lefigaro.fr/societes/2018/06/18/20005-20180618ARTFIG00391-les-syndicats-d-air-france-levent-leur-preavis-de-greve-sauf-les-pilotes-du- spaf.php

Le Figaro (2018d, October 1). Air France: les syndicats saluent une première rencontre «franche et directe» avec Ben Smith. Retrieved December 20, 2019 from Le Figaro: https://www.lefigaro.fr/societes/2018/10/01/20005-20181001ARTFIG00011-air-france-les-syndicats-vont-parler-salaire-avec-leur- nouveau-patron.php

L'Opinion. (2018, April 17). Grève Air France: la direction fait un geste et présente un projet final. Retrieved December 19, 2019: https://www.lopinion.fr/edition/economie/greve-air-france-direction-fait-geste-presente-projet-final-147423

Nussbaum, A. (2018, December 4). Air France-KLML could gain ground in labor talks after union leadership change. Retrieved from Bloomberg: https://skift.com/2018/12/04/air-france-klm-could-gain-ground-in-labor-talks-after-union-leadership-change/

Oliver, J. (2018, May 7). Air France slides on CEO resignation and labour concerns. Retrieved December 19, 2019, from Financial Times: https://www.ft.com/content/e0cc4cce-51ce-11e8-b3ee-41e0209208ec

RFI. (2018a, February 10). Air France to strike 22 February. Retrieved December 19, 2019, from http://www.rfi.fr/en/20180210-air-france-strike-22-february

RFI. (2018b, February 21). Air France passengers grounded by strike. Retrieved December 19, 2019, from http://www.rfi.fr/en/france/20180221-air-france-strike-affect-50-percent-long-haul-flights-22-february

Schalch, K. (2006, August 3). 1981 Stike Leaves Legacy for American Workers. Retrieved from https://www.npr.org/2006/08/03/5604656/1981-strike-leaves-legacy-for-american-workers?t=1576763139446

Shorter, E., & Tilly, C. (1971, January). The Shape of Strikes in France, 1830–1960. *Comparative Studies in Society and History, 13*(1), 60–89.

The Straits Times. (2018, February 23). Air France pilots and stewards strike for pay rise. Retrieved from https://www.straitstimes.com/world/europe/air-france-pilots-and-stewards-strike-for-pay-rise

Thompson, I. B. (2002). Air transport liberalisation and the development of third level. *Journal of Transport Geography, 10,* 273285.

Trat, J. (1996). Autumn 1995: A social storm blows over France. *Social Politics: International Studies in Gender, State & Society, 3*(2–3), 223–236. doi: 10.1093/sp/3.2-3.223

van den Berg, S., & Rivet, M. (2019, February 26). Dutch take stake in Air France- KLM to counter French influence. Retrieved from Reuters: https://www.reuters.com/article/us-netherlands-france-klm-air-france/dutch-government-takes-stake-in-air-france-klm-finance-minister-idUSKCN1QF2J3

Voeth, M. & Herbst, U. (2015). *Verhandlungsmanagement: Planung, Steuerung und Analyse.* Schäffer-Poeschel.

White, S., & Louet, S. (2018, May 6). French government urges Air France to pursue reforms as strikes bite. Retrieved from Reuters: https://www.reuters.com/article/us-air-france-klm-government/french-government-urges-air-france-to-pursue-reforms-as-strikes-bite-idUSKBN1I70AU

Whitney, C. R. (1998, June 11). Air France pilots settle strike, accepting 7-year pay freeze. Retrieved December 18, 2019, from The New York Times: https://www.nytimes.com/1998/06/11/world/air-france-pilots-settle-strike-accepting-7-year-pay-freeze.html

5
WALT DISNEY'S ACQUISITION OF 21ST CENTURY FOX

Valentin Steinhauser, Georgia Sofia Botsis, and Robin-Resham Singh

> ### KEY OBJECTIVE OF THE CASE STUDY
>
> *The key objective of this case study is for the student to identify four main reasons for the uncomplicated conduct of the negotiation between two industry giants, which easily could have spun out of hand.*

Introduction

Indeed, the Walt Disney Company has been on a literal shopping spree. After buying Pixar in 2004, Marvel in 2006, Lucasfilm in 2012, it recently completed its biggest and most complex acquisition. In March 2019, Disney closed a deal with 21st Century Fox [21CF]. The size of the deal becomes clear by just looking at the sum Disney has invested. The three main acquisitions set them back at a total of $15.7 billion. 21CF cost the media giant almost five times as much: roughly $71.3 billion.

While the intentions behind the previous three purchases were to mainly acquire movie franchises like Star Wars, characters from the Marvel Cinematic Universe and production capabilities as in the case of Pixar, the latest acquisition of 21st Century Fox also serves as a long-term oriented maneuver for Disney, creating opportunities for it to expand its streaming business into Europe and Asia.

Bob Iger, Walt Disney's CEO and world-famous negotiator, has executed all of Disney's acquisitions since 2004. The 21CF merger has been his last big project. He even decided to withdraw his position as CEO in order to oversee and safeguard the post-acquisition integration of 21CF until the end of the year 2021.

This chapter will first elucidate the general market situation in the entertainment industry and expound both parties' intentions regarding the acquisition. Second, the detailed procedure of the negotiation will be described with a timeline including the side deal around Sky and Hulu before concluding with the end result of the negotiation. Third, the negotiation will be analyzed in depth with the five steps of the NGM model (negotiation management model). Finally, the conclusion will reflect the entire negotiation and its effects.

Pre-negotiation

The following section will describe the general market situation as well as the challenges the entertainment industry faced at the time of the negotiation. Furthermore, it will deal with both sides intentions before entering the negotiation process.

Market situation

The entertainment industry has changed tremendously during the last decades. Thanks to the digitalization, billions of people are now able to stream entertainment content practically anywhere and anytime. With the rise of YouTube, Netflix, Amazon Prime, HBO and others came the collapse of physical video distributers like Blockbuster. Shortly after, cinemas and TV networks saw their audience decline and profits shrunk that had a striking effect on movie production companies.

Fuelled by the fear of further declining box office revenues and financial difficulties, this change in the industry has promoted rapid consolidation growth and mergers of big production companies in the recent years (Schwartzel & Flint, 2019). AT&T Inc. acquired Time Warner in June 2018, Comcast invested in their NBCUniversal and Universal Pictures subdivisions and purchased the animation studio DreamWorks. CBS and Viacom just merged in December 2019.

With increasing numbers of more diverse consumers, companies must expand their portfolio of franchises and characters and exploit them the right way. Disney for example knows how to make the most revenue out of their assets with its reliable different business models: On top of producing shows and movies it also incorporates their characters and universes into their theme parks, sells toys and capitalizes on consumer product licensing (Schwartzel & Flint, 2019). A successful strategy that its competitors have copied, but that cannot secure the long-term survival of Disney with the change in fundamental trends in this industry.

Disney's strategy

In recent years, Disney followed a pioneering "direct-to-consumer" strategy that strives to increase its library of films and shows, further expand the production capacity in order roll out even more content and establish ways to deliver their content to consumers all around the world (Faber, 2017). The direct-to-consumer strategy is considered to be the main driver of the deal and culminates in a diverse streaming service that offers far more content than its rivals (Schwartzel & Flint, 2019). The final product consists of three essential pillars:

The first being its family-oriented service Disney+ that offers content from Disney, Pixar, Marvel, National Geographic and Lucasfilm. It launched in mid-November 2019 in North America, Oceania and the Netherlands. Most remaining European countries are set to follow by the end of March 2020 (Faber, 2017).

The second pillar consists of their sports network ESPN that was launched in 2018. The regional TV networks of 21CF will complement the more national structure of ESPN, meaning that more local content will be added to ESPN while the regional networks will get more national sports content from ESPN (Faber, 2017).

The final pillar is a more adult-oriented service named Hulu that will offer content that does not fit into Disney's family friendly image (Faber, 2017). Disney already owned 30% of the company's shares before the acquisition with 21CF and Comcast each holding an additional 30% and Time Warner (later AT&T) possessing the remaining 10% that it later sold to Disney and Comcast.

In addition, the three platforms will all share one consumer acquisition and retention system as well as the same technological engine to cut costs (Faber, 2017). The price strategy is set as a bundle and available for $12.99, the same price as its biggest competitor Netflix (Clark, 2019).

Disney is joining a very contested market almost a decade later than its competitors so it must catch up and add an additional offering. Netflix for example, was able to steadily build its consumer base and reinvest into its production capacities churning out more and more "Netflix Originals." Iger, Disney's last CEO was very aware of Disney's competitive disadvantage regarding content production in both quantity and quality as well as its profitable distribution, he expressed: "Consumers are consuming far more content and entertainment experiences than ever before. Quality really matters but so does the means of access. It has to be user-friendly, […] navigable [and] accessible in frictionless ways" (Faber, 2017).

In order to have a chance against established rivals in the highly saturated market, Disney faced the need to win new customers. Since it has been offering its pre-existing content through the platforms of its rivals, it started pulling most of its movies and shows off these sites to make them available on its own streaming services exclusively, hoping to rake in more profits and stealing loyal Disney customers from its competitors (Schwartzel & Flint, 2019). However, this was not sufficient, as the company also had to acquire new customers in both Europe and the United States but especially in unchartered territories. The latter would be more accessible to Disney without 21CF's knowledge and assets in content delivery in Asia and India, specifically the Star India and Tata Sky network. Apart from building valuable networks in Asia, Fox has also mastered online content delivery in Europe through British Sky Broadcasting [Sky].

21st Century Fox's intentions to sell to Disney

Due to the changes in the media industry, Fox had suffered from stagnant and declining revenues in recent years. By selling valuable assets to its competitor, Fox and Rupert Murdoch got a chance to rid themselves of a business unit that, in light of the anticipated death of the cinema industry, was predestined to generate less profits that would eventually have to be offset by disinvestments. The Fox Corporation is left with assets and content believed to be less threatened by online ads and streaming, giving the Murdoch family (21CF's main shareholders) an opportunity to reorient their business and set a new focus. Analysts at Moffett Nathanson also pointed out that 21CF had to rethink its asset mix regarding their weak content output during the last few years (BBC, 2017).

Fox shareholders – especially the Murdoch's with their 39% ownership – will profit from the deal in the future due to the fact they sold their company for both stock and cash (BBC, 2017). 21CF additionally does not want to see its characters be discontinued, while Disney offers them an opportunity for them to keep their reputation. There were rumors that Rupert Murdoch's son James would take over a position at Disney (BBC, 2017). Although he later decided not to join, the rumors were taken very seriously since it would not have been unlikely for him to take over as Disney's CEO in order to replace Iger after his retirement in 2021 (Barnes, 2018; BBC, 2017).

Moreover, Fox could simply not refuse the deal. Their stock price has increased by 30% since the beginning of the negotiations (BBC, 2017). The company has been struggling for years after various scandals regarding Fox News, Rupert Murdoch's right-wing political position, his newspapers' hacking attacks on celebrities and politicians as well as a failed acquisition of Time Warner in 2014 (BBC, 2017; Heise, 2018).

Negotiation procedure

This section will sum up the negotiations and the process of the deal that took place from the Summer of 2017 until March 2019. The involvement of Comcast regarding Sky and Hulu will be examined before the outcomes and effects of the deal for both parties will be laid out.

Description of major events

Discussions began in Summer 2017 at a Los Angeles winery owned by Rupert Murdoch. Him and Iger had casual meeting and talked about the disruptive forces present in the market. Iger had the impression that Murdoch would be open to shifting Fox's focus and orientation. He later called Murdoch to ask if he would consider a merger or an acquisition of Fox's assets by Disney. Murdoch decided to take some time investigate the benefits of such a deal while Disney crunched the numbers in order to come back to him with a concrete offer (Faber, 2017).

The first media reports of Disney's motives to buy Fox date back to early November 2017. Shortly after the official announcement in mid-December, Comcast, Sony and Verizon expressed their interest in Fox and joined the bidding war forming strategic alliances in order to grow stronger. Comcast, who later proved to be Disney's biggest competitor in the race, initially withdrew its bid in order to evaluate the potential benefits of the acquisition (Shaw-Williams, 2019).

Shortly after, Disney publicly announced its first all-stock offer of $52.4 billion ($28 per share) in December 2017 (Gartenberg, 2018). On December 14, 2017, the two companies already announced to have reached a "definitive agreement" on Disney's acquisition of 21CF's entertainment division, its stock in Sky and Hulu as well as its TV business (Shaw-Williams, 2019). That deal would exclude Fox News and Fox Broadcasting and was still far from being sealed but it concretized that assets Disney would acquire.

Comcast, considered to be Disney's archnemesis, also wanted to build an online streaming service and was thus interested in the same assets, most importantly the stakes in Hulu and Sky as well as the TV channels and 20th Century Fox (Welch, 2018). At the time of Disney's and 21CF's negotiations, the merger of AT&T and Time Warner was examined by the U.S. Department of Justice [DOJ]. Concluding that such a deal would be anti-competitive and break antitrust laws lead to the DOJ filing a lawsuit. (Hood, 2018; Lecher, 2018). The issue directly impacted Disney, 21CF and the other bidders, leaving all parties worried whether a deal would be approved by the authorities. Disney also entered a tremendous regulatory risk, since they would have to pay a reverse breakup fee of $2.5 billion if the antitrust authorities refused a deal (Faber, 2017). A U.S. federal judge finally ruled to allow the merger on June 12, 2018 (Lecher, 2018). The following morning Comcast immediately announced an all-cash counteroffer of $65 billion ($35 per share) after already meeting with investment banks in May 2018 in order to secure enough financial backing (Hood, 2018; Welch, 2018). If Fox had chosen to abandon the negotiations with Disney, they would owe them 1.525 billion, which Comcast offered to cover if the Murdoch's decided to merge with them (Welch, 2018).

The offer was topped just a week later by Disney on June 20, 2018, with $71.3 billion ($38 per share) (Gartenberg, 2018). Although Comcasts all-cash offer might have been more appealing to the Murdoch's, Disney now offered 21CF stockholders the choice to receive their part of the sale in the form of either cash or Disney stock instead of their previous all-stock offer. Comcast officially withdrew its $65 billion bid, left 21CF to Disney and said it would shift its focus on acquiring Sky (Comcast Corporation, 2018; Gartenberg, 2018).

In a statement, 21CF called Disney's offer "superior" and Rupert Murdoch commented: "We remain convinced that the combination of 21CF's iconic assets, brands and franchises with Disney's will create one of the greatest, most innovative companies in the world" (Williams, 2018). Although the board of Fox was still concerned that the deal could be scuttled by regulators, it decided to send out a letter to its shareholders at the end of June, containing detailed information about the upcoming acquisition (Bacon, 2018; Shaw-Williams, 2019; Welch, 2018). One month later, on July 27, 2018, 21CF's shareholders voted to accept the deal (Shaw-Williams, 2019).

The deal was approved by the U.S. Department of Justice on July 27, 2018, after just one month compared to AT&T's monthlong struggle. Nevertheless, several countries still had to approve the deal in order for it to move forward. China, one of the last major regulatory hurdles, granted its approval on November 19, 2018 (Shaw-Williams, 2019). The completion of the deal was briefly interrupted by the U.S. federal government shutdown in December and January (Schwartzel & Flint, 2019). In a conference call on February 5, 2019, Iger stated that Disney and Fox would be starting to "effectively combining [their] businesses" as soon as the final few markets granted approval (Shaw-Williams, 2019).

He says that him and Murdoch both are pleased with the price and the assets they agreed on although the terms were somewhat delicate. Iger was pleasantly surprised and expected the negotiations to last much longer than just a few months (Faber, 2017).

Comcast's strategy and the side deal

21CF held 39% of shares of Sky and Rupert Murdoch initially planned to acquire the rest of it before merging with Disney (Shaw-Williams, 2019). Iger, who called Sky "a crown jewel," supported the Murdoch's efforts for the acquisition (de la Merced, 2018). Comcast and Murdoch have been in a bidding war for Sky since 2010. Murdoch's attempts were obstructed multiple times by regulators and his media scandals, specifically the News International phone hacking scandal (BBC, 2017; Heise, 2018). Sky would offer the opportunity for both Disney and Comcast to expand their streaming business and conquer new markets in Europe (Welch, 2018).

While still bidding for Sky, Comcast joined the bidding war in order to acquire 21CF's stock in Sky as well as their Asian TV network with Tata Sky and Star India and thus made its all-cash offer. Disney followed with a counteroffer that exceeded its original all-stock offer by $18 billion and would be paid in equal parts stock and cash. Instead of raising its bid and having to secure more financial backing, Comcast decided to withdraw from the race and focus on the ongoing battle over Sky.

On September 20, 2018, British regulators ordered an auction for Sky, giving Fox and Comcast a chance to make new bids (Waterson, 2018). Two days later Comcast emerged the winner of the battle with its final offer of $39 billion on September 22, 2018 (Barnes & Lee, 2018a). It gained a remarkable European outpost and could now pose a serious threat for Disney since it also owns NBCUniversal in addition to a remarkable array of franchises that compliments Sky's shows and sports network (de la Merced, 2018).

Despite this enormous setback for Iger and Murdoch, losing a tremendous European customer base to one of its biggest competitors, they would not give up and refused to leave the table empty handed (Barnes & Lee, 2018b). Just one week later, on September 26, 2019, they announced that 21CF would sell its 39% of Sky shares to Comcast for a total of $15 billion (Barnes & Lee, 2018b). 21CF sold them on behalf of Disney, which also got the proceeds of the sale (Barnes & Lee, 2018b). Instead of entering yet another bidding war, Disney decided to sell the shares at same price Comcast paid for them at the auction, most likely keeping in mind that Comcast still owned 30% of Hulu, one of Disney's most important pillars in their direct-to-consumer strategy. The distribution of content in Europe would have been far easier for Disney if they had managed to acquire Sky since it was already widely known and had an impressive consumer base.

Nevertheless, after increasing its ownership of Hulu from 30% to 60% by acquiring 21CF's stakes, it managed to make a side deal with Comcast, most likely connected to Disney selling 21CF's stock in Sky to them. This deal allowed Disney to take over full control over Hulu. Comcast agreed to sell its remaining shares to Disney in 2024. All NBC Universal shows (owned by Comcast) will stay available on the platform, making it even more attractive for potential customers and giving Disney enough time to produce content to fill the gap, once it buys out Comcast in 2024.

Disney made the best out of the lost battle for Sky and might have even ended up with a better result since it gained full control over Hulu and was able to keep all the content owned by Comcast. The latter can now focus on its own streaming service while still profiting from the work Disney will be doing until 2024. If Disney had acquired both Sky and 21CF, Comcast would have had a hard time competing with Disney in the European market. In the end, consumers will probably benefit from this new situation as well since the competition between the two media giants will most likely drive content development and a price war.

End result

The merger reduced the Big Six Hollywood studios down to the Big Five (Disney, Universal, Warner Bros. Entertainment, Sony Pictures Entertainment and Paramount Pictures) with Disney now controlling almost 40% of the box office (Shaw-Williams, 2019).

Key assets acquired by Disney were Hulu (30%), National Geographic (73%), 20th Century Fox, Star TV, Tata Sky (30%), FX Productions and the Fox Networks Group. Disney also purchased all of Fox's TV assets except the Fox Broadcasting Company, Fox News Channel, and several other smaller TV networks which are now managed by the newly founded Fox Corporation. The 20th Century Fox studio lot was also not sold and will be rented out to other content producers like Netflix or Amazon. Although Disney did acquire Fox's regional sports networks, it is obliged to sell them to a third parties in order to comply with the conditions set by the DOJ. The European Commission also ruled that Disney had to sell A&E Networks Europe. Several other assets like the 50% stake in the Endemol Shine Group had to be divested as well (Shaw-Williams, 2019).

According to Iger, Disney gets high quality content, global reach, production capabilities, access to new technologies, markets and talent out of the deal (Faber, 2017).

The deal made the Murdoch family, previously major shareholder of 21CF, Disney's second biggest shareholder with a 25% stake in the company. According to Forbes, Rupert Murdoch's net worth has risen from $14.1 billion on December 13, 2017 when the two parties first announced the deal to $18.4 billion on March 20, 2019 after the deal was closed (Berg, 2019).

Analysts speculate that the Murdoch's are positioning themselves to take over Disney, possibly already in the coming years when current CEO Bob Iger is planning to retire. Nevertheless, these rumors are partially refuted because James Murdoch, former CEO of 21CF, who was initially anticipated to join Disney in a high-ranking position, decided to separate from his former company (Barnes, 2018; BBC, 2017).

The negotiation management model: an in-depth analysis

In order to better understand the steps that lead to the final deal between Disney and 21CF, this section will present a deeper analysis of the negotiation steps using the negotiation management model (NGM) (Herbst & Voeth, 2015, pp. 149–151). Due to the secrecy that comes along with such deals the following analysis is composed of facts revealed in the media and assumptions concluded along.

Negotiation analysis

Crossnegotiation analysis

In order to start analyzing the cross negotiation, one must first look at the significance of the resulting negotiation. In this case the negotiation is very high in significance for both parties. One can see the significance with the economic power of the deal in the long-term changes the negotiation would lead to. Indeed, Disney needed a change in its strategy in order to a adapt to the changes in the movie industry environment and fulfill the three different main market segments in the movie industry. As previously mentioned, Disney had already completed three big purchases before entering the negotiation with 21CF. The motives behind the previous three deals were mainly to acquire movie franchises or production capabilities. Thus, the aim of the conclusion of this contract was acquiring 21CF's core competencies in the streaming and technological advantage.

The deal differs from Disney's previous negotiations since in the case the two companies work toward the same goal but remain independent in their core competencies and structure. Disney needed this deal to go through in order to follow up with the new strategy that had to be incorporated within the company in order to keep its strong market share. On the other side, 21CF was not doing great either. The company had been facing losses during the past year and it would either have to divest assets or rid themselves of the ones that were not profitable anymore. Nevertheless, not all assets of 21CF were acquired. The remaining assets were spun off into Fox Corporation. Therefore, it is technically considered a merger. Nevertheless, a respectable amount of assets was transferred to the Fox Corporation right before Disney merged with 21CF. The latter still owned these assets during the negotiation, so it can also be viewed as an acquisition of the original 21CF's assets.

The brand reputation Disney owns due to its consumer image and horizontal diversification in products and services leads to the assumption that Disney partly had the power on this negotiation.

Thus, Disney did face some competition during the conclusion of the deal from Comcast, which had also placed a bid for 21CF but later withdrew the offer in order to better analyze the companies' situation (Shaw-Williams, 2019). Despite Comcast posing a threat to the competition in acquiring 21CF, Disney's strategy and offer as well as Iger's relationship with the Murdoch family were stronger, leaving Disney in the power position.

In addition, Disney's negotiation history has proven to be successful. The deals it has closed so far were very strategic, and the investment was always within the scope and followed up with good returns quickly. Such history also gives an additional power to Disney for the negotiation of such.

Finally, there were no fundamental changes of circumstances in the important environments where and when the negotiation took place. Thus, in order to protect the stakeholders affected, fundamental agreements must have taken place in order to safeguard viability in the future. Usually, in order to safeguard such security for the stakeholders, the actors put in place a negotiation portfolio to understand the model and take the necessary steps to change the environments. The investigation must be done and taken into consideration for all subparts of the company where important actors may be affected, such portfolios don't only protect the actors but also give a directive outline on the common goals such have to focus on in order for the post negotiation situation to be sustainable.

Negotiation-related analysis

The negotiation-related analysis looks at the main actors of the negotiation from and what the original subjects of negotiation rise from in depth. In order to do so we will analyze what is in the hands of one party as a "we" and in the hands of our negotiation opponent as a "them."

This part will introduce an in-depth analysis on the negotiation in order to close a deal that both firms would agree on. In order to do so, one must understand the importance of the consequences of the deal for each respective firm.

Bob Iger, CEO of the Walt Disney Company and world-famous negotiator executed all of Disney's acquisitions since 2004. In this case he was the only representative of Disney and lead the most important steps of the negotiation under the companies' name.

The opposite partners of the present negotiation are the principal shareholders of 21CF being the Murdoch family. The company is primarily family owned and the management is passed by through generations. The CEO of the company at the time was Lachlan Murdoch but it has already been expressed that the patriarch of the family, Rupert Murdoch will run the business in the future. The result and consequences and some burdens of the negotiation will be carried by the next generation. Therefore, the deal must be sustainable for the long-term reputation and survival of the company.

Many negotiation processes do face distributivity until a final deal is accepted by all parties. This deal faced different prices before the final contract. Such may be explained by the ongoing side deals that were happening while the negotiation between Disney and 21CF took place and the DOJ not accepting the first terms of the deal. One should keep in mind that the longer the negotiation or the project at hand takes, the more costly it becomes. One should also make sure they don't lose money and power by making a negotiation longer and if one does so assure that the end result of the negotiation will allow to position oneself with more advantages.

Side deals often come along major negotiations, especially in the important corporate deal. The side deal that has mainly influenced this acquisition is Comcast trying to acquire Sky and later also trying to acquire 21CF, partially because of their 39% stake in Sky. The fact the Murdochs had not achieved to find a conclusive deal for the merger or acquisition of both was a burden that Disney was willing to take even if it meant it had to find its way into the European market by other means.

Furthermore, one must also take into consideration if any restrictions could affect the scope of the negotiation. The scope of the negotiation may be affected if one party decides to exclude some previously set criteria from the negotiation or some things may be split down immediately. We take out of the negotiation whatever item is not useful and might become too time consuming for the relevant negotiation. Fox still developed projects in case the negotiations took longer, or no agreement was reached. But it was illegal for Fox to work on projects with Disney before the deal was made because it would have resulted to regulatory issues or fines (Hood, 2018).

Negotiation organization

In this part, the aim is to understand how the negotiation was organized to achieve a sustainable path in order to arrive at its end goal in the planned time.

Influencing the opposite team

In such deals, there are often statutory rules of game that join the negotiation due to the fact that the negotiation wishes to settle price and assets.

The principal team being Disney, starts by questioning themselves who they shall negotiate with to gain access, in the case at hand both CEOs meeting at a winery for their first discussion is not a coincidence. Bob Iger wanted to introduce the idea to Rupert Murdoch in a pleasant environment and get a better insight on the situation of 21CF. 21CF was selling a part of their brand and thus the brand reputation was at stake, both companies wanting to keep their good reputation in their customers mind in addition to acquire more customers needed to make sure the deal goes down smoothly in order not to cause any scandals that could affect their customers or partners.

Staffing the negotiation team

While a serious negotiation takes place, one has to make sure they undertake the process positioning themselves with the most advantage possible. In order to do so the teams who undertake the deals must be selected. Such selection may be within the company or outsourced by hiring consultants, mediators, arbitrators or delegators. The Disney and 21CF deal did not need to hire and external consultants that investigates the strategies behind the deal. The change in strategy the companies aimed for was set before the deal, merging was merely the last step for both parties. A bigger negotiation team usually results in a lower performance. This can be considered to be an additional advantage of the negotiation between Disney and 21CF. It also affected the duration of the negotiations positively.

Furthermore, the sociodemographic, psychographic, organizational, situational circumstances, gender and country culture specific subareas may play a role in the negotiation. In this case the negotiation process took place within the United States and the United Kingdom by two men in similar positions in two respective companies that worked in the same industry. The fact that the two main parties of the negotiation were so similar, allowed for a very smooth communication during the negotiation. Furthermore, since there was no major power difference among both partners the risks coming along with decisions reflecting ego problems did not occur.

Division of tasks and management of negotiation teams

As with many mergers and acquisitions, a large part of information remains secretive in order to protect both parties in the deal. The negotiation was in the hands of the principle leaders of both countries. Nevertheless, a deal like this cannot be closed by just two men. In order to conclude such a contract, the actors had to outsource and get advice from many corporate lawyers and required the expertise of investment banks. For Disney to set the prices and terms of contract they hired the Guggenheim Partners and JP Morgan that helped to do the price valuation. On the other side, 21CF hired Goldman Sachs and Centerview Partners as sales advisors (Haggerty, 2018).

Place, duration and procedure of the hearing

In order to conclude a deal with such great importance, solely one hearing is not sufficient. Apart from the first meeting at the winery being public, the rest of the negotiations remain very secretive to this day. Thus, the deal was closed way faster than both parties expected. 21CF being primarily family owned and the low number of participants in the negotiation allowed for decisions to happen at a faster pace. As previously mentioned in the timeline the deal solely took a few months, which is very rare for a deal of such importance and with such a big impact. Despite AT&T having issues with the DOJ, the Disney and 21CF deal was approved in a timely manner. Many hypotheses are claimed for the reasons of such a rapid disclosure but the most probable assumption one may conclude is that the negotiation teams were set early and both Iger and Murdoch had the same vision.

Negotiation preparation

The next subtask of the negotiation management is the negotiation preparation. According to Thompson (2005, as cited in Herbst & Voeth, 2015, p. 147), the negotiation preparation is four times as significant as the following negotiation itself. Nevertheless, its effects are mostly highly underestimated. The main objective of the negotiation preparation is to work out a plan for one's own behavior during the negotiation, but it must also try to predict the behavior of the opposite site as accurately as possible (Herbst & Voeth, 2015, p. 147). In this part, the negotiation preparation is analyzed with different concepts from this subtask.

Motives, objectives and strategies

The first concept that will be adapted from the negotiation preparation subtask shows the relationship between the motives, the objectives and the strategies of the negotiation. The negotiation objectives are the results, that a party wants to achieve in the end of a negotiation. These objectives can either be end results or process results. On the other hand, there are negotiation motives. The motive is the greater purpose behind the objectives, for example, the long-term vision of a company. When the motives of your negotiation partner are known, it is possible to derive the objectives from them, which can lead to an enormous advantage during the negotiation. The last aspect, the negotiation strategy, is the way from the motives to the results. It is not an accurately worked-out plan, but rather a general guideline. The detailed negotiation strategy of both Disney and 21CF will not be analyzed extensively in this part, since it will be covered in part 4.4 (Herbst & Voeth, 2015, pp. 149–151).

Disney had several different motives to acquire the different parts from 21CF. One of the main motives for Disney was to expand its direct-to-consumer strategy (see part 2.2). With the acquisition of 21CF and especially Hulu, Disney was able to gain an adequate market share in the fast-growing and highly competitive direct-to-consumer market. Especially with the synergies from its content, Disney hoped to reach an acceptable market share. Disney's CEO Iger expressed, that such will be vital in the media business in the future (Bhargava & Hovenkamp, 2018). Another motive, that goes together with the motive to strengthen the direct-to-consumer market, is to gain control over additional content. If this content is added to the streaming service, Disney could win even more customers (LicenseGlobal, 2018). From these motives, the objectives for Disney can be derived. Disney's main objective was to gain control especially over 21CF's streaming service Hulu and a broad range of content for the least possible price. This shows that mainly result objectives were important for Disney.

As well as Disney, 21CF had several motives to enter the negotiation. Since several parts of its business suffered from declining revenues, it had the possibility to focus on its parts which are less affected by the direct-to-consumer trend. Another motive, at least for the main shareholder of 21CF, the Murdoch family, were the shares of the Disney company, which they got through the acquisition. The possibility of James Murdoch becoming the future Disney CEO might have been another argument to sell large parts of 21CF. However, the main motive was that Disney's offer was simply too good to refuse, especially considering the declining revenues and the fact that 21CF's stock price had increased tremendously since the public was informed about the negotiation (BBC, 2017). For 21CF, the main objective of the negotiation was to achieve a high price. It was essential, especially for the Murdoch family, that the price would be paid at least partially in shares. In addition to this result objective, it can be assumed that 21CF and the Murdochs also had a process objective during the negotiation in the form of the importance put on having a relation-oriented and cooperative negotiation, hoping to reduce friction and problems when becoming Disney's major shareholder.

The SMART-requirement

According to Herbst and Voeth (2015, p. 153), the objectives should follow the SMART-formula, meaning that the goals for the negotiation should be specific, measurable, acceptable, realistic and tough.

Since Disney's objective was to purchase 21CF and mainly its entertainment business, the objective was specific. Disney paid the price in both cash and stock. Since stocks have a certain value it makes them a measurable unit, the criteria of measurability was fulfilled. The fact that 21CF agreed to Disney's offer shows that it was acceptable for both parties. The price Disney paid was in the range of the share price and higher than the offers from other interested parties, making the offer realistic. Considering that Disney offered this price also shows that 21CF demanded price was not exaggerated. It can also be assumed that both main negotiators, Bob Iger and Rupert Murdoch, had ambitious and tough goals, since both are experienced and hard negotiators (Miller, 2015).

The bargaining zone

The range, within which a price can be negotiated, is called the bargaining zone. To determine the bargaining zone, the term reservation price must be introduced. It is the worst outcome, that would still be acceptable for one party. The opposite is the aspiration price, which is the best possible option that the opposite side would realistically accept. A negotiation can only be successful if the reservation price of the buyer is higher than the reservation price of the seller. Otherwise there is no bargaining zone and no agreement can be reached. Ideally, the own aspiration price is equal to the reservation price of the other party. A broader bargaining zone increases the possibility that an agreement can be reached (Herbst & Voeth, 2015, pp. 157–160).

The fact that the negotiation between Disney and 21CF was successful shows that there was a bargaining zone in the negotiation. Disney's aspiration price was most likely the price it offered in their first bid which was $52.4 billion (Shaw-Williams, 2019). Disney's reservation price can only be estimated, because it leaked no information about the maximum price it was willing to pay for the assets. However, it must have been at least the $71.3 billion it paid for 21CF in the end. Neither the aspiration, nor the reservation price of 21CF can be determined with absolute certainty. Even though it looks as if the first offer over $52.4 billion was lower than the reservation price, it is also possible that 21CF did not accept the offer out of tactical reasons. This means that their reservation price could have been below Disney's aspiration price. What can certainly be said is that the reservation price of 21CF was below Disney's reservation price, and that the result of $71.3 billion lied between them.

BATNA analysis

The reservation price is often equal to the BATNA, which stands for the Best Alternative to Negotiated Agreement. An option is only an alternative, when it is certain that the option exists. If the result of a negotiation is less satisfying than the BATNA of a party, it should leave the negotiation and make use of their best alternative. If the BATNA of the opposite side is known, the party can better prepare for the negotiation and thus gain an advantage. The reason for this is that an offer slightly above the other party's BATNA can be made without making unnecessary concessions. In addition, it makes bluffing for the other side almost impossible. Since the BATNA has such an impact on the end result, having a good BATNA is essential in every negotiation (Herbst & Voeth, 2015, pp. 161–162).

Since Disney's motive was to strengthen its direct-to-consumer business and expand its content, it had the possibilities to develop the competences themselves or to acquire a company that already had these competences. Finding a company like 21CF that is willing to sell to Disney was very unlikely since the only comparable options were to acquire one of the remaining Big Six Hollywood studios. This means, that Disney's best alternative was to develop the competences themselves. The fact that it raised their bid from $52.4 billion to $71.3 billion without much hesitation leads to the assumption that developing the competences themselves would have been even more expensive and time consuming (Shaw-Williams, 2019). Summarized it can be said that Disney's BATNA was rather a bad one compared to the actual deal made.

21CF on the other hand, had a more concrete BATNA: selling to Comcast. In addition to its $65 billion all-cash offer, Disney's competitor would have even covered the breakup fees, making it a real alternative for 21CF (Sherman, 2018). Comcast made a public offer, so it could have been assumed that Disney's counteroffer would be just slightly higher than $65 billion. But since Comcast might have responded in a similar way, this would have led to an even more intense bidding war, continuously strengthening 21CF's BATNA. To avoid this, Disney overbid Comcast by more than $6 billion (Palmeri, 2019). In contrast to Disney's best alternative, 21CF's BATNA was certainly more powerful, despite the fact it was well known by Disney.

Relation-oriented approach

A relation-oriented approach is part of the process objectives and is used to make not just the result itself, but also the way to it successful. According to Herbst and Voeth (2015), the relation-oriented approach consists of factors such as co-operativeness, honesty and fairness. The relation-oriented approach is also strongly connected with the cooperation strategy, which is one of the four basic negotiation strategies. In a cooperation strategy, the significance of both the own and the partners interest, is high (Herbst & Voeth, 2015, pp. 174–177).

In the Disney-21CF negotiation, a relation-oriented approach was used. Already the fact that the first meeting was held at Murdoch's winery in Bel-Air is a sign for the friendly atmosphere of the negotiation (Littleton, 2017). According to MasterClass (2019), Iger likes to negotiate with all cards on the table. He is known for his honest and candid negotiation style, which leads to a more time efficient result in end because the time can be spent on more important things. In an interview, Iger described the negotiation as smooth and cordial (Faber, 2017). He even mentions that Murdoch and he liked and respected each other already before the start of the negotiation (Littleton, 2017). These are strong indications for a relation-oriented negotiation approach. In the end, the openness of the negotiation was also key for the fast agreement between the two parties.

First offer

One of the most important parts in the negotiation preparation is the first offer. The reason being is that first offer works as a cognitive anchor, to which all following offers are compared to. For the party receiving the first offer it is recommended to reply as rapidly as possible with an answer or a counteroffer, in order to weaken the effect of the anchor (Herbst & Voeth, 2015, pp. 181–183).

Disney was the party making the first offer in the negotiation. It made its all-stock offer on December 14, 2017. Because both Disney and 21CF were uncertain if the deal would be approved by the DOJ, the two companies could not seal the deal immediately, giving the anchor of the first offer time to settle until Comcasts bid in June weakened the effect of Disney's first offer (Shaw-Williams, 2019).

Concessions

When the first offer is not accepted by the other party, concessions must be made to reach an agreement. According to Herbst and Voeth (2015, S. 184), things that are not as relevant for one party as for the other party should be given up first.

Especially after Comcast's bid for 21CF, which was more than $12 billion above Disney's offer, Disney had to make concessions. Its second offer was significantly higher than the first one. Disney raised the price from the initial $52.4 billion directly to $71.3 billion. The reason for this extraordinary rise was to outbid Comcast in the first place, but also to minimize the amount of further concessions (Palmeri, 2019). Another concession made by Disney was to change its all-stock offer into a bid with both cash and stock (Hayes, 2019). Disney additionally had to agree to sell 22 regional sport channels to third parties after the acquisition to get approval for the deal by the DOJ (Mitchell, 2018). Since Fox had the possibility to accept the Comcast offer, it was in a more comfortable position and had to make less concessions.

Conduct of negotiation

This part covers the negotiation itself. This includes not only the result, but also how it was reached. The way the result is reached should economically be as efficient as possible while still leading to the best possible outcome (Herbst & Voeth, 2015, p. 195). The focus of this part is on the offer design, the negotiation style and the negotiation tactics.

Offer design

According to Herbst and Voeth (2015, p. 199) every offer can be designed in two ways. The first possibility is that each component of the deal is negotiated on its own. This can be useful when a large information asymmetry exists, but it also leads to a more complicated negotiation. The other possibility is to make a package offer, where different components are bundled into one single offer. The main advantage of a package offer is that it is easier to make concessions and trade-offs. When there are too many components, usually more than three, included in one single bundle, it becomes difficult to keep an overview (Herbst & Voeth, 2015, pp. 199–201).

Looking at the negotiation between Disney and 21CF it becomes visible that both sides made a package offer. Disney offered Fox a package of two components, cash and stock, which were bundled together to an amount of $71.3 billion (Hayes, 2019). 21CF on the other hand sold Disney a package of its stake in Hulu, rights to different franchises and several TV networks (VanDerWerff, 2019). The number of components that 21CF offered was a lot higher than the recommended maximum of three, what made the negotiation difficult. But since an acquisition of a 71-billion-dollar-company is hardly ever a simple business, it did not make a big difference. One possible reason for the bundled offer is that the different components together were more valuable for Disney than each component on their own.

Negotiation style

Another aspect of the conduct of negotiation is the behavior during the negotiation, which is determined by different factors such as the negotiation experience or the type of the negotiation. Another important factor is how significant the own interests and the interests of the other party are. If the interest of both parties is insignificant, an avoiding negotiation style is used and confrontation is avoided. When only the own interest is significant, a dominant style is used, which can lead to confrontation and uncooperativeness. When only the interests of the other party are significant it is talked about a compliant negotiation style. This style can be used when the relationship with the negotiation partner is more important than the end result. The most successful negotiation style is usually the integrated style where the interests of both parties are highly significant. This style is characterized by cooperativeness (Herbst & Voeth, 2015, pp. 202–203).

Considering the relation-oriented approach that was used during the negotiation, it is most likely that an integrated style was used by Disney and 21CF (see part 4.3.5). They tried to reach a win-win situation with an acceptable result for both parties. The fact that they were ready to make compromises is also an indication for the integrated negotiation style (see part 4.3.7).

Furthermore, the two main negotiators, Robert Iger and Rupert Murdoch, had a reasonable impact on the negotiation style. Miller (2015) describes Iger as a fearless dealmaker that is experienced in the field of acquisitions. Murdoch was called a consummate dealmaker by Tryhorn (2007) and formidable negotiator by Sebenius (2019, p. 12). The long negotiation experience together with their honest and open negotiation style was certainly benefited their good relationship during the negotiation. A person close to Murdoch said that Murdoch loves Iger, despite their completely different politics (Hagey & Ramachandran, 2018). Both are also known to focus on long-term visions rather than short-term financial results (Sebenius, 2019, p. 6). The high hierarchy level of the two, together with their focus on the end results are additional indicators for the use of an integrated negotiation style (Herbst & Voeth, 2015, p. 209). The integrated style also led to a fast negotiation, especially considering the size of the two firms (Bhargava & Hovenkamp, 2018). However, the problems with the DOJ delayed the final agreement.

Negotiation tactics

One aspect closely linked to the negotiation behavior is the negotiation tactics. They have the objective to strengthen the own negotiation position and to reach a better end result. Examples for negotiation tactics are time games, bluffing, roleplay, promises or the use of derived powers, however, many more tactics exist (Herbst & Voeth, 2015, p. 212).

One possible tactic that was applied during the negotiation between Disney and 21CF was the use of promises. It is said that Rupert Murdoch's son James will succeed Iger as CEO of Disney, which would be a promise from Disney's side (BBC, 2017). However, James Murdoch later decided not to join Disney and started his own company.

After receiving the offer from Comcast, 21CF could have told Disney that Comcasts offered something they in reality did not. If this was the case, CF could have bluffed, however, there is no evidence for this. One indicator could be the second offer from Disney, which was a lot higher than Comcasts offer. But the fact that a relation-oriented negotiation approach was used leads to the assumption that tactics did not play a major role in the negotiation between Disney and Fox.

Negotiation controlling

The last part of the negotiation management is the negotiation controlling. The main objectives are to get information for future negotiation and to investigate if the outcome of the negotiation is as expected. When there are differences between the expected and the actual outcome, the reasons for these must be identified (Herbst & Voeth, 2015, p. 248).

One indicator for the success of the negotiation is Disney's stock performance. According to Littleton (2019), the negotiation result was acknowledged positively by the Wall Street. Since the acquisition, Disney's stock price increased by roughly a third (Finanzen.ch, 2019), meaning that most shareholders were satisfied with the result of the negotiation. 21CF offering their shareholders to choose whether they want to be paid in stock or cash was also a success. The shareholders that chose cash got a high price for their shares, the ones choosing Disney stock profited from their good performance since the acquisition. However, it is too early to comment on the long-term success of the negotiation. In the future, it will become visible if both, only one or even no party profited in the end. If a discrepancy between the actual and the expected result occurs, the reasons behind it must be investigated in order to minimize errors in the future.

Closing remarks

Negotiations occur in our daily tasks in order to position ourselves and the parties we represent in the most favorable position and get the wished outcome. In most negotiations, knowing the partner or the team we negotiate with allows for one to know how to act consequently. Knowing the precise goal, we are aiming for must also be set before the procedure takes place. Depending on the time the ongoing negotiation takes, changes in the environment must also be acknowledged and the person on the team negotiating must always be ready to act consequently and ready to make concessions if needed. In this case the negotiation was done in order to achieve a contract for Disney to acquire some of 21CF assets. Such deals affect many internal and external stakeholders of the company such as employees, customers, partners or shareholders. Furthermore, both companies have a strong brand image in their consumer minds with loyal customers that they cannot risk losing. One can see that the negotiation aimed at Disney acquiring new customers in different markets and complying with their direct-to-consumer strategy in order to compete with their strong rivals in the online streaming market that Disney entered very late.

Top learnings

The negotiation between Disney and 21CF happened in a very smooth way. The main reasons can be seen in the following aspects:

- *The fact that the negotiation mainly occurred among the companies' owner and CEO respectively allows the communication process to take place without a high probability of misunderstanding.*
- *The deal was made among two companies that were working in the same industry with assets that were easy to combine. This allowed both parties to know all the relevant frameworks to close a deal. The relevant environments important to both companies were well known by both parties, allowing them to solve whatever controversy occurred in a timely manner, such as the legal issues the deal faced from the DOJ.*
- *Both companies have a strong economic power allowing them to hire highly skilled external advisors in order to support them with the process of the negotiation.*
- *The time pressure was of importance for both parties, since both had to adapt their strategies within their environments in order to stay competitive in the rapidly changing market. Disney had to acquire know how in order to stay ahead of its competitors and 21CF was already facing losses. Such pressure obligates parties to settle for a deal that will allow them to survive putting many «ego» issues often arising in negotiation processes.*

References

Bacon, T. (2018, June 10). New Disney-Fox merger details emerge in shareholder letter. Screenrant. Retrieved from https://screenrant.com/disney-fox-merger-new-details/

Barnes, B. (2018, May 9). James Murdoch will not join Disney if Fox deal is completed. *The New York Times*. Retrieved December 3, 2019, from https://www.nytimes.com/2018/05/08/business/media/james-murdoch-disney-fox-deal.html

Barnes, B., & Lee, E. (2018a, September 23). In beating Disney for Sky, Comcast remains in the game. *The New York Times*. Retrieved December 8, 2019, from https://www.nytimes.com/2018/09/23/business/media/comcast-disney-sky.html

Barnes, B., & Lee, E. (2018b, September 26). Fox, acting on behalf of Disney, sells its stake in Sky to Comcast. *The New York Times*. Retrieved December 8, 2019, from https://www.nytimes.com/2018/09/26/business/media/sky-comcast-fox-disney.html

BBC. (2017, December 14). Five reasons for the Fox-Disney deal. BBC. Retrieved December 8, 2019, from https://www.bbc.com/news/business-42329731

Berg, M. (2019, March 20). What the Disney-Fox deal means For Rupert Murdoch's Fortune. *Forbes*. Retrieved December 18, 2019, from https://www.forbes.com/sites/maddieberg/2019/03/20/what-the-disney-fox-deal-means-for-rupert-murdochsfortune/#54bb8d34312e

Bhargava, H., & Hovenkamp, H. (2018, July 10). The Disney-Fox deal: Why it's about going directly to the consumer. Wharton University of Pennsylvania. Retrieved December 16, 2019, from https://knowledge.wharton.upenn.edu/article/the-impact-of-disney-fox/

Clark, T. (2019, September 6). We compared Netflix, Hulu, Amazon, and HBO to find the best service for every kind of viewer. Business Insider. Retrieved December 3, 2019, from https://www.businessinsider.com/netflix-vs-Hulu-vs-amazon-vs-hbo-which-is-better-2019-9?r=US&IR=T

Comcast Corporation. (2018, July 19). Comcast corporation statement on twenty-first Century Fox [Press release]. Retrieved December 8, 2019, from https://www.businesswire.com/news/home/20180719005432/en/Comcast-Corporation-Statement-Twenty-First-Century-Fox/

de la Merced, M. J. (2018, September 22). Comcast outbids Fox for control of British Broadcaster Sky. *The New York Times*. Retrieved December 8, 2019, from https://www.nytimes.com/2018/09/22/business/dealbook/comcast-beats-fox-for-control-of-british-broadcaster-sky.html

Faber, D. [CNBC]. (2017, December 14). Disney's Bob Iger Thought Fox Deal Was A 'Longshot' [Video file]. Retrieved December 3, 2019, from https://www.cnbc.com/video/2017/12/14/disneys-bob-iger-thought-fox-deal-was-a-longshot.html

Finanzen.ch. (2019). Walt Disney Aktie [stock data]. Retrieved December 16, 2019, from https://www.finanzen.ch/aktien/disney-aktie

Gartenberg, C. (2018, July 19). Comcast gives up on buying 21st Century Fox assets and leaves Disney as the winner. The Verge. Retrieved December 8, 2019, from https://www.theverge.com/2018/7/19/17590058/comcast-21st-century-fox-bid-withdrawn-disney-rights

Hagey, K., & Ramachandran, S. (2018, June 21). Two Titans' Rocky Relationship Stands Between Comcast and Fox. The Wall Street Journal. Retrieved December 16, 2019, from https://www.wsj.com/articles/standing-between-comcast-and-fox-media-titans-rocky-relationship-1529617091

Haggerty, R. (2018, November 13). Disney and Fox: How bankers merge giants. Medium. Retrieved December 13 from https://medium.com/banking-at-michigan/disney-and-fox-how-bankers-merge-giants-338b68d90f0d

Hayes, D. (2019, March 15). Fox shareholders favor getting cash over stock when Disney deal closes. Deadline. Retrieved December 16, 2019, from https://dead-line.com/2019/03/fox-shareholders-favor-getting-cash-over-stock-when-disney-deal-closes-1202576644/

Heise. (2018, June 5). Comcast vs. Fox: Britische Regierung macht Weg frei für Bieterwettbewerb um Sky. Heise. Retrieved December 8, 2019, from https://www.heise.de/newsticker/meldung/Comcast-vs-Fox-Britische-Regierung-macht-Weg-frei-fuer-Bieterwettbewerb-um-Sky-4069467.html

Herbst, U., & Voeth, M. (2015). *Verhandlungsmanagement: Planung, Steuerung und Analyse* (2nd ed.). Stuttgart: Schäffer-Poeschel Verlag.

Hood, C. (2018, May 7). Comcast takes first steps towards making another bid for Fox. Screenrant. Retrieved December 8, 2019, from https://screenrant.com/comcast-fox-bid-disney/

Lecher, C. (2018, June 12). AT&T and Time Warner can complete massive merger, judge rules. The Verge. Retrieved December 8, 2019, from https://www.theverge.com/2018/6/12/17452870/att-time-warner-merger-decision-judge

LicenseGlobal. (2018, April 6). What the Disney-Fox acquisition means for licensing. LicenseGlobal. Retrieved December 16, 2019 from https://www.licenseglobal.com/in-dustry-news/what-disney-fox-acquisition-means-licensing

Littleton, C. (2017, December 14). Disney-Fox Deal: How Secret, 'Smooth and Cordial' Negotiations Drove a Blockbuster Acquisition. Variety. Retrieved December 16, 2019, from https://variety.com/2017/biz/news/disney-fox-deal-bob-iger-rupert-murdoch-in-side-the-deal-1202641771/

MasterClass. (2019, November 14). Bob Iger's tips for successful negotiation. Masterclass. Retrieved December 16, 2019, from https://www.masterclass.com/articles/bob-igers-tips-for-successful-negotiation#quiz-1

Miller, D. (2015, June 6). How Robert Iger's 'fearless' deal-making transformed Disney. *Los Angeles Times*. Retrieved December 16, 2019, from https://www.latimes.com/entertainment/envelope/cotown/la-et-ct-disney-iger-20150607-story.html

Mitchell, R. (2018, October 15). Disney offers concessions to secure E.U. approval of Fox deal. Variety. Retrieved December 16, 2019, from https://variety.com/2018/film/news/disney-offers-concessions-calm-e-u-competition-concerns-over-fox-deal-1202980119/

Palmeri, C. (2019, November 15). Bob Iger Shares Tips on Negotiating Big Deals for Master-Class. Bloomberg. Retrieved December 16, 2019 from https://www.bloomberg.com/news/articles/2019-11-14/bob-iger-s-masterclass-includes-tips-on-negotiating-big-deals

Schwartzel, E., & Flint, J. (2019, March 20). Disney Closes $71.3 Billion Deal for 21st Century Fox Assets. Wallstreet Journal. Retrieved December 13, 2019, from https://www.wsj.com/articles/disney-completes-buy-of-foxs-entertainment-assets-11553074200

Sebenius, J. (2019). How Rupert Murdoch Outfoxed Larry Tisch: Ten Enduring Lessons from the Negotiations that Wrested the NFL from CBS. Harvard Business School. Retrieved December 16, 2019, from https://www.hbs.edu/faculty/Pages/item.aspx?num=55878

Shaw-Williams, H. (2019, February 9). A complete timeline of the Disney-Fox Deal. Screenrant. Retrieved December 13, 2019, from https://screenrant.com/disney-fox-deal-buyout-timeline/

Sherman, A. (2018, June 13). Comcast bids $65 billion for 21st Century Fox assets, topping Disney. CNBC. Retrieved December 16, 2019, from https://www.cnbc.com/2018/06/13/comcast-bids-65-billion-for-21st-century-fox-as-sets.html

Thompson, L. (2005). *The mind and heart of a negotiator* (3rd ed.). Upper Saddle River, NJ: Prentice-Hall.

Tryhorn, C. (2007, July 18). Rupert Murdoch – A lifetime of deals. The Guardian. Retrieved December 16, 2019, from https://www.theguardian.com/busi-ness/2007/jul/18/citynews.pressandpublishing

VanDerWerff, E. (2019, March 20). Here's what Disney owns after the massive Disney/Fox merger. Vox. Retrieved December 16, 2019, from https://www.vox.com/cul-ture/2019/3/20/18273477/disney-fox-merger-deal-details-marvel-x-men

Waterson, J. (2018, September 20). Sky takeover battle must go to auction, orders regulator. The Guardian. Retrieved December 16, 2019, from https://www.theguardian.com/business/2018/sep/20/sky-takeover-battle-fox-comcast-auction-regulator

Welch, C. (2018, June 13). Comcast makes $65 billion offer to steal 21st Century Fox away from Disney. The Verge. Retrieved December 13, 2019, from https://www.theverge.com/2018/6/13/17457244/comcast-21st-century-fox-film-tv-studios-acquisition-deal-announced

Williams, J. (2018, June 20). Disney ups bid for 21st Century Fox to $71.3 billion. Washington Examiner. Retrieved December 13, 2019, from https://www.washingtonexaminer.com/business/disney-ups-bid-for-21st-century-fox-to-71-3-billion

6
THE LUFTHANSA STRIKES

Max-Philip Dirk, Leon Guckelberger, and Patrick Eschler

KEY OBJECTIVES OF THE CASE STUDY

The key objectives of this case study are for the student to evaluate the following questions:

1. *What negotiation style has been put on display?*
2. *What were the main drivers for the deconstructive manor in which the negotiation was lead?*
3. *What can be said about the integrative potential of the negotiation?*
4. *Which future outlook on the relationship between the negotiation parties can be given, based on the negotiation in 2019?*

Introduction

Taking the plane in Europe has never been so cheap before. The result of a long development of a single European aviation market and a long process of privatization has led to an increasingly large range of direct and indirect flight offers for customers into, inside and out of the European Union (European Commission, 2019). However, while customers have seen the number of flights to choose from rise and the prices to pay for decline, there are a number of disputes going on between employers and employees in the airline industry. With a long history for strikes to achieve better compensation and employee benefits the labor union UFO and Lufthansa have clashed once again in 2019. This case study examines the Lufthansa strike in the year 2019 that has led to thousands of customers stranded and huge economic losses for Lufthansa. It explores different perspectives on the negotiations of Lufthansa and the labor union UFO and evaluates them using the negotiation management approach by Voeth and Herbst. Building an analysis on their concepts of economic and behavioral negotiation management. The chapter further uses the Harvard negotiation concept that allows for a slightly different perspective, that focuses more on the interests and positions of the individual parties. The balancing of these approaches, allows for a balanced perspective and an objective analysis of the Lufthansa strike that has been ongoing for most of 2019. It further can explain and shed light especially on those factors that have led to the escalation of the negotiation that have failed to materialize into an agreement. Emotions, personal relationships and one-style negotiations embedded in hard-bargaining tactics have led to a deterioration. Including attacks on personal matters. This also shows as the case study takes a Harvard negotiation concept perspective, which clearly shows that negotiations were overshadowed by positional bargaining rather than interest based integrative negotiations. A trend of escalation can be identified throughout that originates in long-term differences on personal as well as institutional levels. That this need not be is shown by the analysis presented.

In order for the case study to offer the best possible analysis, it first explores the most important descriptive facts, players and timeline regarding the Lufthansa strike of 2019. This is done through a descriptive analysis using secondary literature. First, the aviation industry is shortly introduced before the case study turns to the parties of the negotiation, Lufthansa and UFO. In addition, important third parties are analyzed, and their positions and interests within the negotiation process are shortly presented to allow for a deeper analysis later on. The chapter then continues to a descriptive presentation of the dispute in more detail. Following this, the chapter turns toward the conceptual approach of the negotiation management approach by Herbst and Voeth. Looking at the economic conduct of the dispute further allows the chapter to develop insight into the negotiations and present the economic grievances of the parties. To add, the case study takes a behavioral-based perspective, which gives further insight into the individuals and their (problematic) conduct of negotiation styles and the role of emotions as well as the negotiation tactics employed by the parties. From here, the chapter continues to assess positions and interests of the involved parties using a more detailed analysis of events through the application of the Harvard negotiation concept of Ury and Fisher. By differentiation positions from interests and looking at the sought for objectives by the negotiation parties, the Harvard negotiation concept is used to show a number of flaws that can contribute to explain why the negotiations failed. The chapter goes even further, using the previously given analysis, to provide a possible four-step improvement plan built on the events and the Harvard negotiation approach employed. Overall both approaches allow the case study to identify a number of factors ranging from economic and emotional factors, to positions over interests that have dominated the negotiation process from the very beginning. This further helps us to spot and assess problematic behavior, conduct and tactics and provides for a theory-based solution and improvements at certain steps of the way. In order to allow for the best possible understanding, the chapter now turns toward an introduction of the airline industry and the negotiation parties involved.

Aviation industry

With record numbers in flight operations in 2018 and growing demand for low-budget direct travels, the market has been dynamic. 2018 was the fourth consecutive year in which the Airline industries net profits exceeded $34 billion worldwide (Oliver Wyman, 2019, S. 4; PWC, 2018). Average airline profitability has reduced to around 8.5% due to higher operating costs and in light of recessionary fears (Oliver Wyman, 2019, S. 4). Profitability has been particularly high in the 2010s, due to low fuel costs and has since declined due to increasing competition and scaling effects (The Economist, 2019). Low oil prices and the correspondingly low costs for fuel, which continue to account for 25% of operating costs, have led to high profitability and factors of scale such as hedging of fuel prices, buying food as well as other products and services increase in importance for the competitiveness of airlines (KPMG, 2019; Oliver Wyman, 2019; PWC, 2018).

The European Airline Industry remains a highly competitive oligopoly, with the largest five airlines taking more than 50% of the market share (Aviator, 2019). Though still less than the 70%+ that the largest carriers in the United States have been able to capture. Lufthansa's market share in European aviation has grown to 12.3% in 2018 due to the integration of AirBerlin, making it the biggest operating airline in Europe (Aviator, 2019). Still, further consolidation is on its way and has been for the last two years, with a number of airlines having to announce bankruptcy as they are failing to stay in business as operating costs rise steadily. In 2018, a total of 18 airlines went out of business. New regulatory environment in the European Union as well as political uncertainty, most importantly Brexit has also weighed on uncertainty for airlines and the aviation industry in the European Union. To add public and government pressure for tackling emissions have specifically in the European Union led to increasing scrutiny of environmental impacts of airlines and air traffic. European operations have especially in the last couple of years been strongly affected by higher emission standards. This pressure is likely to continue to grow and further regulation is likely to be passed in the coming decade. This puts further pressure on the airlines and increases the value of scale and hence size. Micheal O'Leary, CEO of RyanAir, expects the largest five players to dominate more than 70% of the market in the near future (The Economist, 2019).

However, the European marketplace remains highly competitive. Current market structures date back to the privatization of the European aviation space in the 1990s (European Commission, 2019). Specifically, the unification of the European aviation space since 1992 has led to reduction in prices accompanied by stronger competition (European Commission, 2019). New players entered the market in the 1990s and have put state-owned and previously subsidized airlines under immense pressure for reform. Since then, the aviation industry has been marked by network and alliance strategies. Most airlines can be categorized into three distinct profiles; (1) low-budget, (2) network and (3) value airlines (Oliver Wyman, 2019, S. 7). State-subsidies are mostly forbidden and have seen a retreat from the European market. Nonetheless state-support via direct subsidies, loans as well as ownership tend to enter when "national treasures," as was the case with AirItalia, run into financial trouble. Multiple Airlines have had difficulties as trends have been miscalculated and cost-structures have eroded some of the biggest players. To name but just a few examples, AirItalia, AirBerlin, Azur, Cobalt, Monarch, Primera, PrivatAir, Small Planet, VLM as well as ThomasCook have all had to shut parts or all of their operations down (The Economist, 2019). Some operations have been taken over by other, larger airlines, or ended in massive job-losses and routes being dropped, despite heavy state intervention. Nevertheless, the general market remains stable, with huge benefits being created for customers. The European markets have seen lower prices and more choice grow.

Parties to the negotiation

In the following parts, a detailed analysis of the interests and challenges of each party, namely Lufthansa and UFO, as well as third parties, will be conducted.

Lufthansa group

The Lufthansa group is an internationally operating aviation company including more than 550 subsidiaries. With more than 135,000 employees worldwide, revenues of €35,8 bn in 2018 and a European market share of 12.3%, it is the largest operating airline company in Europe (Aviator, 2019; Lufthansa, 2019e). Lufthansa's group strategy is to "take on a key role in shaping the global aviation market and to remain the first choice for shareholders, customers and employees" (Lufthansa, 2019e). The business model consists of two basic pillars. The first being aviation services, which consists of Logistics, MRO (Maintenance, Repair and Operations) and Catering. The second pillar is the operation of the airlines (Lufthansa, 2019e). Recent take overs of the insolvent AirBerlin as well as the previous take over and ongoing integration of Eurowings has created a European airline giant. Reaching beyond its traditional network Airlines (Austrian, Lufthansa and Swiss Airline), to include low-budget airlines such as Germanwings and Eurowings. With a relatively broad strategy that aims not only at a single market segment but rather focuses on network as well as low-cost travel, Lufthansa is trying to achieve the highest possible presence in all of the airline and aviation supply chain across the board. Lufthansa's expansion has additionally been based on network strategies that have led to Lufthansa establishing itself as one of the largest players worldwide, sitting at the center of the star alliance network, one of the largest airline networks worldwide. According to Lufthansa the focus for future growth is set in the airline sector, especially low-cost direct traffic across Europe. This market segment is especially hard fought for with strong competitors in the form of EasyJet and RyanAir. Lufthansa on the other hand, can benefit from its far-reaching network alliance, making use of the associated scale advantages.

Lufthansa's attention has shifted towards a more cost-competitive structure as the newly integrated low-cost segment in the form of the subsidiaries Germanwings and Eurowings has expanded. Next to the scale in purchasing and hedging agreements for fuel costs, another area with a high-cost structure that is important for Lufthansa's competitiveness are wage and salary costs. High competition from EasyJet and RyanAir are likely, especially due to their location in anglo-saxon countries to benefit of slightly less strict and cooperative collective action institutions. Adding to this, in 2018, Lufthansa started a lean program for the entire Lufthansa group with the aim of better being able to address the quick changes in technological and supply chain shifts of the airline industry (Lufthansa, 2019e). Seeking for higher efficiency across the board of operations, lower costs and more intuitive work for the employees. This is likely also to have an effect on cabin crew member wages and salaries and hence is of concern to the labor representatives.

Management on the other hand has a number of interests it needs to balance. While first and foremost, management is interested in a financially successful development of the company, it must balance personal goals and achievements with interests of financial markets, tax collectors, customers as well as employees. Further and in particular related to the negotiations, management also wants to come across as strong in public (and for financial markets), and preserving their power position. This is particularly of interests when looking at personal relations between previous negotiators. With Carsten Spohr (CEO) having been in member of the executive board since 2011 (Lufthansa Group, 2019), personal relationships and particularly emotions play an important role. However further one could argue that management also has an interest in achieving the highest possible corporate valuation for financial markets and tends to push labor costs as much as possible.

UFO (Unabhängige Flugbegleiter Organisation)

Since the beginning of the 1990s, UFO has established itself as the foremost important player for flight attendants' collective action in Germany. Founded in 1992 as the answer to "not sufficient representation" (UFO, 2019h) by the larger labor unions such as SAG and ÖTV. UFO has since developed from a typical registered association with no specific association rights to a recognized and registered labor union. The status was granted in 2000, allowing UFO the right under German law to represent and most importantly to represent employees on the management board as well as directly negotiating with the management board of Lufthansa. In 2002, UFO was subsequently recognized by the Lufthansa group as the main employee representative body and has since been intertwined with the most important labor related negotiations. It has become one of the strongest labor unions in Germany, due to their high organizational degree of up to 70% in some cabins (UFO, 2019h). Which in comparison to most labor unions, where the average organizational degree remains around 18%, is very high (Fink, 2015). This high organizational degree is one of the reasons, that has made UFO one of the strongest labor unions of the last two decades, which have been accompanied by lower levels of organizational degree and declining collective action. Until today, UFO remains the largest specialized labor union in Germany, representing around 30,000 cabin crew members' interest across the globe (UFO, 2019h). The first and largest strike was organized by UFO in 2012. Followed by another large labor dispute in 2014, which resulted in the agreement "Agenda Kabine," which was directly co-authored by UFO and the Lufthansa management. In 2015, Lufthansa came under increasing pressure by investors to start a restructuring, as Lufthansa's expansion and integration of Eurowings increasingly weighed in on profits (Der Spiegel, 2019a). The subsequent restructuring with the goals of attaining lower costs across the board, as well as more efficient processes along the whole supply chain of the Lufthansa group led to increasing pressure on employee salaries and benefits. As a result, UFO engaged in the next negotiation including a strike. The dispute was then for the purpose of avoiding larger across-the-board-strikes arbitrated by the external former prime minister of the state of Brandenburg, Matthias Platzeck (UFO, 2019h). He was able to mediate and settle the dispute (Tagesschau, 2016). Increasing pressures by Investors to move forward with further cost-cutting and regaining a higher profitability in the low-budget sector then led to a further dispute the following year. Once again, an outside mediator was brought into the dispute, this time Klaus Wowereit, former mayor of Berlin (Bürgermeister a.D.). UFO's interests lie in continuing to be able to represent as many cabin crew members as possible, in order to leverage their bargaining position. In addition, UFO is also interested in seeing their members' wages, salaries as well as working conditions (e.g. part-time work) improve, for it to remain a legitimate broker and representative of the cabin crew members paying their monthly contributions to UFO. In the past, UFO has demonstrated being a determined force in achieving higher salaries and improving working conditions for cabin crew members. While it has demonstrated this power, UFO itself has recently been struck by internal disputes for positions and differences in interests (FAZ, 2019). Furthermore, labor unions, such as IGL and Ver.di have expanded their reach into the cabin and have hence put pressure on UFO for remaining the single most important labor union for cabin crew members. The next section will shed more light on those third parties that have come to play a significant role in the most recent negotiation.

Third parties to the negotiation

The role of labor unions in Germany remains strong, but has seen a systematic decline in power due to structural shifts in the work force across sectors

(Specht, 2017). Though flight operations and cabin crew members have been affected comparatively mildly. Organizational degree remains high and outsourcing has only been managed by few airlines, especially in countries with less stringent collective action rights, such as England and Ireland, home to EasyJet and RyanAir respectively. Germany remains one of the countries where strike is avoided most of the time, as cooperation between employers and employees is historically strong. Correspondingly low number of strike days per year in comparison to other European countries, support this (Himmelrath, 2015). However, the underlying structural changes have also led to higher competition among labor unions in Germany (Helfen & Nicklich, 2014). With the Lufthansa group facing higher union pressure and more threats of strike, a number of subsidiaries have started to negotiate labor related compensation, benefits and conditions with unions that are competing with UFO. One of these is Ver.di, being the largest labor union in Germany and representing more than two million employees in labor disputes in the service sector reaching across the German economy (Ver.di, 2019). The second important competitive player here is the IGL, which, rooted in the production of the aviation industry and has only recently started to expand and joined the competition for labor representation for cabin crew members (Koenen, 2018). The entry of Ver.di and IGL into competition for cabin crew members has meant that UFO's bargaining power is in decline as Lufthansa tries to undermine and weaken then labor unions by employing a variety of them across their distinctive subsidiaries (Koenen, 2018).

An important individual to recognize for the negotiation process is also Mathias Platzeck and Klaus Wowereit. Mathias Platzeck, politician and member of the SPD, has been an active mediator in labor union disputes in Germany. Platzeck has also previously negotiated an agreement between Lufthansa and UFO in 2016, in which the two parties managed to find a compromise that settled a dispute that expanded over one and a half years (Tagesschau, 2016). Previously Platzeck had also been a successful mediator in another labor dispute between the Deutsche Bahn and the GDL (Die Zeit, 2017). Bringing his personal skills to the table, Platzeck has a good hand for labor dispute negotiations, which made him a viable and attractive option for UFO and Lufthansa. Further one needs to also closely look at the individuals at the table of the negotiations. Carsten Spohr, CEO, has been a long-time member of the executive board of Lufthansa and hence has developed a personal relationship with UFO members. To, Nicolas Baublies, head negotiator of UFO, applies the same logic. As he gets made redundant as the negotiation goes on, has had previous long-term experience with the negotiations and Carsten Spohr (Der Spiegel, 2019b). The next section will set the negotiation timeline.

The negotiation timeline

For the understanding of the negotiation the employee–employer relationship, as well as the high degree of digitalization in the nonservice sector are important factors. As more and more processes in the aviation industry become digitalized there is a divergence of pay in the different professions. Those of air traffic controllers have become more specialized and higher paid, whereas service-oriented jobs and in particular those of cabin crew members have seen declining real wages and outsourcing across the industry. As pointed out, the organizational degree of cabin employee's remains high and hence labor unions retain strong bargaining powers. Whereas some airlines, particularly in the low-budget segment (EasyJet and Ryanair) have managed to avoid high labor union involvement, or profited from outsourcing, Lufthansa remains and hence retains its legal headquarters in Germany. Which unlike the Anglo-Saxon countries still has relatively stricter labor law standards and rights for collective action and organization (Thelen, 1999, S. 141).

The most recent bargaining dispute of the Lufthansa group and UFO cannot be understood with a broader historical perspective. UFO being the recognized collective bargaining partner of Lufthansa since 2002 has repeatedly negotiated with the Lufthansa group and their respective subsidiaries for higher wages, part-time and other benefits packages. In 2014–2016, UFO and Lufthansa saw their biggest stand-off end in an arbitrated compromise that was reached under the experienced labor dispute mediator Matthias Platzeck (Tagesschau, 2016). Ever since, UFO and Lufthansa's relationship has been rocky. As UFO and Lufthansa failed to agree on a settlement for their subsidiary, Eurowings in 2018 (Figure 6.1).

As a consequence, and as huge aggravation for UFO, in March 2019, Ver.di, a labor union in direct competition with UFO signed a deal with Eurowings (Reuters, 2019). In April 2019, the planned expansion of Eurowings started to get held up, by negative growth and profitability numbers of the low-budget airline. Then in August 2019, internal fights for posts of functionaries and their different views at UFO were made public and hindered a strike at Lufthansa going forward. On the 16 of the same month, Lufthansa further escalated the already dire situation, as it tabled a court filing asking the court for labor relations to withdraw UFO's labor union status (Der Spiegel, 2019b). On September 30, the highest level of escalation was reached as Nicolas Baublies, former and long-term head negotiator of UFO is made redundant for misconduct and failure to give notice to Lufthansa of his secondary consultancy services, while on sick leave (Handelsblatt, 2019). Going forward, UFO made a short-term announcement for a strike that was to take place only two days later, as Lufthansa refuses to opt-in to the demands for a 1.8% salary increase as well as still sticking to a cut in the employee-profit-sharing scheme. Neglecting any communication with UFO, just before the strike is about to get started, Lufthansa announced that for those employees with Lufthansa Airline a 2% wage increase was set in place. Followed by a strike by UFO. While Lufthansa in return tries to enforce a legal restraining order, the situation escalated further, with no direct lines of communication open at this stage. For the next two weeks, airline traffic resumed to its normal at Lufthansa, as passengers grew increasingly impatient and news coverage of troubles at UFO as well as the difficulties of UFO and Lufthansa to find a compromise increased.

100 Max-Philip Dirk et al.

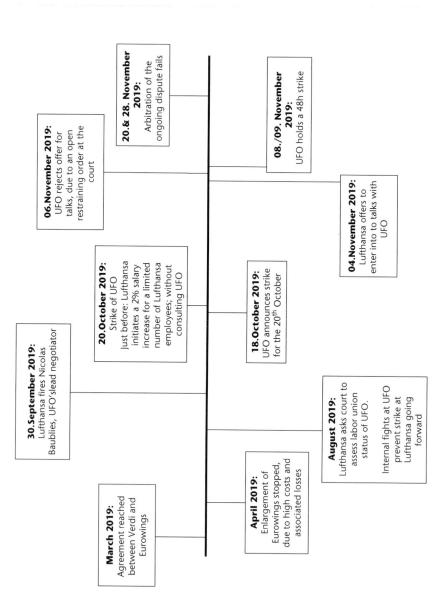

FIGURE 6.1 Illustration of the timeline of events unfolding (illustration of the Authors).

Then on November 4, Lufthansa backed-down from its noncommunication track offering to enter talks with UFO. For a day it looked as if Lufthansa and UFO might be back to a less confrontational and more integrative negotiation process, before UFO comes out and rejected Lufthansa's offer for talks and announces a 48h strike for November 8 and 9, pointing to an at that point still pending restraining order at the court. Two days later, Lufthansa faces its biggest logistical challenge yet, as UFO sets out for a 48-hour strike, resulting in cancellations of 1,400 flights. As communication channels reopen, an arbitration is sought for November 20, which turned out to be unsuccessful nonetheless. Pressure of UFO that Lufthansa should concede to their demands by November 28, otherwise further strikes would follow turned out to be a threat without consequences.

Economic conduct of negotiations

In order to achieve your own negotiation objectives there are two distinctly different approaches to conduct negotiations. The first one being "power-based negotiating" where a higher leverage of one's own negotiation position is based on an asymmetrical power distribution between the involved parties. The disadvantage of such an approach however, is its limited integrative potential or effects. Secondly, a "value-based negotiating" approach can be applied. By using this approach, a party will focus on the potential benefit of settlements. Thus, negotiators must be well informed about consequences and potential benefits of negotiated issues and anticipated results ("objective control"). This implies that own offers must be beneficial for the own objectives and interests ("offer design") (Voeth & Herbst, 2015, pp. 195–196).

In the negotiation referred to, "power-based negotiating" can certainly be identified. Interestingly, Lufthansa assumed it was in a superior negotiation position due to the – in their view – questionable labor-union status of UFO. Lufthansa was hence not willing to negotiate with UFO and thus rejected every single invitation for negotiations by UFO. In reality, however, UFO was the largest labor-union of Lufthansa's employees, representing more than 30,000 members (UFO, o. J.). This resulted, in a superior negotiation position of UFO, with a large power imbalance tilted towards UFO. The labor-union made use of this power imbalance by way of announcing and executing two strikes, which in total led to 1,400 cancelled flights within three weeks (Plück, 2019e; Rheinische Post, 2019e). It has to be added, though, that those strikes were executed as a consequence after Lufthansa announced a "discussion embargo." The incorrectly assumed superior position of Lufthansa backfired and was therefore the trigger for "power based negotiating" of UFO, which in the end, led to first concessions of Lufthansa, such as (i) a one-off payment of 1,500€, (ii) a salary-increase of 2% as well as (iii) new seasonal working models (UFO, 2019b). This "power-based negotiating" approach can be observed throughout the ongoing negotiations between both involved parties. Another example for the application of this approach is the threat of UFO that further strikes will be staged during the Christmas holidays-period, as a consensual result couldn't be achieved by November 28 (Die Zeit, 2019). In the aftermath, UFO used its factual superior power position to exert additional concessions by Lufthansa.

Behavior-based negotiation

The individual and organizational behavior during negotiations is a substantial factor which influences the process and outcome of negotiations: "The course and outcome of negotiations are also influenced by factors such as the respective negotiation culture, the negotiating style of the negotiators, the emotionality of the participants, and the negotiating tactics used in negotiations" (Voeth & Herbst, 2015, p. 195). In the negotiations between Lufthansa and UFO, those factors were crucial for the failing to reach an integrative deal in the end. In the following parts an analysis of negotiation styles, emotionality as well as the negotiation tactics of both, Lufthansa and UFO, will be presented. Due to the identical cultural background of both parties involved and their long-term entanglement, cultural aspects will not be part of this analysis.

Negotiation styles

First, the different negotiation styles of the involved parties will be analyzed in detail. This will also include an analysis of the concession behavior of each party.

According to Voeth and Herbst (2015, p. 204), there are five negotiation styles:

- First, there is a so-called "avoiding negotiation style" that implies minimal adherence to opposing as well as own interests.
- If, second, own interests are deemed more important than those of the opposite party, one speaks of a dominant negotiation style, also known as "win–lose" style.
- If the issues of the opposing party are more significant than the own issues, a compliant negotiation style is the key for a successful negotiation.
- Fourth, if both, the interest of the opposing party and the own interests are deemed to be of high relevance for achieving the objectives, an integrating negotiation style ("win–win") is being observed.
- Finally, a hybrid negotiation approach is an approach in which all negotiation styles referred to above are being applied simultaneously (Voeth & Herbst, 2015, p. 204).

As regards concession management, there are two different strategies. On the one hand, a "reciprocity strategy" is possible. This results in a reciprocal behavior of both negotiation parties where a "give and take" mechanism is essential. On the other hand, an "aspiration level strategy" can be part of the concession management. Here, concessions are not made reciprocally but only small or no concessions at all are being made. This often results in a higher risk of arriving at a standstill of the negotiations or even the entire abandonment (Voeth & Herbst, 2015, pp. 187–189).

The negotiations between Lufthansa and UFO can be divided into two phases. The first phase, dating until October 20, can be described as aggressive, non-communicative and distant. In this period, each party particularly tried to demonstrate its (alleged) bigger power as compared to the opposite side which, eventually, even resulted in the abortion of further talks. Lufthansa was negotiating aggressively and tried to make use of legal and judicial tricks, e.g. even declining the legal status of UFO (Plück, 2019a). Drug tests against members of the negotiation teams of UFO, dismissals of the head negotiator Nicolas Baublies, and several threats are examples for Lufthansa's attempts to weaken the opponent's position (Plück, 2019b; UFO, 2019b). In addition, the German airline was not prepared to negotiate with the labor union due to the (allegedly) formal and legal questionable status of UFO's Board of Directors and threatened employees with consequences in case of them participating in the announced strikes (Plück, 2019a; Plück, 2019b). Lufthansa's main objective was, therefore, to leverage its position by utilizing assumed and actual internal problems and predicaments at UFO and pushing them (Plück, 2019c). Hence, Lufthansa's own interests were of higher importance than the opposing interests, resulting in an initial competition strategy. And yet, just before the start of the first strike on October 20, the airline agreed to a salary increase of 2% for employees of the core company Lufthansa being 0.2% higher than what was demanded by UFO (Plück, 2019b). This however did not include any concessions for the subsidiaries of Lufthansa, which were also part and parcel of the overall negotiations. Due to the missing concessions given towards the subsidiaries and the ongoing lawsuit against UFO, an "aspiration level strategy" can be identified as regards Lufthansa's concession management. UFO on the other hand, called for a more cooperative approach from Lufthansa in the beginning. Due to the uncooperative, if not hostile, practices of Lufthansa and in particular the denial of UFO's labor-union-status, this changed to a decidedly more aggressive and threatening approach. Since no concessions at all were made for Lufthansa-subsidiaries, first strikes were staged at four of Lufthansa's major and most important subsidiaries, namely Germanwings, Eurowings, Sun-Express and CityLine, on October 20, 2019 (Rheinische Post, 2019a). The strikes were even expanded by 13 hours that can be interpreted as an attempt of the labor union to demonstrate its strength and therefore leveraging its own negotiation position (Rheinische Post, 2019b). Due to both, the cooperative and competitive components of the negotiation strategy of UFO, a compromise strategy can be identified. Still, UFO's concession behavior can be described as an "aspiration level strategy" due to missing concessions, which were made. Especially the collision of both concession strategies shows the high risks of an "aspiration level strategy" that lead to a standstill of negotiations in the end.

The second phase however, dating from October 20 to November 28, can be described as partially more communicative and integrative. Lufthansa, on the one hand, negotiated based on a distinctly more cooperative approach. For example, it first offered to enter into talks with UFO on November 4 (Plück, 2019d). After UFO announced further strikes targeting Lufthansa's core company, the German airline even invited UFO and further labor-unions to first meetings because, according to Lufthansa's CEO Carsten Spohr, "a solution can only lie in dialogue" (Lufthansa, 2019a). It has to be added, though, that Lufthansa, on a parallel track, filed for a temporary restraining order against the strikes due to the – in Lufthansa's mind still - questionable status of UFO. Such lawsuit was later dismissed by the labor courts. However, the filing of such was reason enough for UFO rejecting Lufthansa's invitation for meetings on November 6 (Rheinische Post, 2019c). Additionally, Lufthansa made it clear that it would uphold its option of possibly suing members of UFO for the compensation of losses stemming from the strikes (Kotowski, 2019a). However, in opening the window for entering into a dialogue (see above), a first step towards a change of its negotiation style can be identified, given that Lufthansa initially entirely denied the legal status of UFO. As an additional, even stronger signal towards UFO, Lufthansa withdrew the lawsuit regarding UFO's status as a labor-union altogether. Such step was touted as "a sign of de-escalation" by Lufthansa (Lufthansa, 2019b). The German airline also conceded that UFO may still call for a strike while the negotiations were ongoing (Lufthansa, 2019c). On the other hand, Lufthansa did not agree to withdraw from the mentioned potential lawsuits against members of UFO as regards compensation for losses incurred through the strikes. Overall, the negotiation style of Lufthansa in the second phase can be described as more integrative as it made several concessions towards UFO, although they still threatened to sue UFO for the strike action; the opposing and own interests were of high relevance at the same time. UFO on the other hand was still threatening and actually executing strikes at Lufthansa due to missing concessions of Lufthansa regarding its subsidiaries. This resulted in a 48-hour strike at the Lufthansa core company and additional threats that the strikes could be expanded onto Lufthansa-subsidiaries (Plück, 2019d). Ultimately, these strikes and the additional threats led to further concessions of Lufthansa and a partial change of their perception of UFO, now viewing them as an acceptable party to the negotiations plus a reassessment of the overall situation with a change in rhetoric of the CEO. This resulted in an offer of Lufthansa to enter into negotiations encompassing any and all open items. On top of that, Lufthansa offered (i) a one-off payment of 1,500€ for every employee of Lufthansa, (ii) no disciplinary consequences for employees that went on strike and (iii) a minimum stay of two nights when flying into Japan or Korea (UFO, 2019b). The negotiation style of UFO at this stage can be deemed as being dominant given that it was solely Lufthansa that had to concede to various offers of UFO. Regarding the concession management of both parties, only minor changes can be identified. While Lufthansa was forced to make various major concessions, such as the withdrawal of the lawsuit regarding UFO's status, UFO had to make only minor concessions, such as no further strikes at the Lufthansa core company during the negotiation phase. As a consequence, "give and take" mechanisms cannot be identified.

Emotionality

Emotions of the involved parties were essential for the course and outcome of the negotiations. Lufthansa had just announced that its EBIT decreased by 8% in the third quarter, resulting in an overall reduction of EBIT of 30% in the first nine months of 2019 (Drebes, Kowalewski, & Plück, 2019). Furthermore, UFO threatened that strikes could be called during the Christmas holidays period that would be tantamount to even higher losses in EBIT, given that this period of the year is one of the most active ones in the airline industry (Die Zeit, 2019). This threat substantially increased the pressure on Lufthansa as fourth quarter sales were crucial for Lufthansa's profitability. The fact that Lufthansa wanted to re-organize the structure of its Board of Directors and that it was also due to replace various members of it added to a change in emotionality at this juncture of the negotiations (Kotowski, 2019b). The situational emotion and reaction of Lufthansa on strikes can be described as being driven by anger and aggression which resulted in a highly competitive negotiation: only minor concessions were made whilst numerous threats were made against the labor-union. UFO threatening and additionally staging strikes has to be seen as a direct response to Lufthansa's initial dominant negotiation style which included the denial of UFO and their completely noncommunicative approach. For UFO the negotiations were of existential importance. On the one hand, internal problems such as accusations of illegal embezzlement of its Board members led to a decline of trust of its members (Plück, 2019c). On the other hand, the legal infight with Lufthansa and their threat to simply not enter into negotiations with UFO jeopardized the status of the latter. To add to that, Ver.di, Germany's biggest union for service industries, increasingly put UFO's status to represent Lufthansa's organized employees into doubt. This even also included separate negotiations between Ver.di and Lufthansa, a new labor contract for Eurowings agreed upon between Ver.di and Lufthansa, and statements of Ver.di criticizing UFO (Rheinische Post, 2019c; UFO, 2019e). All this led to a more pronounced and even aggressive negotiation approach and a dominant negotiation style of UFO, by way of which it wanted to demonstrate its actual legitimacy, strength and power. Due to the fact that the personal situation of each party was tense, a competitive negotiation with negative emotions including threats and small concessions can be observed. Because of the negative and competitive emotions, mediators were nominated for each party.

Negotiation tactics

According to Voeth and Herbst (2015, p. 211), negotiation behavior is also determined by the tactics used during negotiations. A negotiation tactic can be defined as "a situational plan of action for negotiations" (Voeth & Herbst, 2015, p. 212) and must be differentiated to a negotiation strategy that can be described as the overall plan for target achievement. There are numerous negotiation tactics such as time games, threats, aggressiveness, and derived power that can be identified in the negotiation between Lufthansa and UFO. In the following parts these tactics shall be analyzed in detail.

In case of time games, time can be used as a parameter for negotiations that can lead to substantial advantages for one party (Voeth & Herbst, 2015, p. 216). During the negotiation between Lufthansa and UFO, both parties were using time games to leverage their own negotiation position. Lufthansa, for example, increased the time pressure artificially by allowing members of UFO only one 20-minute talk with members of the Board of Lufthansa to discuss essential issues (UFO, 2019d). This also included talks between UFO and officials of Lufthansa's subsidiaries who were not even empowered to make any decisions, resulting in a waste of important time for the preparation of the negotiations for UFO officials (UFO, 2019c). UFO also used time games amply by way of executing strikes shortly after announcements. The first strike on October 20, for example, was announced only two days prior to its start and required fast responsive action of Lufthansa, for example, to develop alternative flight schedules (UFO, 2019a). Furthermore, the strike was then expanded by 13 hours. Also the 48-hour strike on November 8 and 9 was announced only three days before, leading to the cancellation of 1,300 flights and 180,000 affected passengers (Plück, 2019e; Rheinische Post, 2019d). Another example is the statement of UFO that strikes would be staged during the Christmas holidays-period, if an agreement could not be reached by November 28 (Die Zeit, 2019). UFO set the timeline and increased time pressure on Lufthansa's side that, as a consequence, reduced the risk of postponement.

It is fairly obvious that this announcement was also a threat. As a result, Lufthansa's demand of a ban of strikes at its subsidiaries during negotiations was not heard and the German airline had to agree that this issue will not be part of further negotiations (Lufthansa, 2019c). Furthermore, first concessions were made from Lufthansa such as a one-off payment of 1,500€ for each employee (Rheinische Post, 2019f). The negotiation tactic of threats was used extensively by the labor union during the negotiations. This was, for example, manifested in respective statements of Mr. Nicolas Baublies on German TV such as "our committees are now preparing for labor disputes again" (Tagesschau, 2019a) after an "overall settlement" was not reached. Those threats also led to further issues ("side deals") being added to the negotiation mass. UFO, for example, at the outset demanded particular issues for Lufthansa employees such as a salary increase of 1.8%, higher expenses and allowances, as well as a new seasonal working model (Plück, 2019e). Even though those issues were of high importance, the main issue was an "overall settlement" where numerous points of the Lufthansa core company and its subsidiaries should be negotiated. Furthermore, the cancellation of the lawsuit on UFO's status as a labor union was of high importance for UFO. As a result, by applying the negotiation tactic of threats, UFO was successful in exerting numerous concessions out of Lufthansa, for example, the withdrawal of the lawsuit regarding its status, and to enter into negotiations with the objective to arrive at an "overall settlement." A possible reason for the aggressive and threatening approach of UFO is the negotiation history between Lufthansa and UFO which, according to UFO, in the past was characterized by unfair and dishonest practices by Lufthansa (Kotowski, 2019a). In the past, threats were the only instrument available to UFO so as to overcome Lufthansa's refusal to negotiate with them. In addition to that, the existential crisis of UFO led to time pressure where fast action was needed. UFO was therefore not in a position to agree on Lufthansa's first offer which included talks on an interim deal in November 2019 that was supposed to last until the new Board of UFO is elected in February 2020 (Plück, 2019d). In the end, UFO's negotiation tactic of aggressiveness and threats led to immediate negotiations regarding an "overall settlement" between both parties. If a strong negotiation position is at hands, threats and aggressiveness can be a useful negotiation tactic in serious and existential situations.

Beyond threats, derived power was a further negotiation tactic used by UFO. In case of the lawsuit regarding the legality of strikes on November 8 and 9, for example, UFO weakened the arguments of Lufthansa by winning the lawsuit and adding that UFO "make[s] use of [their] basic right to strike" (Rheinische Post, 2019c). This statement refers to the decision of the court and weakens the arguments of Lufthansa. Furthermore, this statement is also essential to legitimize the announced strikes in public.

Harvard approach to the negotiation

In the following parts, the four components of the Harvard Business Approach, namely separate problems from people, interests, generate options and objective criteria will be theoretically deduced. In a second step, the ongoing negotiations between Lufthansa and UFO will then be analyzed based on the Harvard Business Approach.

Separate problems from people

Personal and emotional involvement can aggravate the progress of the negotiation. The tendency of feeling personally attacked when the opponent criticizes one's position increases with it. To prevent this type of over involvement it's of utmost importance that the negotiators understand each other's problems and point of views. It is only possible to find an appealing solution if this is understood by them. Because emotions are mostly hard to control or suppress the main goal shouldn't be to avoid emotions entirely, because that's not realistic. Emotional outburst should be acknowledged and taken seriously. The worst thing to do in such a situation is to dismiss the importance of the opponent's emotions. This most certainly provokes an even higher emotional involvement. Over-emotional reactions can also be triggered by a simple miscommunication which leads to a misunderstanding. Therefore, it is important that the parties give their full and undivided attention to each other. In doing so, it is also important not to confuse understanding with agreement. A good relation can prevent this sort of "people problems" all to getter, by not letting them arise in the first place (Fischer & Ury, 2011, pp. 13–18).

Lufthansa and UFO haven't focused on interests at all. Throughout the entire time of the negotiation numerous people problems can be identified. For example, the head of HR at Lufthansa, Bettina Volkens, was fired because of her willingness to cooperate with UFO, people familiar with the matter said. This incident shows how emotionally charged the situation between the airline and its trade union was (Schnabel, 2019).

A possible reason thereof is the miscommunication between the two parties. Throughout the negotiations from the end of November, there is a lack of proper communication. UFO accused Lufthansa of not taking the negotiation seriously and that they aborted the last negotiations prematurely. Lufthansa on the other hand, denied the accusations and offered a big arbitration plan but never communicated it properly. UFO got informed by the media of the existence of this proposal (Tagesschau, 2019d). They further refused to accept the offer due to low legal certainty. UFO also complained that during the last three days of negotiation they only had 20 minutes to talk to the airline's representatives. Lufthansa again denies all the accusations. All mentioned incidents show how easily the personal relationship and the different egos got tangled up with the problem itself. This endangers the relationship between the two negotiators as the example of Bettina Volkens demonstrates (Fischer & Ury, 2011, p. 15).

The dismissal of former UFO boss Nicoley Baublies resembles another escalation of the people problem between Lufthansa and UFO. After 15 years as employee of Lufthansa he was fired. He organized the longest strike in the airline's history and initiated one of the most expensive and complicated tariff agreements. Lufthansa claimed that his involvement with UFO jeopardized his work for them. The conflict escalated when Lufthansa demanded a drug test from him. After all his history with Lufthansa he remained highly involved in the negotiations (Deckstein, 2019).

Astonishing was that after these incidents both parties were still willing to negotiate and eager to find a solution. They agreed upon the use of moderators for a small settlement plan. Frank-Jürgen Weise and Matthias Platzeck will execute this challenging role. This strategy is an optimal way, considering the circumstances, to clearly separate substantial problems from people problems (Die Zeit, 2019). It can be observed that the relationship between the two negotiation partners was negatively preloaded. People like Baublies shouldn't have been involved as much as they were in the discussions. Their opinion and experience should and must be acknowledged, however they shouldn't take on leading roles in the process. It is not realistic for people like Baublies to be objective and unbiased, even with his level of experience. The optimal lead negotiator should be someone that is not that emotionally connected to the case.

Focus on interests rather than positions

As Fisher and Ury wrote "Your position is something you have decided upon. Your interests are what caused you to so decide" (2011, p. 24). Lufthansa's interests in this negotiation, as already mentioned in part 3, is the financial stability and success of the company as well as to obtain a good public image. Due to high fuel costs and the ongoing price wars caused by low-cost airlines, Lufthansa had to correct its expected EBIT downwards from 2.4–3 bn to 2–2.4 bn (Tagesschau, 2019a). Based on the economic circumstances, Lufthansa's position is to cut costs. Lufthansa is not willing to lower their expectations by any means. Even after the announcement of a potential strike by UFO they held on to their expected profit targets. This behavior shows that Lufthansa will do everything in their power to reach the desired goal and was not willing to diverge from its position (Tagesschau, 2019b). UFO's main interest is to represent as much of their members in the best way possible. In their position, they demanded better working conditions for cabin crew members as well as a salary raises for employees of Lufthansa and their subsidiaries (UFO, 2019a). As mentioned in part 4, Lufthansa offered a 2% increase of the salary which wasn't accepted by UFO because it wouldn't meet the tariff demands. It resembled a voluntarily raise instead (Manager Magazin, 2019). Both examples further amplify the stubbornness of the two parties. Even when one side tried to approach the other or apply pressure, positions were held onto.

Fischer and Ury (2011, pp. 27–30) recommend the following steps for this kind of situation. First, the parties must identify their interests and communicate those. The position is underlined with the different interest of one party. Second, they need to discuss their interests with each other. In this phase, it is important that the negotiators pay attention to the opponent's interest so they can be addressed in a potential proposal. They should also keep their interest in mind while remaining open to different proposals. Regarding the behaviour of Lufthansa and UFO it can be stated that the recommended process wasn't executed as described. Lufthansa and UFO should have focused the negotiations on the interest rather than positions. As this could have helped them to advance from a "win-lose" mentality towards a "win–win" approach.

Generate options

Fischer and Ury (2011, p. 31) describe different obstacles to overcome before generating options. The first one is premature judgment. Due to premature judgment, it is harder to invent creative options. There might be also a fear of disclosing valuable information which will harm the bargaining position. This is very well displayed in this negotiation situation. UFO prejudges Lufthansa by saying that they try to create costs for UFO and waste time with their lawsuits (UFO, 2019f). Other statements from their news blog paint the same picture. Lufthansa is portrayed as a cruel company that tries to make life miserable for the trade unions (UFO, 2019g). Lufthansa on the other hand, prejudges UFO as a nonlegitimate trade union. As mentioned, Lufthansa filed a lawsuit against UFO for this purpose. Nonetheless this lawsuit was ruled in favor of UFO, who hence retained their legal status as a trade union (Lufthansa, 2019d).

Searching for the single answer is the second barrier for diversified options. Most negotiations are dominated by the need of closing the gap between the different positions and not by inventing new options. This is based on the assumption that a wider scope of possible agreement options delays and aggravates the whole negotiation (Fischer & Ury, 2011, p. 32). Again, this specific assumption can be found in the present case. Both parties try to hold their position for any means and attempt to gain power over their opponent by applying pressure. Lufthansa for example, implemented the same strategy as the Deutsche Bahn did a couple of years ago. This strategy tries to lever out the trade unions using legal tricks. The mentioned lawsuit above displays this contra productive behavior (Schnabel, 2019). On the other hand, UFO used the same strategy to apply pressure over and over using the threat and last-option of a strike. This tool gives the trade union good leverage and bargaining power over its employer due to the financial losses that come with it. It is hence obvious that with these tactics no favorable solution nor new options can be explored or found. It also makes the impression that they didn't even try to find a solution, let alone any solution. Rather they strive to overpower their opponent (Tagesschau, 2019c).

The third difficulty is the assumption that can be identified according to the Harvard negotiation process is that of a fixed pie. In this scenario the negotiating parties consider the situation as a zero-sum game, where the profit of one is the loss to the other party. With that in mind there is no stimulus for creating new options (Fischer & Ury, 2011, pp. 32–34). A good example for this type of situation are the negotiations about the tariffs. If one party gives in, it means automatically that it gives up parts of its profit. Why would they voluntarily give up parts of their profits? But as the theory mentions this is exactly the problem. It doesn't have to be this way. If they would broaden their scope of possible solutions, there would be a chance that they find an option where neither of them is worse off.

Another hurdle to overcome, as described by Fischer and Ury (2011, p. 32) is the fact that each side is only concerned by their own interests. But to reach an agreement the solution must be appealing to both negotiation partners. The best way to do so, is by giving in on its low-cost objectives, which have a high benefit for the opponent. Emotions are often the cause of this one-sided view. Lufthansa and UFO clearly didn't align their procedure with these recommendations. They were not able to overcome the different obstacles for generating different options. They mainly focused on their own positions without thinking about mutual beneficial solutions.

Objective criteria

Insisting on an objective criteria-based agreement is the fourth pillar of the Harvard negotiation concept. The main goal of the objective criteria is an agreement which rests on principles rather than pressure. There are no universal criteria which guarantee a successful negotiation. They must be individually found for the specific situation of the negotiation. Scientific findings, professional standards or legal precedent are potential indicators for such criteria. The best way to confirm that the criteria are reasonable is by assuring that both sides are willing to stick to them. If that's the case, there is a high chance to a fair solution process. As already mentioned, the finding of these criteria is highly subjective and therefore requires an interactive cooperation. It is crucial to understand the reasoning behind the counter party's suggestions. This specific reasoning can also be used to support the own position. In addition, to the interactives the negotiation partners should keep an open mind and be open to reconsider their position if there is a plausible reason for it. Pressure and threats on the other hand are counterproductive and destroy the relationship (Fischer & Ury, 2011, pp. 33–36).

Applying pressure and trying to out-power each other have massively damaged their relationship and sabotaged the negotiations multiple times. Especially the lawsuit regarding the legal status of UFO has harmed the already bad relationship. UFO as a result, claimed that Lufthansa is trying to blame UFO for the failed talks, because of a lack of preliminary conditions. However, they are trying now to restore the last positive fragment of their relations by the use of mediators. This strategy is a good approach in a tense situation like this. It helps to lower the emotional involvement and increases simultaneously the objectiveness (Handelsblatt, 2019). It would be recommendable for both parties to form objective criteria for the negotiation. Lufthansa could therefore assure that UFO doesn't walk over them by gaining too much power. UFO on the other hand, could assure that they get treated fairly and that their interests are represented as desired. A cooperative long-term relationship would also be supported by the objective criteria, as it helps to maintain focus on the core interests by setting the ground rules for the negotiation (Schnabel, 2019).

Recommendations

As the previous part has demonstrated, there were major problems regarding a variety of aspects in the negotiation. This part shows an alternative approach to the identified problems of the previous section.

The mixing of personal and substantial interests is the first big challenge to overcome. Due to the long negotiation history of the two parties, it is especially hard to untangle these and confront them separately. One clearly identifiable factor is the long-term (personal) relationship(s) that have shaped the negotiation process. It has led to a number of prejudgments and aggravated emotional factors. This was further accelerated as the company has come under increasing pressure from the financial markets. From a perspective of UFO, the law suit, against their labor union status, was a personal attack on the highest level. An open discussion, possibly with the help of a mediator would have had a better chance at resolving and calming the negotiations down from the very beginning. The emotional commitment could have been lowered and controlled from the beginning and thus provocations and attacks would have been prevented or at least minimized.

Mediators would have also supported the understanding of the opponent's point of view, which would have led to a better communication process. A big behavioral flaw can additionally be identified in the communication process. Even though they tried to negotiate various times, concerns and opinions couldn't be addressed directly. The failed proclamation of the "large settlement" proposal stands symbolically for the inefficient communication. It was also said, that Lufthansa tried at one point to address the problem directly, involving the public and the affected workers (Tagesschau, 2019a). This can't simply be a valuable strategy because of the dependency and long-term involvement of the two parties. The problem won't dissolve itself if the solution finding doesn't involve the party addressing them in the first place. It is hence likely that future negotiations will get caught up in this personal and emotional process once again.

Further, the Harvard negotiation approach also finds support for focus on positions rather than interests. This resembles another big problem in the course of this negotiation. As already mentioned in part 10, it is extremely important that both sides define their interests first for themselves and then make them understandable for the other one by explaining why it is important and how the position reflect these needs and demands. The best way to understand the opponent's interests is by asking why this is so important for them. The answer to that question shouldn't be a generic justification. Rather it should help the understanding of the hopes, needs and fears. Another way is to ask the opposite question, why not? Why did the counterparty not accept our proposal? What interest is blocking an agreement? By asking these questions, one can figure out the current state of mind of the negotiation partner, which is crucial if one wants to change the opponent's mind.

Lufthansa and UFO should have first asked these questions before starting to bargain over their position and tried to close the gap between them. Another important factor that could have helped the negotiation is to investigate the human needs behind the interests. Both positions are mostly of financial nature but that doesn't mean that it is only about the money. One could have asked because of what UFO demands higher salaries? Is it because accommodation got more expensive? Is it to feel financially secure? Are they concerned about their financial wellbeing? Do they have a sense of belonging to a different type of group they are currently in? If these questions remain unanswered or even never were asked finding a solution gets really complicated because no group will agree upon something that doesn't consider their basic human needs (Fischer & Ury, 2011, pp. 25–27).

In addition, the two organizations failed to let the past be in the past. A possible way to overcome this problem is to be hard on the problem and soft to the people. Being hard on the problem doesn't automatically mean to be closed-minded about possible proposals of the opponent rather than advocating strongly one's personal interest. If the negotiators push their interest strongly, they often can stimulate each other's solution finding process (Fischer & Ury, 2011, p. 30).

The process of generating options for mutual gains was also not implemented the way Fischer and Ury proposed. The source of this issue is the fact that an actual negotiation, where possible solution would be created, most certainly never took place. If an approximation was made it was declared as insufficient and the conversation got cancelled. By following the recommendations to separate the creation and valuation of potential solutions as described by Fischer and Ury (2011, pp. 33–37), this dilemma could have been resolved as follows (Figure 6.2):

Step 1.
Lufthansa and UFO should have defined their problems not only on their own but together. For UFO the issues are mainly the raise of the tariffs and better conditions for the seasonal workforce. Lufthansa is concerned with their financial profits and the public image.

Step 2.
These problems can be separated into two categories: financial issues and working condition issues. The causes for the financial issues are linked to each other. If Lufthansa has to pay higher tariffs, their profit will necessarily decline, which embodies the fixed-pie mindset. The reason for the working condition issues can also be connected to financial circumstances. To resolve

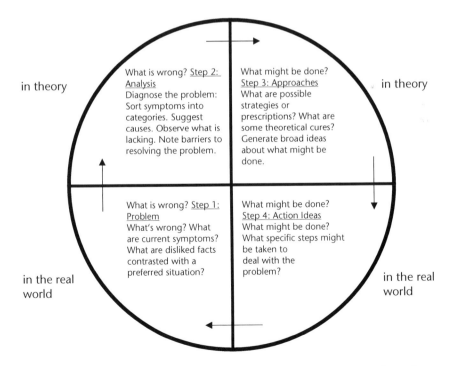

FIGURE 6.2 The four basic steps in inventing options (in accordance with Fischer & Ury, 2011, p. 37).

this, it is essential to understand the other side and to work with them rather than against them.

Step 3.
Only if the negotiation partners understand the problems of the counterparty, they can come up with possible solutions. A possible solution regarding a "small settlement" could have been the attempt to link the tariffs to the financial performance. By this, the two main interests are connected and both sides would have an incentive to increase their personal profits and commitment. The financial interest issues are clearly connected to each other and should therefore also be connected in the solution.

Step 4.
A potential manual of the forthcoming negotiation could have help course of the negotiations. The main problem in the encounter between Lufthansa and UFO was that the negotiations didn't follow a certain roadmap. At first, they didn't even talk, then they did, then they stopped and so on and so on. This process costs a lot of nerves and forces the parties to start from scratch every single time. If there would have been a clear agenda in which was defined when, what and how would be discussed the opponents would have known exactly what they can expect and perpetrate accordingly.

This strategy would also have helped to lower the emotional involvement. If the negotiation is focused on hard facts, the potential emotional involvement can be prevented, as the facts leave no room for it. By addressing the different interests positional bargaining can be avoided and the solution finding gets more interactive and cooperative. This would have also helped the relationship between Lufthansa and UFO. They also should have separated the process of generating possible agreements and the evaluation process of those possible solutions. A way to do so is by collective brainstorming. If this was implemented accordingly, the different interests could have been addressed directly and even made compatible. As already mentioned, this would have facilitated an agreement by creating a mutual gain solution and addressing them directly towards the decision makers.

Concluding remarks

If Lufthansa and UFO would have left their strong history in the past and therefore also most of the emotional tension, a lot of people problems wouldn't have come up from the very beginning. It was furthermore not smart to involve people who had a strong personal noncooperative relationship with the other party such as Baublies and Spohr. This only leads two prejudgments, which are very harmful not only for the negotiation but also for the ongoing and long-term relationships. They should have also focused more on the interests and the reasons that lay behind. Only if each other's problems are understood, multiple integrative and win-win solutions are possible.

Top lessons learned

- *The negotiations between Lufthansa and UFO show an aggressive negotiation style, to a large extent driven by anger.*
- *Lufthansa's wrong assumption as regards UFO's negotiation position and the resulting "power-based negotiating" approach of the labor union led to a situation in which the negotiations required mediators so as to arrive at a consensual outcome. Numerous factors such as negotiation styles, negotiation history and emotions involved led to negotiations characterized by threats and time games as well as minor concessions ("aspiration-level strategy").*
- *Instead of focusing on the interests of the opposing party, for example, both parties were highly affected by personal problems such as the dismissal of Nicolas Baublies and the fraught negotiation history. Problems and people were not separated decisively, leading to additional tensions during negotiations.*
- *The interests of each party, being financial stability for Lufthansa as opposed to labor related and status related demands of UFO were only partially considered. An intensified focus on opposing interests could have eased existing tensions, leading to more focused negotiations with respect to an "overall settlement."*
- *After first obstacles between Lufthansa and UFO, namely premature judgement, searching for a single answer, the assumption of a fixed pie, and the consideration of own interests, were overcome, both parties added further issues to the negotiation mass resulting in additional options (e.g. "overall settlement").*
- *Objective control, however, and its main goal of an agreement based on principles rather than pressure, was overlooked throughout the negotiations. Both parties unduly pressurized the opposing party, for example, by applying time games and the negotiation tactic of threats.*
- *The clash of all these factors led to negotiations with limited integrative potential. Both parties negotiated in a one-off manner where consequences on future negotiations were certainly not taken into consideration.*
- *This approach is particularly questionable because a long lasting and mutually beneficial business relationship is favorable for both parties.*
- *Future negotiations will be negatively affected by the path laid out by the fraught negotiations of autumn 2019.*

References

Aargauer Zeitung. (2019, November 8). Flugbegleiter streiken weiter – hunderte Lufthansa-Flüge gestrichen. Aargauer Zeitung. Retrieved December 2019 from: https://www.aargauerzeitung.ch/wirtschaft/flugbegleiter-streiken-weiter-hunderte-lufthansa-fluege-gestrichen-135941210

Aviator. (2019, February 20). Europe's big five take more than half of region's air travel market as small airlines struggle. Aviator. Retrieved December 17 from https://

newsroom.aviator.aero/europes-big-five-take-more-than-half-of-regions-air-travel-market-as-small-airlines-struggle/

Deckstein, D. (2019, September 30). Lufthansa schmeißt Ex-UFO-Chef raus. Spiegel Online. Retrieved December 9 from https://www.spiegel.de/wirtschaft/unternehmen/nicoley-baublies-lufthansa-schmeisst-ex-ufo-chef-raus-a-1289347.html

Der Spiegel. (2019a, November 29). Lufthansa startet neue Billigmarke für Langstrecken. Spiegel Online. Retrieved December 17 from https://www.spiegel.de/wirtschaft/unternehmen/lufthansa-plant-nach-verlusten-mit-eurowings-neue-langstrecken-billigmarke-a-1298860.html

Der Spiegel. (2019b, August 16). Lufthansa lässt Gewerkschaftsstatus von UFO gerichtlich prüfen. Spiegel Online. Retrieved November 29 from https://www.spiegel.de/wirtschaft/unternehmen/lufthansa-laesst-gewerkschaftsstatus-von-ufo-gerichtlich-pruefen-a-1282382.html

Deutsche Welle. (2019, November 12). Keine weiteren Streiks bei Lufthansa – rersteutsche Welle. Retrieved December 11 from https://www.dw.com/de/keine-weiteren-streiks-bei-lufthansa-vorerst/a-51215797

Die Zeit. (2017, March 10). Schlichter wenden Streiks bei der Bahn ab. Zeit Online. Retrieved December 11 from https://www.zeit.de/mobilitaet/2017-03/deutsche-bahn-gdl-tarifgespraeche-schlichtung-bodo

Die Zeit. (2019, November 26). Lufthansa-Schlichtung mit prominenten Vermittlern. Zeit Online. Retrieved December 18 from https://www.zeit.de/news/2019-11/26/lufthansa-schlichtung-mit-prominenten-vermittlern

Die Zeit. (2019, November 28). Lufthansa macht Ufo Angebot für Schlichtung. Zeit Online. Retrieved December 18 from https://www.zeit.de/wirtschaft/unternehmen/2019-11/lufthansa-luftverkehr-flugbegleitergewerkschaft-ufo-streik-schlichtung-abbruch

Drebes, J., Kowalewski, P., & Plück, M. (2019, November 8). Die Lufthansa vollzieht die Kehrtwende. RP Online. Retrieved November 20 from https://rp-online.de/wirtschaft/lufthansa-streik-airline-chef-carsten-spohr-zur-schlichtung-bereit_aid-47011749

European Commission. (2019, December 21). EU Aviation: 25 years of reaching new heights. Mobility and Transport. Retrieved December 21 from https://ec.europa.eu/transport/modes/air/25years-eu-aviation_en

FAZ. (2019, August 8). Querelen bei Ufo verhindern Streik. Frankfurter Algemeine FAZ.net. Retrieved December 18 from https://www.faz.net/aktuell/wirtschaft/querelen-in-gewerkschaft-ufo-verhindern-weiter-streik-16323590.htmlabgerufen

Fink, A. (2015, May 5). Von Lohnquote und gewerkschaftlicher Organisationsgrad Gewerkschaften ohne Einfluss auf Lohnquote in EU-15 Ländern? IREF. Retrieved December 15 from https://de.irefeurope.org/Diskussionsbeitrage/Artikel/Lohnquote-und-gewerkschaftlicher-Organisationsgradabgerufen

Fischer, R., & Ury, W. (2011). *Getting to yes* (3. Aufl.). New York: Penguin LCC US.

Handelsblatt. (2019, September 30). Lufthansa kündigt Ufo-Gewerkschafter Nicoley Baublies. Handelsblatt Online. Retrieved December 15 from https://www.handelsblatt.com/unternehmen/handel-konsumgueter/fluggesellschaft-lufthansa-kuendigt-ufo-gewerkschafter-nicoley-baublies/25071932.html?ticket=ST-39607060-GtjCafKffdpwhJjQp5JZ-ap2

Handelsblatt. (2019, December 20). Tarifkonflikt zwischen Lufthansa und UFO geht in nächste Runde. Handelsblatt Online. Retrieved December 20 from https://www.handelsblatt.com/unternehmen/handel-konsumgueter/neue-verhandlungen-tarifkonflikt-zwischen-lufthansa-und-ufo-geht-in-naechste-runde/25357316.html?ticket=ST-35490055-QcytpgX9rUFA24TIYNdC-ap3

Helfen, M., & Nicklich, M. (2014, April). Gewerkschaften zwischen Konkurrenz und Kooperation? Inter-organisationale Beziehungen in der Facility Services-Branche. *Industrielle Beziehungen, 21*(2), 181–204.

Himmelrath, A. (2015, November9). Die Deutschen mögen's zahm. Spiegel Online. Retrieved December 17 from https://www.spiegel.de/karriere/streik-kultur-arbeitskaempfe-in-deutschland-und-anderen-laendern-a-1060119.html

Koenen, J. (2018, August 19). Neue Konkurrenz für die angeschlagene Ufo: IGL will Kabinenpersonal vertreten. Handelsblatt Online. Retrieved November 22 from https://www.handelsblatt.com/unternehmen/handel-konsumgueter/luftverkehr-neue-konkurrenz-fuer-die-angeschlagene-ufo-igl-will-kabinenpersonal-vertreten/24919510.html?ticket=ST-39672364-KdbSz0mckeAWlgKfcd5N-ap2abgerufen

Kotowski, T. (2019a, November 28). Die Versöhnung bleibt aus. Frankfurter Allgemeine Zeitung FAZ.net. Retrieved November 30 from https://www.faz.net/aktuell/wirtschaft/lufthansa-und-ufo-die-versoehnung-bleibt-aus-16508698.html

Kotowski, T. (2019b, December 3). Lufthansa Aufseher bauen Vorstand um. Frankfurter Allgemeine Zeitung FAZ.net. Retrieved December 5 from https://www.faz.net/aktuell/wirtschaft/lufthansa-aufsichtsrat-krempelt-vorstand-um-personalchefin-geht-16517426.html

Kotowski. (2019c, October 18). Warum Ufo nun Eurowings statt Lufthansa bestreikt. Frankfurter Allgemeine Zeitung FAZ.net. Retrieved December 7 from https://www.faz.net/aktuell/wirtschaft/ufo-bestreikt-nicht-lufthansa-sondern-eurowings-16440004.html?premium

KPMG. (2019). The aviation industry leaders report 2019. Abgerufen am December 2019 von https://assets.kpmg/content/dam/kpmg/ie/pdf/2019/01/ie-aviation-industry-leaders-report-2019.pdf

Lufthansa. (2019a, November 5). Carsten Spohr lädt Ufo, Verdi und CU zu Spitzengespräch ein. Lufthansa Newsroom. Retrieved December 4 from https://newsroom.lufthansagroup.com/german/newsroom/all/carsten-spohr-l-dt-ufo--verdi-und-cu-zu-spitzengespr-ch-ein/s/f3d0e037-8987-4dfd-a7ab-605469fa0c33

Lufthansa. (2019b, November 22). Lufthansa zieht Klage im Statusverfahren gegen Ufo zurück. Lufthansa Newsroom. Retrieved November 30 from https://newsroom.lufthansagroup.com/german/newsroom/all/lufthansa-zieht-klage-im-statusverfahren-gegen-ufo-zur-ck/s/8838e9ce-284a-4c27-b839-5a7c712cab03

Lufthansa. (2019c, November 28). Lufthansa bietet Ufo an, auch ohne Friedenspflicht bei Tochter Airlines in „große" Schlichtung zu gehen. Lufthansa Newsroom. Retrieved December 4 from https://newsroom.lufthansagroup.com/german/newsroom/all/lufthansa-bietet-ufo-an--auch-ohne-friedenspflicht-bei-tochter-airlines-in--gro-e--schlichtung-zu-ge/s/eb772cf2-ab47-414a-99ba-bb77b7c520bb

Lufthansa. (2019d, August 16). Lufthansa lässt Gewerkschaftsstatus der Unabhängigen Flugbegleiter Organisation (Ufo) überprüfen. Lufthansa Newsroom. Retrieved December 6 from https://newsroom.lufthansagroup.com/German/Newsroom/lufthansa-l-sst-gewerkschaftsstatus-der-unabh-ngigen-flugbegleiter-organisation--ufo---berpr-fen/s/5e327e18-b175-4c7a-9ad2-8245e8e5591b

Lufthansa. (2019e). Lufthansa Group, Star Alliance and partner airlines. Lufthansa Group. Retrieved December 10 from https://www.lufthansa.com/de/en/lufthansa-group-star-alliance-and-partner-airlines

Lufthansa Group. (2019). Biography Carsten Spohr. Investor relations. Retrieved December 7 from https://investor-relations.lufthansagroup.com/fileadmin/downloads/en/corporate-governance/Biography-Carsten-Spohr-2019-03.pdf

Manager Magazin. (2019, October 19). Streiks bei Lufthansa jederzeit möglich. Retrieved December 7 from https://www.manager-magazin.de/lifestyle/reise/gewerkschaft-ufo-droht-ausweitung-der-lufthansa-streiks-moeglich-a-1292349.html

Oliver Wyman. (2019). Oliver Wyman. Abgerufen am December 2019 von Airline Economic Analysis: https://www.oliverwyman.com/content/dam/oliver-wyman/v2/publications/2019/apr/APRIL262019_Airline_Economic_Analysis_2018–2019vFweb.pdf

Plück, M. (2019a, October 15). Der eskalierte Lufthansa-Konflikt. RP Online. Retrieved November 30 from https://rp-online.de/wirtschaft/unternehmen/lufthansa-streik-am-sonntag-am-flughafen-frankfurt-und-flughafen-muenchen_aid-46485553

Plück, M. (2019b, October 18). Ufo verlagert Streik auf Lufthansa-Töchter. RP Online. Retrieved November 30 from https://rp-online.de/wirtschaft/unternehmen/lufthansa-streik-im-oktober-2019-ufo-weitet-streik-auf-eurowings-und-co-aus_aid-46593147

Plück, M. (2019c, November 4). Ufo will Lufthansa bestreiken. RP Online. Retrieved December 1 from https://rp-online.de/wirtschaft/unternehmen/ufo-bei-lufthansa-und-eurowings-drohen-wieder-streiks_aid-46876499

Plück, M. (2019d, November 5). Gewerkschaft Ufo kündigt zweitägigen Ausstand an. RP Online. Retrieved December 2 from https://rp-online.de/wirtschaft/unternehmen/lufthansa-streik-november-2019-auch-eurowings-und-co-betroffen_aid-46940713

Plück, M. (2019e, November 7). Lufthansa-Streik trifft 180.000 Passagiere – Was Betroffene jetzt wissen müssen. RP Online. Retrieved December 2 from https://rp-online.de/wirtschaft/unternehmen/lufthansa-streik-trifft-180000-passagiere-fragen-und-antworten_aid-47006439

PWC. (2018). PWC. Abgerufen am December 2019 von Tailwinds Report – 2018 airline industry report: https://www.pwc.com/us/en/industrial-products/publications/assets/pwc-tailwinds-report-2018-airline-industry-trends.pdf

Reuters. (2019, March). Verdi einigt sich mit Eurowings über Flugbegleiter-Tarife. Reuters Online. Retrieved December 15 from https://de.reuters.com/article/deutschland-lufthansa-idDEKCN1QL15A

Rheinische Post. (2019a, October 14). Flugbegleiter wollen Lufthansa am Sonntag bestreiken. RP Online. Retrieved December 2 from https://rp-online.de/wirtschaft/unternehmen/lufthansa-flugbegleiter-kuendigen-streiks-fuer-sonntag-an_aid-46485353

Rheinische Post. (2019b, October 21). Flugbegleiter-Streik beendet – Ausfälle in Düsseldorf und Köln. RP Online. Retrieved December 1 from https://rp-online.de/nrw/staedte/duesseldorf/flughafen-duesseldorf-ufo-flugbegleiter-streik-beendet_aid-46614499

Rheinische Post. (2019c, November 6). Gericht erlaubt Flugbegleiter-Streik bei Lufthansa. RP Online. Retrieved November 25 from https://rp-online.de/wirtschaft/unternehmen/lufthansa-gericht-erlaubt-flugbegleiter-streik-donnerstag-und-freitag_aid-46986317

Rheinische Post. (2019d, November 6). Lufthansa streicht Donnerstag und Freitag insgesamt 1300 Flüge. RP Online. Retrieved November 26 from https://rp-online.de/wirtschaft/unternehmen/lufthansa-streik-2019-1300-fluege-am-donnerstag-und-freitag-gestrichen_aid-46990525

Rheinische Post. (2019e, November 6). Wie Lufthansa den Flugbegleiter-Streik verhindern oder auffangen will. RP Online. Retrieved November 26 from https://rp-online.de/wirtschaft/soll-will-lufthansa-den-flugbegleiter-streik-verhindern-oder-auffangen_aid-46982005

Rheinische Post. (2019f, November 20). Lufthansa strebt weiterhin grosse Schlichtung an. RP Online. Retrieved December 1 from https://rp-online.de/wirtschaft/unternehmen/tarifstreit-mit-ufo-lufthansa-strebt-weiterhin-grosse-schlichtung-an_aid-47304247

Schnabel, C. (2019, December 11). Es macht keinen Sinn, die Gegenseite zu bekämpfen. Aero Luftfahrtnachrichten. Retrieved December 12 from https://www.aero.de/news-33452/Interview-Prof-Claus-Schnabel.html

Specht, F. (2017, January 31). Von Die schwindende Macht der Gewerkschaften. Handelsblatt Online. Retrieved November 26 from https://www.handelsblatt.com/politik/deutschland/mitgliederzahlen-schrumpfen-die-schwindende-macht-der-gewerkschaften/19328554.html?ticket=ST-39685741-xfoWKcdgzSho4bfErlm6-ap2abgerufen

Tagesschau. (2016, June 30). Lufthansa und Flugbegleiter finden Kompromiss. Tagesschau.de. Retrieved December 19 from https://www.tagesschau.de/wirtschaft/lufthansa-flugbegleiter-tarifstreit-beigelegt-101.html

Tagesschau. (2019a, June 17). Lufthansa rechnet mit Gewinneinbruch. Tagesschau.de. Retrieved December 8 from https://www.tagesschau.de/wirtschaft/boerse/lufthansa-gewinnziele-101.html

Tagesschau. (2019b, November 11). Lufthansa hält an Gewinnziel fest. Tagesschau.de. Retrieved December 8 from https://www.tagesschau.de/wirtschaft/boerse/gewinnziel-lufthansa-101.html

Tagesschau (2019c, November 12). Vorerst keine Streiks bei der Lufthansa. Tagesschau.de. Retrieved November 22 from https://www.tagesschau.de/wirtschaft/lufthansa-ufo-streik-159.html

Tagesschau. (2019d, November 28). UFO kippt "grosse" Schlichtung. Tagesschau.de. Retrieved December 18 from https://www.tagesschau.de/wirtschaft/lufthansa-ufo-tarife-101.html

The Economist. (2019, April 27). Going American – Europe's airline industry is consolidating. *The Economist*. Retrieved December 13 from https://www.economist.com/business/2019/04/27/europes-airline-industry-is-consolidating

Thelen, K. (1999). *Die deutsche Mitbestimmung im intenationalen Vergleich*. In W. Streeck, & N. Kluge, Mitbestimmung in Deutschland (S. 135–223). Frankfurt a. M.: Campus Verlag.

UFO. (2019a, October 18). Streikaufruf bei Eurowings. Retrieved from https://ufo-online.aero/de/themen/eurowings/item/1324-streikaufruf-eurowings.html

UFO. (2019b, November 14). Gemeinsam stark – Die Kabine redet wieder mit. Retrieved from https://ufo-online.aero/de/themen/lufthansa/item/1376-gemeinsam-stark-die-kabine-redet-wieder-mit.html

UFO. (2019c, November 28). Lufthansa beendet trotz inhaltlicher Einigung Gespräche mit UFO. Retrieved December 4 from https://ufo-online.aero/de/presse/item/1394-lufthansa-beendet-trotz-inhaltlicher-einigung-gespraeche-mit-ufo.html

UFO. (2019d, December 3). Zwischenstand zur "Schlichtungssituation": Was ist passiert?. Retrieved December 4 from https://ufo-online.aero/de/themen/lhconcern/item/1397-zwischenstand-zur-schlichtungssituation-was-ist-passiert.html

UFO. (2019e, December 6). Ver.di Klappe besonders weit aufreisst, der wird schon Recht haben. Retrieved December 8 from https://ufo-online.aero/de/themen/lgw/item/1399-ver-di-klappe-besonders-weit-aufreisst-der-wird-schon-recht-haben.html

UFO. (o.J.). Über Ufo Wer wir sind. Retrieved November 29 from https://ufo-online.aero/de/ueber-ufo/wer-wir-sind.html

UFO. (2019f, September 25). Gericht entscheidet: Tarifverträge seit November und Januar wirksam gekündigt. Retrieved December 7 from https://ufo-online.aero/de/themen/lufthansa/item/1292-gericht-entscheidet-tarifvertraege-seit-november-und-januar-wirksam-gekuendigt.html

UFO. (2019g, September 27). Tarifverträge wirksam gekündigt, Infotour zur Streikvorbereitung. Retrieved December 7 from https://ufo-online.aero/de/themen/lufthansa/item/1296-tarifvertraege-wirksam-gekuendigt-infotour-zur-streikvorbereitung.html

UFO. (2019h). Über die UFO: Historie der UFO. Retrieved December 9 from https://www.ufo-online.aero/de/ueber-ufo/geschichte.html

Ver.di. (2019). Über Ver.di. Retrieved December 8 from https://www.verdi.de/ueber-uns/mitglied-werden

UFO. (2019i, July 26). Erste Infos zum Tarif-Forderungspacket 2019. Retrieved December 7 from https://ufo-online.aero/de/themen/lufthansa/item/1237-erste-infos-zum-tarif-forderungspaket-2019.html

Voeth, M., & Herbst, U. (2015). *Verhandlungsmanagement – Planung, Steuerung und Analyse* (2. Aufl.). Stuttgart: Schäffer-Poeschel Verlag.

7
BAYER VS. MONSANTO

Luca Franziscus, Julia Reis Coury, and Luca Loris Gerini

KEY OBJECTIVE OF THE CASE STUDY

The key objectives of this case study are for the student to give judgment on three main aspects of the negotiation:

1. *What judgment can be made on the merger negotiation over all?*
2. *What were the direct and indirect costs of the negotiation for Bayer?*
3. *What can be said about the integrativity of the negotiation?*

Introduction

The Merger of Bayer (German company) and Monsanto (U.S. American chemical corporation) was the biggest acquisition in Germany's economic history. The $66 billion merger, that started in May 2016, was an important step regarding the sector of agriculture and caused major impacts on the economics of food, farming, and the environment. The new company not only became the world's largest vegetable seed and cottonseed company, but also the world's largest manufacturer and seller of herbicides. Besides that, Bayer (who did not keep the name of Monsanto) is now the world's largest owner of the intellectual property, patents, and researcher for herbicide-tolerant seed traits. The acquisition was aimed to boost agriculture research and innovation for doubling the world's food supply by 2050 (Kumar, 2018).

According to some researches, total synergies of approximately $1.5 billion after 3 years of merger were expected along with additional integrated benefits. As an

DOI: 10.4324/9781003105428-7

example, the return for the period of the acquisition process (−5 to +531 day) for Bayer was approximately 6.72% and the cumulative return for Monsanto stock during the same time window 0- to +25-day period was approximately 19.50% (Kumar, 2018).

As it was well-known during the period of the deal, with two major companies involved in discussions in order to achieve common ground, the negotiation process was characterized by multiple phases of agreements and deadlocks. The companies had to deal with trust issues in terms of willingness to disclose information, as well as willingness to achieve higher and better prices to offer. Furthermore, the deal required approval from regulators in 30 countries.

In order to understand the negotiation process, this case focuses on (1) discussing the importance of the merger to the sector of agriculture, (2) analyzing the process steps of negotiation management and its outcome in the Bayer Monsanto case and (3) learning about the outcomes of the merger for both companies.

Bayer

In the following part, the company Bayer will be introduced. This is achieved by presenting the history and evolution of Bayer and by showing its present corporal structure, the affected markets and intellectual property.

Origin and growth of Bayer

The Bayer Group has its headquarter in the German city of Leverkusen and is comprised of 420 fully consolidated companies that are located all over the world and employs approximately 117,000 people. The company is managed as a Life Science enterprise consisting of the Pharmaceutical, Consumer Health and the Crop Science division. The main objective of the Bayer Group is the research and development of solutions to some major challenges like the growing population and the involved problems (Bayer AG, 2019a).

The history of Bayer as a company started in the year 1863 when the dye salesman Friedrich Bayer and the master dyer Johann Friedrich Weskott founded the partnership "friedr. Bayer et comp." with the goal of manufacturing and selling dyestuffs. The target market of Bayer in the early years was the textile industry, which was starting to make a change from natural dyes to industrially produced chemical dyes. The technological milestone of the chemical dyes had the consequence that many companies emerged in this new market and only the most innovative companies like Bayer survived (Bayer AG, 2019b).

In the late 19th century, the company made big investments into new research facilities. These state-of-the-art facilities enabled the development of modern types of dye and also pharmaceuticals. Pharmaceuticals were a new Market for Bayer but with the invention of the "drug of the century" Aspirin, which became the most used pain reliever in history, they had a very successful start into the new market. But the successful expansion was soon stopped by the outbreak of the First World

War when it got cut off from its export markets. During the war, Bayer started to produce war materials including explosives and chemical weapons. The consequences of the war have been devastating for the company because they lost a great percentage of their foreign assets, trademarks, patents and markets were not accessible anymore (Bayer AG, 2019b).

After the First World War, the company merged into the I.G. Farbenindustrie AG to joined forces with other German chemical Companies to be able to survive. This enabled the invention of new pharmaceutical drugs, despite the problems of the big depression. The big depression was followed by the Second World War, which again meant difficult times for the I.G. Farbenindustrie AG. After the War, the merged companies were split and controlled by the allied forces and the Farbenfabrik Bayer AG was established (Bayer AG, 2019b).

The reconstruction and the reestablishment of the company were facilitated by the German "Wirtschaftswunder," which enabled them to grow their foreign assets again. The growth of Bayer led to the development of the new Crop Science division. The growth continued for the company in the late 20th and the early 21st century that lead to many acquisitions in growing markets to enable the globalization of Bayer, which finally lead to the acquisition of Monsanto in 2016 (Bayer AG, 2019b).

Today the Bayer Group is built up in four divisions. The pharmaceutical division focuses on the production of prescription drugs for cardiovascular diseases, woman's healthcare and on therapeutics in the area of oncology. Furthermore, the pharmaceutical division works on solutions for radiology with the necessary technical equipment and contrast agents. Another division of Bayer is the Consumer Health division that specializes on nonprescription drugs and ointments in different categories of treatments, with well-known products like Aspirin. The third division is the Crop Science division that specializes in seeds, crop protection and non-agricultural pest control. The fourth business unit of the Bayer Group is the Animal Health division. This division develops and sells products for the prevention and treatment of diseases in companion and farm animals (Bayer AG, 2019a).

Monsanto

Origin and growth of Monsanto

Monsanto has been founded in the United States, by John F. Queeny in 1901. He named the company by the name of his wife, Olga Monsanto Queeny. At this time, his main activity was to produce saccharin. This chemical product, which is used to sweeten aliments has been later sold to Coca-Cola.

In the 1920s, Monsanto expanded through industrial chemicals and drugs. While the company was the world's larger maker of aspirin and acetylsalicylic acid, they invented PCBs. This chemical product is under the form of oil with the particularity that it does not burn. Many uses have been found to this oil before the government found out it was toxic and prohibited its use.

During the following decade, Monsanto came to the field of agriculture with their first hybrid seed corn. This will be the premise to their future success, 40 years later. Nevertheless, they continued to produce other products, such as detergents, soap, industrial cleaning products, synthetic rubber and plastic.

During the 1950s, they built the house of the future in the Walt Disney park of California. This house was entirely made of plastic, from the walls to the different daily utensils. The house stayed for almost 10 years a famous attraction of the park, before being removed. This operation gave many difficulties to destruction teams, as the house was so robust that many usual destruction technics failed.

The decade before this presence on Walt Disney, Monsanto began research on uranium for the Manhattan Project. Which gave birth to the two atomic bombs dropped to Hiroshima and Nagasaki.

In the continuation of this collaboration with the U.S. government in a military manner, Monsanto created in the 1960s the agent-orange. This chemical defoliant has been used during the Vietnam war by the U.S. army. This agent was used as a defoliant in the Vietnamese fields, preventing the army to be fed. Moreover, this defoliant has also been used by farmers for their private use.

During the same period, they commercialized Aspartame, which is a derivative of sugar, 200 times sweeter and used as complement in different food or beverage. This product is used because using it instead of sugar would reduce calorie intake and body weight in adults and children.

In 1997, they commercialized the product which will make their success but will also bring many controversies, The Roundup line which two products are used together. The first product is an herbicide composed of glyphosate, and the second is genetically modified seeds, chemically produced to resist to this herbicide. The combination of these two products makes the life of farmers easier. They can plant the seeds closer one from another than with usual technics, increasing their return. Furthermore, this process requires less work, as by spraying the herbicide on the seeds it will enable them to grow without risking illness or invasions of weed, which decreases the amount of work required. Farmers need fewer employees and have higher revenues. The Roundup line was therefore sold as the dreamed product that every farmer needs. Later on, it has been discovered that this product could be a cause of cancer and other serious diseases.

After this discovery, Monsanto focused on agroindustry and from 2000 to 2018, the date of the purchase by Bayer, bought other companies related to this field of activity. An antitrust lawsuit has then been brought against the company for monopoly over the industry.

As one can imagine, the company was ethically questionable. This point will be discussed in the next section.

Ethical position

Monsanto has been very controverted, due to the fact that a large number of their products were extremely toxic or pollutant. Furthermore, in many cases, the company knew the destructive power of its products and hid the result of their experiences to the authority to continue to sell their products.

As example, we can take products mentioned in the section above. In the 1920s, they invented the PCBs (Polychlorinated Biphenyls). This product was presented under the form of heavy oils with a good electrical insulating property but had also other interesting properties and therefore many other uses. According to (Carpenter, 2006, pp. 4, 5), "PCBs are carcinogens; alter immune system functions; cause adverse alterations of the nervous system, skin, thyroid and sex steroid hormonal systems; liver, kidney, pancreas, and the cardiovascular system." One could be exposed to these illnesses by ingestion, inhalation or even by eating fish coming from contaminated water. As a result, it is not rare for a resident of a developed country to have a certain amount of PCBs in one's body (Carpenter, 2006).

By creating this product, Monsanto poisoned thousands of people and still today, a century after its discovery, people and animals all over the globe are still contaminated.

PCBs were only forbidden in 1979. This means that between the invention of the product and its removal, PCBs were freely used. But according to (industry, 2009) early as 1937, Monsanto knew about the danger of these products and tried to keep the secret of this danger. Going as far as "manipulate[ing] scientific studies by urging scientists to change their conclusions to downplay the risks of PCB exposure" (industry, 2009).

According to (Richard Gale, 2015), the same happened with the Roundup herbicide, for which Monsanto has been in trial. They hide the truth to continue to sell their products, even if these same products gave serious sickness to consumers.

This is not the only ethically disputable decision they made. They also helped the U.S. military power by carrying on researches on uranium, which led to the two atomic bombs at Hiroshima and Nagasaki, with millions of deaths, people intoxicated, as well as enormous damages to the environment. They were also one of the companies working for the agent orange used in the Vietnam war. This defoliant was highly toxic and has contaminated over three million people, killed half a million and the same number of babies are born with birth defects. Even the U.S. military veterans who were in charge to spread it around Vietnam are affected.

We can, therefore, conclude that Monsanto was not an ethical company. They had less interest in what was happening to consumers, and to the nature which were in contact with their products than about the money these products will bring to the company.

Due to this unethical behavior, many people hate Monsanto. This has, therefore, a consequence for Bayer, as a purchaser.

Process steps of negotiation management

The following part has the goal to give some insights on the agricultural supply industry in the time of the initial deal and on the reasons why Bayer wanted to buy Monsanto and what the initial deal consisted of. Furthermore, the characteristics of the negotiation will be analyzed based on negotiation management theories to get an overview of the processes of the biggest merger in the history of the German industry.

Reasons for Bayer to merge with Monsanto

One of the most important questions concerning the merger of Bayer and Monsanto is, why Bayer wanted to buy the American company Monsanto and what were the incentives behind the effort to make such a big expense. Prior to Bayer's first offer to Monsanto, the agriculture supply industry was going through big changes. There were already two big mergers going on in the time when Bayer made its first offer, the consolidation of the American companies Dow Chemical and DuPont which resulted in the company DowDuPont and the merger of the Chinese ChemChina and the Swiss company Syngenta (Kumar, 2018, p. 283). Therefore, the market which earlier consisted of seven big companies started to consolidate into only five agriculture supply companies. This development of the Market can be seen as reason why Bayer was opting to buy its competitor, because of the synergies that can be taken advance of and because of the possibility to offer advanced customized agronomic solutions to their costumers (Bayerr Investor Relations, 2018, p. 12). Bayer wanted to achieve this by combining their crop protection portfolio with Monsanto's market-leading portfolio of seeds and traits (Bayerr Investor Relations, 2018, p. 12). This merger would result in the company Bayer being the biggest company in the agriculture supply industry and therefore having a by far bigger influence on the Market.

Another strategical reason for Bayer to buy its competitor was the geographical focus of Monsanto on North and South America (The European Commission, 2018, p. 20). This was an opportunity for Bayer to facilitate the entry into these foreign markets by using existing marketing and sale channels of Monsanto to make use of sales synergies (Bayerr Investor Relations, 2018, p. 20). The other kind of synergies that would be possible to achieve by merging the two companies are cost synergies. Cost synergies consist out of financial advantages, that can be achieved for example by consolidating functions of the business units, consolidation of IT infrastructure or IT platforms, the application of best Practices of both organizations and by saving on in production, warehouse and distribution costs (Bayerr Investor Relations, 2018, p. 19). One of the most promising synergies for Bayer was the consolidation of the two R&D departments because their knowledge and patents it would enable them to develop products in a lot smaller time horizon (Kumar, 2018, p. 284). These and also other synergies were consequently also an important reason why Bayer considered buying Monsanto. These previously mentioned Points were the most important factors that played a role in the decision making of the Bayer executives when they were evaluating if they should go ahead and make an offer to Monsanto to buy the company and merge with Bayer or if they should continue with their business and see how the Industry evolves.

Initial deal

The decision to make an offer for Monsanto was then finally made by Werner Baumann at the beginning of May 2016, only 10 days after he became the CEO of the Bayer AG (Bender, 2019). Prior to the first offer of Werner Baumann, the chief executive of Monsanto, Hugh Grant was also discussing alternative mergers with three other companies, which were similarly interested in negotiations with Monsanto (United States Securities and Exchange Commission [SEC], 2016, pp. 27–29).

The two CEO's first met on May 10, 2016, when the Monsanto Executives invited the newly elected CEO of the Bayer AG to visit one of their research facilities to meet the new CEO and discuss possible marketing arrangements. Mr. Baumann then made an unexpected move, by making a non-binding proposal for a transaction in Which the Bayer AG would buy all the outstanding common stocks for $122 per share in cash (SEC, 2016, pp. 28–29). This first offer was then reviewed by Mr. Grant together with the Monsanto board and the board of directors, which came to the conclusion that the proposal was determined to be inadequate. Despite of the inadequate proposal, Monsanto indicated in a press release, that they are still interested in the continuation of the negotiations about the potential merger of the two companies (SEC, 2016, p. 29). Bayer responded to this press release, stating that they were still interested in making a deal with Monsanto and that they would be able to address financing and regulatory matters to the proposed transaction (SEC, 2016, p. 29).

During the following weeks Monsanto and its advisors kept having meetings with other companies to talk about possible mergers, but they also continued to negotiate with Bayer about different aspects of the proposed merger like the financing (SEC, 2016, p. 30). In the next meeting on June 21, 2016, Mr. Baumann stated that Bayer is not willing to increase its price until they had access to due diligence to get more information about Monsanto, but this request was then declined by Mr. Grant because he wanted to achieve a higher price and to introduce a reverse termination fee to have a greater deal certainty (SEC, 2016, p. 30).

At this point of the deal, both parties didn't want to make concessions and for the next weeks the two parties kept negotiating over the price and deal certainty issues (SEC, 2016, p. 31). This situation continued until July 9, 2016, when Mr. Baumann presented a new deal with a share price of $125 per share and reverse termination fee of $1.5 billion with the additional indication, that five banks were prepared to enter a loan agreement (SEC, 2016, p. 31). This second offer was again discussed together with the board of directors, which then decided that the price was still not appropriate but they authorized the management to start a due diligence process in order for Bayer to get more information to facilitate a further price increase (SEC, 2016, p. 32). After a management presentation, Bayer was still not willing to increase the price as Monsanto requested and the negotiation was again blocked as they couldn't find a compromise (SEC, 2016, p. 33).

This standstill continued until August 10, 2016, when Bayer offered a new price of $127.5 per share, the antitrust reverse termination fee of $1.5 billion and they also stated that they will be willing to divest up 12% of Monsanto's net sales to obtain antitrust approvals for the transaction (SEC, 2016, pp. 33–34). This proposal still wasn't accepted by Monsanto's board of advisors, but they decided to let Bayer proceed with its due diligence (SEC, 2016, p. 34). The whole month of August and the beginning of September were used by Bayer to make further due diligence and they also started to let their legal advisors negotiate regulatory matters relating to the potential merger (SEC, 2016, p. 35).

The final negotiation concerning the merger was then made on September 7 and 9, 2016, at this point, both CEO agreed on a price of $128 per share and a reverse termination fee of $1.85billion (SEC, 2016, p. 36). These conditions were then given to the board of directors who met on September 12 and 13 and discussed the proposal with their financial and legal advisors and finally made the decision, that a price of $128 per share is a fair deal for its investors and then resolved a recommend adoption of the merger agreement to holders of shares of the company's common stock (SEC, 2016, p. 37).

Characteristics of the negotiation

The following part focuses on the characteristics of the merger negotiation between Bayer and Monsanto, based on the theoretical background of Markus Voeth and Uta Herbst (2015, pp. 52–146).

Negotiation analysis

As Voeth and Herbst (2015, p. 52) describe, the first step of a negotiation analysis is to check if negotiation management has a high significance for the outcome of a negotiation. They define two factors which make negotiation management is highly important (Voeth & Herbst, 2015).

- The first of those two is the case in which the outcome of the negotiation has a high significance for the company. This means if the negotiation outcome is highly important for a company, they should use negotiation management and invest a lot of time and effort to prepare and plan the negotiation (Voeth & Herbst, 2015, p. 53).
- The second factor that enhances the importance of negotiation management is the level of difficulty of a negotiation. In case of a difficult negotiation, all the involved parties have to prepare themselves for the negotiation. This enables the parties to make the right decisions at the right time. There are many possible reasons for a higher difficulty of a negotiation but the most

important ones are the object of the negotiation, the negotiation partner, the negotiation history and the circumstances of the negotiation (Voeth & Herbst, 2015, pp. 53–58).

Considering these factors, the importance of negotiation management was very high in the case of the merger of Bayer and Monsanto. This assumption can be made by considering the high importance of the outcome of the negotiation for both parties, as both sides would face big organizational or also financial challenges in case of a successful negotiation (Voeth & Herbst, 2015, pp. 54–55). On the other hand, the difficulty of the negotiation is also very high because of the size of the deal and the high number of regulatory hurdles that had to be overcome to make a successful closing on the deal (Voeth & Herbst, 2015, pp. 55–56).

By analyzing these factors, it is possible to create negotiation portfolios. These negotiation portfolios are used to identify which items of negotiation have a high importance and are therefore necessary and which items have a low importance and can be conducted at a later point of time by lover hierarchy levels (Voeth & Herbst, 2015). In case of the merger of Bayer and Monsanto, the merger negotiation clearly was in a portfolio of high importance and consequently it was mainly the board members and the CEO's that made the decisions (SEC, 2016, pp. 27–37).

As a second step, at the time when negotiation will take place, it is important to collect and organize as much data about the opposite party and about the negotiation as possible. These data are then used to prepare for the coming negotiation.

One of the most important information areas for negotiation analysis is the object of the negotiation (Voeth & Herbst, 2015, p. 64). The three most important steps of this analysis are:

1. the identification of the object of negotiation,
2. the examination of the object,
3. the analysis of the integrity of the objective (Voeth & Herbst, 2015, pp. 64–74).

Regarding this theory, it is possible to assume that Bayer was following this concept and started to gather information about Monsanto. In case of the merger of Bayer and Monsanto, the price and the amount of the reverse termination fee to be paid were clearly the main negotiation objectives. These two objectives were clearly bilateral preferences, this means that both involved parties do not want to make compromises and in such a case a win-win situation is not possible. The identification of the main negotiation objects was followed by the analysis of the objects. The analysis of the price for the merger and of the amount of the reverse termination fee to be paid was conducted by making a due diligence during August 2016, where additional information regarding financial information and the company's assets was gathered.

Another interesting addition to the topic of the negotiation analysis is the extension of the scope of negotiations. Such extensions can be achieved by creating different kinds of side deals (Voeth & Herbst, 2015, p. 79). Side deals are used to link the outcome of a negotiation to the outcome of another negotiation and are split into three kinds of side deals. These side deals are used in negotiations to strengthen the positions of certain negotiation parties compared to their opponents (Voeth & Herbst, 2015, p. 79).

During the initial negotiations of the merger of Bayer and Monsanto, side deals were for example used by Monsanto to secure the closing of the main deal. They discussed with Bayer that they will only allow further negotiations if Bayer would consider divestments because Monsanto feared that without divestments the deal would not get approved by the authorities (SEC, 2016, pp. 27–37). This side deal can be categorized as an object-related side deal because of the links to other negotiation objectives (Voeth & Herbst, 2015, p. 81).

Negotiation organization

The analysis of the negotiation is followed by the organization of the negotiation (Voeth & Herbst, 2015, p. 86). In this phase, the companies must identify the rules that are valid during the planed negotiation. Another important decision in this phase is the question of who will negotiate the different negotiations and in addition to that the logistical questions of where to meet and when to meet are also discussed in this phase.

The first phase of the negotiation organization consists of the definition of the rules that are valid during the negotiation (Voeth & Herbst, 2015, p. 86). According to them, there are three kinds of rules that apply to negotiations:

1. Legal rules (e.g. rules by legal authorities),
2. One-sided rules (e.g. e-bidding processes),
3. Mutually agreed rules (e.g. rules that were introduced with mutual agreement of affected group).

During the negotiations of the merger of Bayer and Monsanto, the most important rules were those of the governmental authorities. These rules were extremely important because of the restrictions concerning the market share of the new merged company that would have to be calculated and negotiated properly to get clearance from the authorities (SEC, 2016, pp. A-9, A-17, A-30).

Another important possibility of negotiation organization strategy is trying to influence the other negotiation team (Voeth & Herbst, 2015). This can be achieved by the decision who we want to send to a negotiation or also be defining the size of the negotiation group. By sending different kind of people we achieve that the other party must adapt its negotiation strategy. If one company for example sends the CEO and the CFO the other company should also send high executives to profit most of the negotiation (Voeth & Herbst, 2015, pp. 105–106).

This was also the case during the first meetings between Bayer and Monsanto as both companies negotiated via their top executives. This had the advantage that the rough outline of the merger could be determined in only a few meetings between them and with access to important information and a direct link to the board of directors (SEC, 2016, pp. 27–37). Also, negotiation groups were always quite small due to the hierarchy of the representatives. Most of the meetings during the negotiations consisted only out of two to four people (SEC, 2016, pp. 27–37; Voeth & Herbst, 2015, pp. 104–105).

Phases of negotiation

Usually, negotiations deal with different items. In the case of the Bayer-Monsanto merger, many different items had to be negotiated. As it is a merger, every item composing Monsanto must be disclosed. Monsanto has been founded more than a hundred years ago, therefore, has expanded in different domains, having a lot of different items. The two parties had to find an agreement on all of them. By discussing these items, companies had respective wishes and want to have the best out of this merger. Meaning the maximum amount of money for Monsanto, and well detailed information and processes for Bayer, as well as a small purchase price. A merger, to be efficient, must successfully integrate both companies into one. Meaning, amongst others, a complementarity of products and process. From these elements, the most important items of the negotiation will stand out. In most cases, these elements will be products as well as research and development carried on by the selling company, in which the buying company is interested. The price of those items is often of main importance, and therefore, a subject of discord as both parties want to maximize their own output out of the merger. It is of main importance, for a good negotiation, that both parties can find convergence of interests. Firstly, on the value of the different items, but also on the other important topics. If they cannot find an agreement on prices, they will be in the "No bargaining zone" (Voeth & Herbst, 2015). In this case the maximum price at which the buyer is willing to pay the good (RPB) is lower than the minimum price at which the seller is willing to sell its good (RPs). Therefore, no deal is possible as they will not find any compromise.

Now that the importance of finding convergent points and to minimize issues has been formulated. We can analyze these points on the Bayer-Monsanto merger.

Convergence points

In the following, the points of convergence for the merger of Bayer and Monsanto will be given and analyzed from a negotiation perspective, especially the points that they brought to the negotiation, their importance as well as the willingness of Bayer to pay for Monsanto.

To better understand in which area the two companies found convergence points, one has first to know to which extent the products of Bayer and Monsanto are different and complementary. On one hand, Monsanto was focused on three main fields of activities. Seeds, data science and crop protection (Bayer, 2018, p. 12). On the other hand, Bayer was mainly focused on high- value seeds, innovative chemical and biological pest management solutions as well as extensive customer service for modern and sustainable agriculture (Bayer, 2018, p. 12).

Therefore, according to Bayer annual report of 2016, the two companies are different and highly complementary. Monsanto domain of activity, as a leading global provider of agricultural products, including seeds and seed technologies, herbicides and digital platform, allowed the company to provide agronomic recommendations to farmers (Bayer, 2016, p. 235). The differences between the two companies are present, even if working on the same field of activity, the agroindustry. These two companies are therefore not competitive as Bayer is more focused on plant and soil health, as well as in crop protection. As we can see, Bayer needs the knowledge of Monsanto in order to offer a comprehensive set of solutions to meet current and future needs of food supply in the sector of crop's quality as well as digital farming and crop protection. It is only by using both companies' innovation capabilities and R&D technology platform that they will be able to reach this goal (Bayer, 2016).

One of the items which interested them the most was therefore Monsanto's knowledge in the domain of; – outstanding seeds & traits portfolio, – focus on yield, – breeding and trait development focus and, – advanced digital farming platform. As we can see in the "Monsanto acquisition update" from June 2018 retrieved by Bayer. They planned to combine those newly acquired knowledges with their own ones; – outstanding crop protection portfolio, – focus on plant and soil health, – excellence in chemistry and, – biologics platform, to create what they assess as the future of farming; a "customized agronomic solution." This should be the result of a specialization on three key fields coming from the above-mentioned combination of Bayer and Monsanto respective field of specialization; – seeds and traits, – crop protection including biologics and, – digital technologies and services (Bayer, 2018; Varinsky, 2018).

As the objective of Bayer is to provide added value to the farmer through entire growth process of the farmer's seed, they needed knowledge about data science. As they had no research and development going on in this sector, they saw the opportunity to complement their lack of knowledges by acquiring this company based in St. Louis.

As saw earlier, despite Bayer's willingness to create an extensive customer service for modern and sustainable customer, they did not have the knowledge to create a data science-related product. The knowledge acquired by Monsanto in the domain of data science can therefore be useful for Bayer in this perspective. This is not the only item which Bayer was lacking in order to reach their goal.

It is also important to have in mind that it takes approximately ten years for an agronomic company to create a new herbicide. Beginning from the research and development to the moment the product arrives in the market. After some time in the market, if the product shows grate sales and is likely used by customers, it takes another decade for seed trait responding to the new chemical to be created. Which means that a minimum of twenty-year is necessary to satisfy a need of the market. Therefore, both innovation push and innovation pull require an enormous amount of time. Having the risk to be overtaken by the concurrent companies.

By performing this merger, the two companies are able to share this long process by dividing the work amongst respective companies preferred sector of activity. Using this process, the time is divided by half. Which will instantly give them advantages in terms of innovations and time of reaction to the demand of the market over their concurrent. Which according to Werner Baumann, CEO of Bayer AG, and despite the thoughts of a large party of concerned people who think that Bayer is now the undisputed leader in the sector, is still very strong. On that subject, Bayer wrote:

> We are competing with other very strong companies that offer similar products and have strong R&D capabilities. We will only succeed with pricing and selling our products if our value proposition to our customers is better than that of our competitors and if we continue to innovate. We are also convinced that in a competitive business such as the agriculture industry, the efficiency gains generated by innovation will increase returns for farmers. (Varinsky, 2018)

But not everyone shares this opinion. An example is Mark Connelly, an agriculture analyst. He is of the opinion that "Monsanto has historically sought out partnerships and joint ventures with other companies that are developing innovative products. But that means dividing up profits" (Varinsky, 2018). Therefore, he predicts that the new company will use the possibility to have the entire process to favor in-house production of products of bad quality instead of more promising ones which would require a revenue-sharing partnership. With this proceed, they would spare money and therefore, increase again their revenues.

The main convergence points were therefore linked to a similar vision for the future of farming and a need from Bayer to buy a company able to provide products for which they did not have any knowledge. Now that we have seen the convergence points, one can analyze the issues, as those are the most important topic in negotiation as one has to resolve them in order to avoid lockout.

Main issues

> Negotiation is the process of agreeing on one or more objects of exchange between parties with at least partially different preferences, it the course of which the parties try to influence the generally possible solutions in their favor. Negotiations are thus also to be understood at the joint decision-making process between at least two parties. (Voeth & Herbst, 2015)

According to this definition of negotiation, the aim of a negotiation is to agree on different items of exchange, for which the different parties have at least partially different preferences. Issues are therefore part of negotiation and unavoidable. Furthermore, the parties will try to influence the solutions in their favor, which can bring serious lockout in the negotiation.

In this section, we will analyze the different issues of the negotiation. We will try to reference the items of negotiation on which the two parties did not agree, and why this was the case. An analysis of the method used to resolve the different disputes will also be performed.

First, the "Model Variant of Game Theory" proposes two options of negotiations; "Cooperative Games" and "Non-cooperative Game" (Voeth & Herbst, 2015). The latter by opposition to the "Cooperative Game" involves Nash-Equilibrium, Pareto-optimal solution, as well as "referee solution." Therefore, a model emphasizing equalities amongst the two parties. In this model, a global maximization of the benefits is performed. This is the opposite of the non-cooperative game that happened between Bayer and Monsanto. The merger was characterized by offer and counteroffer. Monsanto refused to disclose information as long as the price offered by Bayer did not satisfy them. Process observation has also been a main component of the negotiation as after each offer, parties discussed internally to look at the different opportunities. The characteristics we have seen in the merger are the different elements characterizing a "Non-cooperative Game." We can, therefore, say that the merger has been performed under this variant of the Game Theory.

Bayer faced two huge issues concerning this merger. One of those was the price. As stated above, the price is often a subject of disagreement in negotiation. Monsanto wanted to sell the company at a good price, to satisfy its shareholders. That is the first reason for which they fought on the price of the company (Monsanto, 2016). Bayer, on the other hand, wanted to spend as little money as possible. But even with these divergent requests, they were able to conclude a negotiation. It is only at the third offer from Bayer that Monsanto agreed to disclose information they hid to this point, and to merge.

Bayer initial offer was to pay Monsanto 122$ by share. This amount was too low according to the thought of Monsanto negotiators. The company refused to disclose any detailed business information until a higher offer is made. This kind of negotiation tactics can be linked to the

U.S. culture. The cultural factor plays a great role in a negotiation (Voeth & Herbst, 2015) (United States Institute of Peace, 2002), the U.S negotiation style, is amongst other categorizations, forceful, explicit and result oriented. Which is exactly what has been done here. By refusing to provide important information, they explicitly shew their opinion over the deal, in a forceful way. They played with a key item of this negotiation to obtain the needed result. This can also be linked to another theory, which is related to the significance of the interest of both parties in the negotiation. Monsanto positioned itself in a winning situation. By having the power to choose under which condition they wanted to give that information, they could have raised the price, leading to a cooperation strategy (win–win). One could even argue that this was a competition strategy (win–lose) from the point of view of Monsanto, as this information could have been useful to Bayer, to evaluate the value of the company as a global company, as well as the different items of the negotiation.

Eight days later, Bayer increase the offer to $125 per share, where it created a deadlock. A deadlock is the increase in the price of did not satisfy Monsanto; as according to Eyk Henning (2016), "investors reaction to the news indicated the market is skeptical the increase will be sufficient to seal the deal." This has been seen in reality as the final deal has been $128 per share, according to Bayer's annual report of 2016 (Bayer, 2016).

To understand the following part, one should have deeper knowledge about this negotiation. The first question we will try to answer is why Bayer wanted to buy Monsanto. As seen earlier, their intention is to provide to their customers, a "customized agronomic solution." The issue Bayer faced with such a product was that it requires a digital platform. Having a recommendation for the farmer, depending on the weather conditions as well as on the seeds to use or other parameters requires a great knowledge in Data Science. A great amount of research and development should also have been performed to provide a usable product. At the time of the merger, Bayer had no products which such characteristics, and developing one from scratch would require a lot of financial and time effort for a company that does not have the necessary knowledge. Monsanto, on the other hand, was a leader in this technology (Bayer, 2018).

With this new technology arriving in their company, the merger will give Bayer the lead in the agronomic industry. Emphasizing the lead, Bayer already bought several agronomic industries before concluding this merger. This led them to issues with antitrust law concerning this lead. As they were able to provide products for the entire process of growing seeds, plus services that no other company is capable to provide. The merger will give Bayer 28% of the market share in this sector. Which is enormous for a single company. Therefore, they had to sell different products to BASF in the sector of crop protection, seed and traits and digital farming. These products were worth $9 billion, but they were obliged to sell those licenses to be able to acquire Monsanto. Furthermore, they also agreed on "structural divestitures" and to sell off "certain intellectual property and research capabilities, including 'pipeline' R&D projects." Without those sells, the merger would have been unlawful (Mangan, 2018). As it would have brought a monopoly from Bayer, leading the entire market.

If they reach their objective to render the life of farmers easier and increase the productivity with their range of product. This would lead to an enormous amount of benefit for this company. According to some critics, it could be possible that the company also take advantage of the technology to collect data from their consumer to use them in a marketing purpose. This would lead to personalized advertisement, increasing the likelihood of the farmer to buy Bayer's products.

The economic perspectives of this merger were therefore interesting. And as they are convinced that the glyphosate, used in Roundup, is not dangerous for human health at the quantity used by farmers, they have the firm intention to change people's mind about this uncertainty. They are therefore not afraid of lawsuits concerning this product. They therefore plan to lose only a negligible amount of money in those lawsuits and reparations, having a net raise of income following the merger with Monsanto.

Bayer is also facing other key issues. As they state in their annual report from 2016,

> Difficulties may arise in connection with the acquisition and integration of the Monsanto business that adversely impact our current business or may prevent the expected benefits of the acquisition from being fully realized. These include the retention of key employees, important customers, suppliers, partners, licensors or contacts to other stakeholders, unexpected challenges in developing and successfully executing a strategy for the combined business, and risks resulting from management being distracted from the operational business by the agreed transaction. Combining businesses, processes and workforces as intended while retaining multiple corporate locations could be more complex than expected, partly in view of different corporate cultures and divergent internal control and compliance systems. (Bayer, 2016, p. 178)

This statement shows that the two parties did not find agreements on every item of negotiation. This could be because these items have been excluded from the negotiation. Meaning that they "deliberately exclude[d] from the negotiation some of the issues under consideration" (Voeth & Herbst, 2015). Those items listed above match the requirements for an exclusion, they are not of main importance as the two companies had more incentive to be focused on the price of the merger or to negotiate on Monsanto's information. As the negotiating parties are not the only concerned parties concerned, as example, Monsanto key employees can also decide by themselves that they do not want to work for Bayer, those people can change opinion, and this will not be under Monsanto's control.

Final deal

In June 2018, Bayer became Monsanto's official owner, however, as required by the Justice Department of the United States, the company was only allowed to manage the business after selling some assets (Bender, 2019).

At the end of the arduous two-year antitrust process, the $63 billion acquisition of Monsanto Co. by Bayer was finalized. By retiring the U.S. seeds maker's 117-year-old name, Bayer doubled the size of its agriculture business and became the biggest seed and agricultural chemicals maker in the world. As said in an official statement at the time of the merger "Bayer will remain the company name.

Monsanto will no longer be a company name. The acquired products will retain their brand names and become part of the Bayer portfolio" (Burger, 2018). In its official investor relations site, Monsanto stated that J.P. Morgan was part of the negotiation by assisting Bayer with processing the purchase price paid for this huge acquisition. Further, the American company shares were not anymore traded on the famous New York Stock Exchange after the purchased and the Monsanto shareholders received $128 per share.

Also, the deal suffered major criticism as Monsanto was pursuing its intellectual property rights with farmers, which depend on its seeds, more intensely than other companies, besides as being decided during a period when U.S. President Donald Trump was criticising Germany's trade surplus with the United States. As said by the Bayer Chief Executive Werner Baumann in a statement, "We aim to deepen our dialogue with society. We will listen to our critics and work together where we find common ground. Agriculture is too important to allow ideological differences to bring progress to a standstill" (Burger, 2018).

As for the next steps, Liam Condon – a member of the Bayer Board of Management, responsible for leading the combined Crop Science Division – has another important task: unify the two companies. As soon as Bayer finished the sale of some of its agriculture assets to BASF, as stated by the Justice Department, already mentioned, they started the integration with Monsanto. The Monheim, Germany was chosen as the combined unit and St. Louis unit held the North American business and seeds division. As for Bayer Chairman Werner Baumann, the company "will be even better placed to help the world's farmers grow more healthy and affordable food in a sustainable manner" (Kresge, 2018).

In the case of the Indian units, Bayer CropScience Ltd. and Monsanto India Ltd., they continue to operate independently, as disclosed in a separate statement (Burger, 2018).

This is the third negotiation in the industry, after Dow Chemical's merger with DuPont Co. and China National Chemical Corp.'s acquisition of Syngenta. In that sense, the Germany company decided to sell its plastic business and focused on becoming a life-science company-oriented: half of the sales now come from health and the other half comes from agriculture.

Also, in terms of making sure that would have been enough competition in the market, as stated by regulation agencies, Bayers sold $9 billion in assets from field seeds and vegetable seeds business, some of the seed treatments and, also, digital farming to BASF.

Regarding future expectations, the German company hoped that the American company would transform Bayer's smaller agrochemicals business into a market leader by combining its pesticides with Monsanto's seeds and high-tech crops. Based on that, it was stated that Bayer could gather $1.2 billion a year in costs, besides being able to develop new products more efficiently and generate more revenue (Bender, 2019).

The main objectives with the deal were to attract long-term growth market, become a leader with broad and complementary agricultural offering and geographic

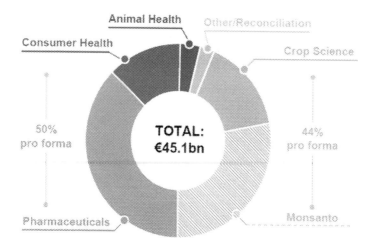

FIGURE 7.1 2017 Pro forma Sales incl. Monsanto ("Bayer Closes Monsanto Acquisition | Monsanto," 2018).

footprint, develop powerful innovation engine, create substantial synergy potential and generate strong value creation for the shareholders. As Figure 7.1 shows, Bayer was predicting a total of €45.1 billion of Pro forma sales including Monsanto in 2017 ("Bayer Closes Monsanto Acquisition | Monsanto," 2018).

Hence, as Monsanto planned, Bayer's best-selling products (Xarelto and Eylea) could cushion a possible decline in pharmaceutical revenues and the extra capacity would shield Bayer from unwanted suitors (Bender, 2019).

Outcomes

Werner Baumann, Chairman of the Bayer Board of Management in the Monsanto's Investor Relations official site at the time of the merger said

> Today is a great day: for our customers – farmers around the world whom we will be able to help secure and improve their harvests even better; for our shareholders, because this transaction has the potential to create significant value; and for consumers and broader society, because we will be even better placed to help the world's farmers grow more healthy and affordable food in a sustainable manner. As a leading innovation engine in agriculture, we offer employees around the world attractive jobs and development opportunities. (Monsanto, 2018, second paragraph)

"Our sustainability targets are as important to us as our financial targets. We aim to live up to the heightened responsibility that a leadership position in agriculture entails and to deepen our dialogue with society" (Monsanto, 2018). However, what were the major outcomes of the merger after almost a year after an apparently integrative deal?

Monsanto

Regarding the outcomes after the merger, besides ending the name of "Monsanto" and relocation of previously mentioned sites, the company's personnel would be the one who will have to deal with major changes, not only in terms of maintaining previous positions, but also regarding the company's culture merger.

As stated by Figure 7.2, the new acquired Bayer sector added some Monsanto workers, but layoffs will happen in several countries until 2021. The industry will make cuts in its agrochemical sector, with the suppression of 4,100 stations, as well as in the production of over-the-counter drugs and research and development. This will result in the removal of 12,000 jobs (Cohen, 2019).

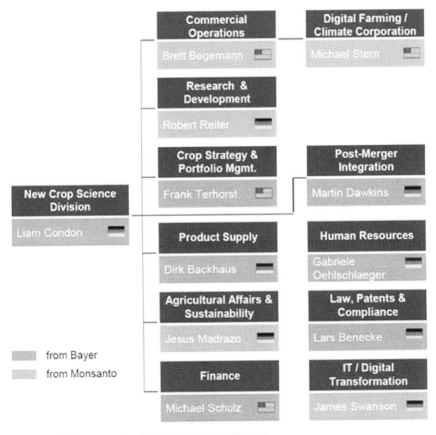

FIGURE 7.2 New crop science executive leadership team in place (Monsanto, 2018).

Regarding the cultural merge, Bayer conducted a cultural assessment and identified the cultural journey for both companies, with Bayer characterized as a long-term viewer (Driven to create lasting stakeholder); and Monsanto being more entrepreneurial (Driven to create new markets value). Based on that, Bayer strategy was to develop but a culture evolution & change process led by senior management, in order to align foundational values and cultural sensitivity was started. The main objective of Bayer is to focus on customers, innovation, execution, stakeholder value and people.

Bayer

Unfortunately, there are still no good news regarding the outcomes of the merger for Bayer. The $63 billion negotiation ranks as one of the worst corporate deals recently and is vividly threatening the good reputation that Bayer conquered over time. Only after some weeks of the conclusion of the takeover, Bayer not only lost a lawsuit regarding Monsanto's Roundup herbicide, as it was allegedly a cancer-causing but also was damaged by more than $190 million payment because of two other subsequent defeats. In addition, according to *The Wall Street Journal* , the problems are just starting, as a total of 18,400 accusers are suing the company (Bender, 2019).

As shares are majorly dropping by 30% since the final deal, Bayer is trying its best to appeal regarding the safety of Roundup. As we can observe in Figure 7.3, the deal is already considered as one of the worst corporate mergers by lost share still and Bayer's market capitalization is almost close to what the company paid for Monsanto, suggesting the dissipation of the value of the company (Bender, 2019). But how can all this happen?

According to Ruth Render, there were major factors that impacted the bad outcomes for Bayer. First, it was the idea.

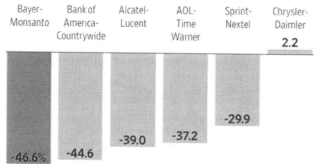

FIGURE 7.3 Change in share price, one year after deal completion (Sherman, 2019)7.

There were some indications that the CEO, Mr. Baumann, wanted to buy Monsanto for a long time, but it was only in 2015 when the Syngenta deal – regarding Monsanto's pursuit of Syngenta that caused a frenzy of agrochemicals transactions – fell through and Monsanto's shares fell that Mr. Baumann took action. Besides that, during a visit to the St. Louis Monsanto's headquarters, being backed by Chairman Werner Wenning, the new CEO with only two weeks in charge made the offer to the Americans executives.

The second point is the meltdown. Despite the disbelief from the investors, as after four months and several improved offers to Monsanto, the CEO could secure Monsanto's approval.

In that sense, with the agreement of Monsanto, Mr. Baumann had to sell the idea to his own shareholders. As stated in a Bayer's Investor Relations Presentation, the German company believed that the acquisition of Monsanto would create a lot of value. By targeting the year of 2022, they expected $1.2billion annual synergies (net EBITDA impact before special items) and envisioned to be accretive to core EPS in 2019. Besides that, they had planned the Integration process and were willing to create a global leader committed to transforming agriculture that could generate industry-leading profitability by combining agriculture business as stated in a Monsanto Acquisition Update in 2018.

Also, the CEO strategy was not to radically change the company, as some investors were pushing for a pharma deal. Further, as he had the concern of the amount of debt that needed to be raised to fund the Monsanto deal, which could lead to a reduction in investments in the pharma side, he stated that other divisions will still continue to be invested. However, in 2017, as the plan to close the acquisition was harmed by the European and U.S. antitrust regulators, the company had to issue a profit warning as Bayer had to deal with high inventories at its own Brazilian crop science business and decreasing sales for consumer health in the U.S. market (Bender, 2019).

However, when Bayer acquired Monsanto in 2018, the company still needed to sell some of its assets first and could not start managing the business right away. In that way, when Monsanto's lawyers were preparing themselves for the first Roundup trial, Bayer executives were not involved. Being defeated in the court, Monsanto had to pay $289.2 million in damages in August 2018, the price later reduced to $78.5 million, but that discouraged Bayer directors and alarmed markets. Besides, new lawsuits were rapidly increasing worsening the situation (Bender, 2019).

As the third point, it was the aftermath. In order to uphold the deal, Bayer, who is still advocating for the security of Roundup, aimed for a company restructuring in 2018 with the intention to raise profits, sell more assets, save €2.6 billion in annual cost and cut 10% of its personnel. For that matter, Bayer sold its animal health business to Elanco for $7.6 billion and had abandoned its sun care line Coppertone and foot care brand Dr. Scholl's (Liu, 2019).

As we can observe, by separating this plan from the Roundup adversities, the CEO had a strategy to recover investor confidence (Bender, 2019). However, in April 2019, in the firm's general meeting, as the share price continued to fall, 55.5% of the shareholders cast a rare no-confidence vote in Mr. Baumann and a third of investors were dissatisfied with the supervisory board led by chairman Werner Wenning, who also endorsed the Monsanto deal. According to *The Wall Street Journal*, more than 90% of those votes were in favor of Bayer's leadership in the five years from 2014 to 2018 (Liu, 2019).

At that time, Mr. Wenning stated that the vote was "an opportunity to support Bayer's Board of Management in its efforts to swiftly and fully restore the confidence of shareholders and other stakeholders in the company and in its strategy," and that the Supervisory board "unanimously stands behind" Baumann and his team (Kresge & Loh, 2019).

Later, in order to manage the pressure from the investors, Bayer added additional legal adviser and improved the failure of its past legal problems. The analysts calculated between €5 billion and €25 billion ($5.5 billion and $27.7 billion) of Bayer's total Roundup liability, based on the, already, three decisions against the German company. Furthermore, lawmakers are already discussing implementing more bans on Roundup's ingredient, as some jurisdictions banned glyphosate, one of the products ingredients (Bender, 2019).

In that sense, is common that analysts and investors question whether the acquisition of Monsanto business, in fact, generated value for Bayer. There is also some speculation that the best for Bayer would be to break up (Bender, 2019).

According to Christopher Perrella, a chemicals analyst from Bloomberg Intelligence, "the loss of a nonbinding confidence vote at Bayer's annual meeting may hasten management changes and the eventual logical split of Crop Chemicals and Pharmaceuticals into separate companies" (Kresge & Loh, 2019). Unfortunately, researchers and analysts do not have information access and even after the data is consolidated, it is still hard to analyze everything and confidently achieve the right conclusions in order to share the results (Liu,2019).

When the deal was finalized, Bayer envisioned a regular rise in sales and gains by 2022 with the acquisition of Monsanto, as previously shown in Figure 7.1 from Bayer's official Investor Relations Presentation of June 2018. However, the results released in July 2019 demonstrated that the crop-science business, containing Monsanto, did not achieve the positive results expected regarding bad weather situation (Bender, 2019).

It is possible to observe that the Monsanto deal improved Bayer's crop science business, however the original intention was that the pharma side (Bayer's growth engine for years) would not be hurt in terms of receiving investments. As Bayer's handle multiple trial defeats, there are apprehensions regarding the debt of the company. The main reason is that, in 2023, Bayer's most famous drugs – blood thinner Xarelto and eye drug Eylea – lose patent protection and analysts believe that Bayer's pharma sector could not afford all the expenses and did not have enough funds to gather other major pharma negotiations (Liu, 2019).

In August 2019, Bayer was still 50% down in comparison with April 2015, when the company was considered the most valuable German enterprise. Nevertheless, the company is getting back on track by achieving a reduction of two more trial verdicts and by getting the investors to believe on a fast settlement. The good news was that shares were slightly increasing from June's seven years low (Bender, 2019).

Top learnings

- *What first was seen as one the most revolutionary and biggest integrative deal in the agriculture sector (together the companies would be the biggest seed and agricultural chemicals producer in the world) now is being considered as one of the worst corporate mergers.*
- *The negotiation process had considerable directly and indirectly linked costs for Bayer:*
  - *Monsanto's asking price of $63 billion.*
  - *An antitrust process, which was settled by selling of $9 billion worth of assets.*
  - *Legal proceedings estimated between $5.5 billion and $27.7 billion.*
  - *A rare and highly reputation damaging no-confidence vote for the management by alarmed and angry shareholders.*
  - *Until long after the negotiation Bayer was still handling stock slump, loss of market space, decline in reputation and low levels of production (culture integration issues, high inventories, etc.).*
- *The deal cannot be viewed as integrative at all and financially severely hurt the German company.*

References

Bayer. (2016). Annual report 2016 augmented version. Retrieved December 12, 2019, from https://www.annualreport2016.bayer.com

Bayer. (2018). Annual report 2018. Retrieved December 12, 2019, from https://www.bayer.com/en/bayer-annual-report-2018.pdfx

Bayer AG. (2019a). History. Retrieved November 28, 2019, from https://www.bayer.com/en/history.aspx

Bayer AG. (2019b). Profile and organisation/at a glance. Retrieved November 28, 2019, from https://www.bayer.com/en/profile-and-organization.aspx

Bayerr Investor Relations. (2018). *Monsanto acquisition update, June 2018*. Leverkusen: Bayer AG.

Bender, R. (2019). How Bayer-Monsanto became one of the worst corporate deals – in 12 charts. Retrieved December 7, 2019, from http://www.vis-am.ch/uploads/allegati/How_Bayer-Monsanto_Became_One_of_the_Worst_Corporate_Deals%E2%80%94in_12_Charts_-_WSJ.pdf

Bender, R. (2019, August 28). *The Wall Street Journal*. Retrieved December 13, 2019, from https://www.wsj.com/articles/how-bayer-monsanto-became-one-of-the-worst-corporate-dealsin-12-charts-11567001577

Burger, L. (2018). With deal to close this week, Bayer to retire Monsanto name. Retrieved December 7, 2019, from https://www.reuters.com/article/us-monsanto-m-a-bayer-closing/with-deal-to-close-this-week-bayer-to-retire-monsanto-name-idUSKCN1J00IZ

Carpenter, D.O. (2006). Polychlorinated biphenyls (PCBs): Routes of exposure and effects on human health. *Reviews on Environmental Health, 21*(1), 1–23.

Cohen, B. (2019). Bayer anuncia supressão de 12.000 empregos após compra da Monsanto. Retrieved December 8, 2019, from https://www.em.com.br/app/noticia/internacional/2018/11/29/interna_internacional,1009107/bayer-anuncia-supressao-de-12-000-empregos-apos-compra-da-monsanto.shtml

Eyk Henning, J. B. (14. July 2016). *The Wall Street Journal*. Retrieved from https://www.wsj.com/articles/bayer-makes-new-offer-for-monsanto-1468512577abgerufen

Gale, Richard. (2015). Online Reference: https://content.sierraclub.org/grassrootsnetwork/team-news/2015/09/monsanto-s-sealed-documents-reveal-truth-behind-roundup-s-toxicological-dangers

Kresge, N., & Loh, T. (2019). Bayer board backs CEO after unprecedented shareholder Rebuke. Retrieved December 8, 2019, from https://www.bloombergquint.com/business/bayer-says-supervisory-board-supports-ceo-baumann-after-vote

Kresge, N. (2018). Bayer closes Monsanto deal to cap $63 billion transformation. Retrieved December 7, 2019, from https://www.bloomberg.com/news/articles/2018-06-07/bayer-closes-monsanto-deal-to-cap-63-billion-transformation

Kumar, B. R. (2018). Bayer's acquisition of Monsanto. In *Wealth creation in the world's largest mergers and acquisitions* (pp. 281–287). Cham: Springer.

Liu, A. (2019). Worst deal ever? Bayer's market cap now close to the total cost it paid for Monsanto. Retrieved December 8, 2019, from https://www.fiercepharma.com/pharma/worst-deal-ever-bayer-s-market-cap-now-close-to-total-cost-it-paid-for-monsanto

Mangan, D. (2018, May 30). CNBC. Retrieved from https://www.cnbc.com/2018/05/29/bayer-will-sell-basf-9-billion-in-assets-to-allow-monsanto-purchase.html abgerufen

Monsanto. (2016). 2016 Annual Report. St. Louis, Missouri. Retrieved December 7, 2019, from http://www.monsantoglobal.com/global/in/Documents/Annual%20Report%202016%20-%202017.pdf

Monsanto. (2018). Bayer closes Monsanto acquisition. Retrieved December 7, 2019, from https://monsanto.com/news-releases/bayer-closes-monsanto-acquisition/

SEC. (2016). Online Source: https://www.sec.gov/Archives/edgar/data/1110783/000110465916145111/a16-12008_39ex99d2.htm

Sherman, M. (2019). Change in share price, one year after deal completion [Graphics]. *The Wall Street Journal*. Retrieved from https://www.wsj.com/articles/how-bayer-monsanto-became-one-of-the-worst-corporate-dealsin-12-charts-11567001577?mod=hp_lead_pos5.

The European Commission. (2018, March 21). europa.eu. Retrieved December 13, 2019, from https://ec.europa.eu/competition/mergers/cases/decisions/m8084_13335_3.pdf

United States Institute of Peace. (2002). *Special report, U.S. negotiating behavior*. Washington, DC: United State Institute of Peace.

United States Securities and Exchange Commission. (2016, October 26). sec.gov/archive. Retrieved December 13, 2019, from https://www.sec.gov/Archives/edgar/data/1110783/000119312516741843/d252304dprem14a.htm

Varinsky, D. (2018, May 29). Von Business Insider France. Retrieved from https://www.businessinsider.fr/us/bayer-monsanto-merger-has-farmers-worried-2018-4abgerufen

Voeth, M., & Herbst, U. (2015). *Verhandlungsmanagement: Planung, Steuerung und Analyse*. Stuttgart: Schäffer-Poeschel Verlag für Wirtschaft Steuern Recht GmbH.

8
THE TRANS-PACIFIC PARTNERSHIP AGREEMENT

Amanda Wegener and Michele Floridia

KEY OBJECTIVES OF THE CASE STUDY

The key objectives of this case study are for the student to conceptualize both context and details of the negotiation with respect to the following areas:

1. *Identify the five main difficulties in the negotiation*
2. *Analyze Japan's motives for joining the TTP*
3. *Identify the lead figure in the negotiation process*
4. *Analyze Japan's outcome of the negotiation*
5. *Evaluate the integrative potential lifted of the negotiation overall*

Introduction

The foundations for the, now defunct, suggested Trans-Pacific Partnership (TPP) were laid in 2011 between 12 countries of both hemispheres in the Pacific Rim namely Chile, Peru, Brunei, Australia, New Zealand, Malaysia, Mexico, Canada, Singapore, the United States, Vietnam as well as Japan (Stanojević & Masadeh, 2017, p. 8). They mark the starting point of a mega free trade agreement (FTA) whose aim was to minimize trade barriers concerning areas, such as tariffs, intellectual property, investment, services, state-owned enterprises (Amari, 2016, p. 12), labor, environment, competition policy and digital trade (Davis, 2017, p. 90).

In short, participating countries would have had a prerogative to an open influx of "people, goods and capital" and information within their borders (Amari, 2016, p. 11). This FTA, had it been ratified by all necessary members, would have

DOI: 10.4324/9781003105428-8

proved its positive worth economically by including countries that, to themselves amass a whopping 40% of the world's GDP (Stanojević & Masadeh, 2017, p. 8). It would also have benefitted immensely from an economical as well as from a geopolitical standpoint. However, it was not brought into effect as the United States withdrew its signature under the Trump administration in 2016 (Ping, 2019, p. 124). Nevertheless, the TPP was no mulligan, in fact it paved the way for the Comprehensive and Progressive Agreement for TPP signed by the remaining 11 signatories that entered into force in December 2018 (Ping, 2019, p. 122). In brief, the TPP has allowed Japan to emerge as a key player on the global scale and has shown its mastery at maneuvering between its national and international interests.

This case study of the TPP veers toward a multilateral approach imbued with clear-cut features of geopolitical framing and its underpinnings. However, it will attempt to assess the steps of the negotiation that took place to give rise to the TPP by taking a partial stance, i.e. a closer look at Japan's role as a negotiator through a wide array of literature ranging from scholarly articles as well as books that address the theoretical matter at hand. In a first step, it will examine the premeditated negotiation through an analytical-prescriptive approach and a cross-negotiation keeping each members' perspective in mind, i.e. from a macro-level. Second, it will evaluate the organization of the negotiation by analyzing contentious obstacles and external circumstances by comparing scenarios including some of the TPP members. The preparation for the negotiation will be discussed in a third step by describing Japan's motives and its objectives through the means-end concept at a micro-level. Finally, the chapter will move on to the conduction of the negotiation by means of assessing the negotiation behavior as well as the verification of authenticity between the conflicting or similar interests of the parties.

Negotiation analysis

Analytical-prescriptive approach

The analytical-prescriptive approach perceives negotiations as a "self-contained interdependent decision-making problem between at least two parties, which should be solved with the help of mathematical-formal models" (Voeth & Herbst, 2015, slide 15). This approach allows for a precise and quantitative examination of the negotiation yet contains in its essence fallacious assumptions. Namely, one of complete rationality and information, one that negotiators behave strictly in their self-maximizing interest as well as one of optimality, meaning that the results of the negotiations are maximum for both parties (Voeth & Herbst, 2015, slide 15).

Indeed, applied to the TPP, these fallacies do appear as it is certain that emotions invariably trump rationality or that the 12 members do not possess the entire set of information regarding each one of them. There are too many contingencies to keep count of. Nevertheless, these fallacies may well be present, but they are also of little relevance, which is why the game theory, a mathematical-formal concept developed by the mathematician John Nash, still acts as an adequate explanatory tool. It determines the strategic interaction of economic parties involved in a specific context making decisions based on preferences resulting in specific outcomes (Ross, 2019). The rules are modelled as Nash theorized, in such a way that all economic agents will maximize their utility according to the subjective welfare (Ross, 2019).

Concerning the TPP and taking the area of investment as an example, such a scenario did arise in the sense that the negotiations had to strive for a middle ground that would put both investor countries and investor host nations in a better position. In this case, the United States and Japan were both investors and the rest were investor host nations. The lengthy discussions that followed this discrepancy were thorny since it was "a two-to-ten split". For this reason, Japan's Prime Minister, Shinzo Abe firmly pushed for "a ban on performance requirements for host nations" (Amari, 2016, p. 16). Consequently, the clauses included in the TPP stipulated explicitly that strict prevention of abuse of process would provide the necessary measure to reduce this imbalance and grant a fair chance to all of the members (Amari, 2016, p. 16). After all, this was about establishing symmetry between the somewhat richer countries, such as the United States, Japan, Canada, New Zealand, Singapore and Australia as opposed to the relatively poorer countries namely, Mexico, Malaysia, Brunei, Chile, Peru and Vietnam (Stanojević & Masadeh, 2017, p. 11). This illustrative example demonstrates that the utility of all was indeed maximized, as stated by the game theory with reference to the subjective welfare of all.

Cross-negotiation

Cross-negotiation deals primarily with the intertwined dynamics that take place when difficulties on contentious matters erupt or to put it simply, it is the analysis of how one's adversary fares. Voeth and Herbst highlighted four main reasons for difficulties in the negotiation: the object of the negotiation, the partner, the history as well as the negotiation circumstances (2015, slide 38). This subpart will assess each criterion concerning Japan along with other key negotiators in relation to their most salient motives related to the TPP.

The first criterion is the object of the negotiation that focuses on the clear definition of the important objectives, which serve as the catalyst for the negotiation to happen in the first place. The goals enumerated in the introduction comprise amongst many the curtailing of tariffs, which are defined by Radcliffe as taxes imposed on imports as a means of trade protectionism (2019). They also include the encouragement of investment and the redefining of intellectual property through the removal of trade barriers (Amari, 2016, p. 12). The lowering of tariffs was the main driver for the creation of the TPP that is why the lobbying concentrated mostly on this point. In the TPP, Japan faced some adversity mainly from the United States to lower its tariffs to 100%, whereas the other members only requested a tariff abolition rate of anything north of 95.9% (Ishiguro, 2016, p. 182).

Indeed, this was a too high demand that Japan could not comply with as it was already facing adversity at a national level from the local agricultural sector claiming that this would lead to a devaluation of the exported goods, therefore a loss of profit on the long term. Still, Japan managed its national complaints by abolishing tariff rates up to 89.9%, namely on fishery, agricultural and forestry imports (Stanojević & Masadeh, 2017, p. 18) that was met with approval by the remainder of the TPP participants (Ishiguro, 2016, p. 182). This compromise was also approved by the local Ministry of Agriculture provided Japan's main commodity, rice, stops being regulated. Rice's farmland acreage would then increase, thus improving price competitiveness and boosting supply (Ishiguro, 2016, p. 173).

The second criterion focuses on the negotiating partner, the resulting relationship between negotiators and how cultural differences, know-how deficits, economic difficulties or lack of negotiation experience may morally wound the prospects of a successful negotiation. Keeping in mind that the 12 participating countries encompass 800 million people on four different continents (Mukhopadhyay & Thomassin, 2018, p. 2), it is of paramount importance to stress that economic difficulties are predominantly responsible for diverging interests. Cultural differences as well as know-how deficits will be discussed in depth in the coming parts.

Why these economic hardships play such an important role is mainly due to the fact that some countries' GDP is significantly higher, therefore creating some interdependences in trade. Canada for instance heavily relies on the United States' participation for its incentives to also participate in the TPP to become economically fruitful (Mukhopadhyay & Thomassin, 2018, p. 3). This acute reliance is not only depicted by Canada but also by most of the members of the TPP, including Singapore, Vietnam, Brunei, Malaysia, Chile and Peru who strongly depend on the import of goods manufactured in China (Sutter, 2017). China's strong exertion of influence in Asia is in fact one of the main reasons why Japan decided to take the lead and most of all, exclude it from the TPP (Katada, 2017, p. 151). This intended estrangement by Japan brokers a solution for the inextricable economic ties of the mentioned countries to China and allows for an open-door policy that will draw in investment like a magnet and invigorate trade between the members, therefore benefitting them all.

The third criterion analyses the negotiation history, i.e. the diplomatic relationship of the countries. Japan and the United States, for instance, have always been interconnected when it comes to international relations given their common participation in a wide range of agreements such as the General Agreement on Tariffs and Trade, as well as post-war international organizations, namely the United Nations (UN) and the Organization for Economic Cooperation and Development (OECD). Naturally, their relationship when drafting the TPP was anything but prejudiced by past misdeeds (Latz & Notehelfer, 2019). Instead, it was encouraged by the virtue of good geopolitical relations toward one another. The rest of the members also reinforced the notion of collective action by having polished their mutual ties, without any apparent shortcomings and upholding current agreements. This is exemplified by the North American Free Trade Agreement (NAFTA) between Canada, Mexico and the United States, all of which consolidated their relations and promoted trade by bridging the gap in tariffs and paving the way for an economic liftoff in the region (Ishiguro, 2016, p. 174).

The fourth and last criterion hinges on the circumstances of the negotiation related to changes in the organizational framework that may be important to make the negotiation process plannable. Japan's aggressive takeover after the abdication of the United States is such an example, given the necessity to reorganize the framework so the TPP would still come to fruition. Ping argues that with the help of the TPP, Japan "endeavoured to shift from an echoer to a shaper in the economic and trade-agenda setting and rule-making process" (2019, p. 128). The former being the result of avoidance of any political expediency of any kind at the national level since Japan is historically known to have been very protectionist about its trading policy and aloof to FTAs (Davis, 2017, p. 91). This is partly due to local opposition whenever political reforms intended on crippling protectionist inward-looking policies (Ishiguro, 2016, p. 194).

Furthermore, as aforementioned, the local pressure in Japan was off the charts, making it all the more tedious to propose a policy that would abate local dissent, mainly from the ruling Liberal Democratic Party, whose views advocated for the protection of Japanese fisheries, forestry and agriculture and simultaneously, please international consent (Davis, 2017, p. 90). According to Davis, a nationally marked anti-China sentiment enabled Japan to pursue the ratification of the TPP fervently and successfully as this sentiment was the only common point the ruling Liberal Democratic Party and the Prime Minister, Shinzo Abe agreed upon (2017, p. 90). By leveraging the geopolitical logic, Abe was able to unite local opinion in favor of the TPP. It can therefore be said that the worry of Chinese hegemony in Asia was in and of itself the driving force that undeniably cast Japan in the leading role, which enabled it to take administrative charge of the negotiation and plough ahead with the launch of the TPP.

Integrativity

Ultimately, it is interesting to notice that the concept of integrativity advanced by Voeth and Herbst in which certain agreements place both sides in a better position than others also comes into play (2015, slide 44). The TPP is indicative of integrativity through the potential it presents as it dealt with a broad array of issues, such as tariffs, regulations concerning investment, intellectual property and labor, this list being nonexhaustive. Moreover, it creates value (Voeth & Herbst, 2015, slide 44), meaning that Japan engineered a situation in which all members of the TPP who relied on Chinese goods would now benefit from the added value of building ties to new trading partners within the TPP. The added value would change the dynamics and usher in a time where "the supply chains" of the members of the TPP "would benefit from transparency of rules" (Davis, 2017, p. 92). This in turn, would strengthen the political commitment and erect a pillar of foreign policy through the TPP that would serve as an example for future mega FTAs.

Organization of negotiations

Psychographic factors as circumstantial obstacles

The organization of the negotiation comprises individual success factors, such as situational, organizational, psychographic and sociodemographic factors (Voeth & Herbst, 2015, slide 67). These tend to influence the conduction of the organization in such a way that can either lead to a successful negotiation if put to good use or to the contrary, draw a wedge between the concerned parties. This subpart will attempt to analyze the reasons why the TPP is so triumphant despite its encompassing cultures from each end of the spectrum by focusing on the psychographic and the organizational factors. It will take a closer look at the two cultures that dominated the landscape of the negotiations, namely the Western and the Asian culture. It can safely be assumed that Canada, the United States, Mexico, Chile, Peru, Australia and New Zealand versus Brunei, Malaysia, Vietnam, Singapore and most of all Japan differed in their negotiating fashion, the former pertaining to the West and the latter to the East.

The theoretical lens of the psychographic factors determines values as its main criteria (Voeth & Herbst, 2015, slide 67). Needless to say, this factor is one of the building blocks of what common knowledge understands under culture, disregarding cuisine, tradition or ideas in the interest of succinct precision. With respect to values, it is clear that the Asian and Western culture have different rationalities in the sense that the West accentuates science and religion as cornerstones of its culture, which accounts for a more "rule-based" society, whereas the East highlights the importance of the imagination and Confucianism, which in turn justifies a more "relationship-based" approach (Rüegg-Stürm & Grand, 2019). In addition, the cultural expressions in business also have a tendency to vary via the expression of honesty, which is more open and brutal in the West and conversely, much more subtle in the East (Rüegg-Stürm & Grand, 2019). The expression of consent or disagreement is argumentative and verbal in the West, as opposed to the avoidance of a direct divergence of opinion in the East. Overall, collectivism reigns in the East and individualism are extolled in the West (Rüegg-Stürm & Granddl, 2019).

Be that as it may, this chapter maintains that parties from both sides were able to overcome these cultural obstacles of the arduous path that led to the TPP, through the rise of globalization as well as through the organizational factors that are yet to be evaluated.

Bridging the gap between cultures

The two factors that allowed both the East and the West to put their cultural differences aside and negotiate for a greater good were globalization as well as organizational factors.

Indeed, globalization bridges cultures and mentalities leading to more open societies where tangible benefits can be safeguarded. McLean and Lewis define culture as "a system of assumptions, values and norms transmitted (…) to the next generation" (2010, p. 31). Through globalization, doors that were previously closed, were now wide open and ready to steer the cultural diversity the world has to offer, toward one another. This would then generate a transcendent flow of values that would successively be molded into basic common understandings each culture has of the other. With reference to the TPP, it is clear that the West was aware of the dos and don'ts in the East and vice versa. McLean and Lewis further argue that the reason why such complex, cross-cultural negotiations are possible is because a working knowledge of cultural diversity, mainly acquired thanks to globalization, lays the groundwork for a "multiethnic, multilingual and multidisciplinary society" (2010, p. 31). In short, both cultures carried out the realization of the TPP and saw it as an opportunity to bridge the gap between both cultures instead of perceiving it as a barrier.

Furthermore, organizational factors also account for the breakthrough of the TPP in spite of the disparities in the psychographic factors. Japan and the United States, as previously mentioned, were among the leading economic powers (Amari, 2016, p. 16), thus possessing the majority of the bargaining power and being placed at the top of the hierarchy. After the United States' withdrawal (Ping, 2019 p. 125) and surrendering of the leverage, the torch was passed on to Japan who utilized it in order to move the negotiating process along (Katada, 2017, p. 151). Katada also claims that the two reasons that promote the progress of a negotiation are issue linkage and foreign pressure (2017, p. 151). On one hand, Japan felt foreign pressure soon after the United States' abdication (Ping, 2019 p. 125) on an internal level, meaning that it felt obliged to take over to bring about the TPP. On the other hand, one of its tactics as a highly ranked member is also the fact that Japan employed issue linkage, such as linking tariffs on imported commodities to various areas, namely fisheries, agriculture and forestry (Ping, 2019 p. 124) as mentioned before, in order to solidify the members' commitment to the TPP and ensure its materialization.

Japan's completion of the TPP is qualitatively measurable in that it is apparent that it strove to climb up the social status ladder at an international level "in the economic and trade field" (Ping, 2019, p. 123). Japan's merit in this sense is particularly remarkable, since some of its regional press was corroding public approval of the TPP (Kagitani & Harimaya, 2017, p. 58) making its leadership beyond challenging and all the more exceptional.

Preparation of negotiation

The pertinence of the groundwork

This part discusses and further analyzes the preparation of Japan in setting the TPP into motion. The essential elements Japan considered during the period of strategizing and organizing the preparation for the TPP will be listed in the following section. It will soon become evident that Japan's careful arrangements were a crucial requirement for its future success. Even more so when the United States decided to stop supporting the agreement.

According to Voeth and Herbst, the preparation of negotiations proved to be a fateful phase in terms of reaching a fruitful conclusion. Moreover, the ratio between the groundwork and the conduct of a negotiation must be distinguished, where the former needs to be considerably longer (2015, slide 92). Japan's methodical involvement in the TPP since 2011, as previously mentioned, already laid the groundwork for the success of the agreement. Despite the fact that the United States abandoned the accord in 2017 and a certain symbol of alliance and cooperation between the United States and the other members of the accord deteriorated, Japan endeavored to keep the promises of the agreement by accepting the role of a leader in these negotiations (Davis, 2017, p. 90). Its success can be attributed to its extensive preparations. Indeed, after years of planning and strategizing, the Japanese decided to give rise to the TPP (Stanojević & Masadeh, 2017, p. 20).

The leading motives and Japan's stratagem

Japan decided to take this role upon itself mainly for two motives. One of them being the revitalization of the Japanese economy that had been staggering over the recent years. The other one is to reach a win-win denouement for all participating members of the TPP while simultaneously not granting too much power to the exporting countries (Amari, 2016, pp. 11–15). To further illustrate the importance of the preparations one must first have an understanding of Japan's motives. Motives as defined by Voeth and Herbst are fundamental forces that pull the strings from behind the scenes (2015, slide 93–96). In other words, motives are the reason for entering a negotiation. The former motive mentioned at the beginning of this paragraph delineates a basic concept of general trade agreements. It is even stated in the preamble of the TPP (2016; TPP Preamble) that one of the main objectives is to bring economic growth to the members. This motive is not as simple as it sounds. Although a cooperation between members might sounds friendly, one cannot neglect the fact that a cooperation spawns not only from gaining benefits from the cooperating partners but also to protect oneself from a common threat. Indeed, Japan saw the benefit of the TPP as a countermeasure against China's rising power in exporting resources (Backer, 2014, p. 65). Furthermore, one can see a clear relation between the two motives that only strengthens the relevance of the issue at hand.

The Means-End-Concept by Voeth and Herbst explains the connection between the different motives and the way to achieve them (2015, slide 96). The Means at the bottom of the model depict a method of one's party. In our case study, it is the participation in the TPP. Participating in the TPP will then lead to the Consequences found in the middle section. They are direct results that spawn from the Means. After the successful introduction of the TPP, small-medium enterprises in Japan would have a better chance to grow internationally. Consequently, it would lead to Japan obtaining a better and secured position as an exporter. The End represents the incentives behind a negotiation. Here we can observe the recovery of the Japanese economy as a protectionist measure against China's trading power. Ergo, after establishing a secured position as an exporter, Japan would eventually be able to improve its economy and at the same time be better shielded against China's aggressive trading power.

To get a better insight on how Japan successfully prepared itself, it is necessary to take a thorough examination at the objectives and strategies. Following the definitions provided by Voeth and Herbst, the concretizations of underlying motives represent objectives, while the strategy characterizes a path on how to reach an objective (2015, slides 94, 97, 98, 100). In addition, a negotiation objective has to be specific, measurable, acceptable, realistic and tough. Applying this theory to our case study, Japan's objectives can be seen at the end result of the negotiated items. According to Stanojević and Masadeh, Japan was the only country that lowered their tariffs less than other members of the TPP (2017, p. 18). Roughly one-third of 586 sensitive agricultural products were not going to have any tariffs. Even though they increased the import quotas on rice as a form of concession, they still kept the tariffs on it. Japan insisted on keeping the tariffs due to the large agricultural sector specialized in rice production. An abolition would have endangered the agricultural economy. In this case study, the achieved tariff levels were the objectives of Japan as they were specific, measurable, acceptable, realistic and quite ambitious. The strategy on the other hand was the offered concession which is closely related to one of the key points of the TPP, which was to promote economic growth. This outcome of the strategy can be perfectly described by using the following diagram which was provided by using the concept of differences between own and opposing payouts by Loewenstein et al. (1989, p. 436). What Loewenstein wants to convey is that the benefit of a party will eventually start to decline when considering a positive relationship or a co-operation between two or more parties. In other words, the more a party gains from a negotiation, the less the other party receives. This in return, has a negative effect on the perceived benefit, despite the increase in pay-out. Therefore, striving for a balanced outcome is the best outcome. That is why, the other parties agreed with Japan on the above-mentioned terms since they only crystallized the integration and cooperation between the members. Moreover, the act of increasing the quota by Japan can be seen as the outcome of the reciprocity strategy by Voeth and Herbst (2015, slide 118). The strategy states that a party that has received concessions from another party will reciprocate that act by also offering a concession. Here, the other members of the TPP accepted Japan's nonabolition of all of their tariffs when the Japanese made a counteroffer with an increase in the quota on rice. Generally, this strategy has a positive influence on the whole process of negotiation as well as its efficiency.

Relation-oriented approach

In the past, Japan has been seen as an isolationist country, as is indicated by its history both old and new. However, one might be surprised to see the co-operativeness and integration efforts of the Japanese with this partnership. The uptake of leadership can be attributed to the Prime Minister Shinzo Abe, as he vigorously pushed for it in order to further support his domestic economic policy, known as Abenomics (Davis, 2017, p. 90). These processes conducted by the Japanese can be explained by using Voeth and Herbst's concept of relation-oriented approach toward negotiations (2015, slide 111). The theory behind it is that cooperativeness, honesty, emotionality, dependability, open-mindedness, demeanor as well as fairness increases substantially more than when parties have a transaction-oriented approach. This is why members of the TPP decided to take a relation-oriented approach for this negotiation. One can see that cooperativeness, fairness and open-mindedness are entirely reflected in the example of the TPP. Lewicki's cooperation strategy, which promotes a win-win situation for all parties, fits perfectly to explain this behavior (1998, p. 64). That is to say that the significance of other members' interests as well as Japan's were viewed as highly relevant. These strategies would eventually lead to an integrative approach for all countries, where everyone was better off. It is therefore noticeable that this FTA was an act of cooperation so as to benefit all members economically and socially, as well as to stimulate sustainability.

Conducting negotiations

Negotiation behavior

"For the Japanese, negotiation is usually a process of reaching a point that is acceptable to both parties. For Americans, it's a competition dividing winners and losers" (Brett & Okumura, 1998, p. 495). This part will convey a deeper analysis of Japan's way of conducting negotiations. By using a model from Voeth and Herbst, this chapter will reveal all factors that influence the negotiation behavior of a party. With the obtained insight, a verification will be performed whether or not Japan was acting authentic or not through its actions.

This analysis will take the prime minister Shinzo Abe as the lead figure in representing Japan. Pursuant to Voeth and Herbst, individual actors can take up to five different negotiation styles: Compliant, avoiding, integrating and dominant negotiation style (2015, slide 128). A negotiation for compromise, however, is a mixture of all the styles. It goes without saying that Shinzo Abe followed an integrating negotiation style since he regarded the interest of the other members and Japan's interest as highly relevant. Japan strove to complete this partnership without any losers whilst leaving doors open for any future members (Davis, 2017, p. 92). Through Voeth and Herbst's Factors Influencing Negotiation Styles model, one can explain the different factors influencing an actor's negotiation style

(2015, slide 129). Said model claims that the negotiation behavior of a person is affected by the actor himself, i.e. his persona and values. Other factors are the general negotiation culture of the country and the situational negotiation, which naturally differs depending on what the nature of the negotiation is, who the negotiating partner is and the importance of the negotiation relationship. All these aspects fused together result in the individual negotiation style that is what ultimately determines the negotiation behavior of a party.

Negotiation style analysis of the different components on a microlevel

Starting with Japan's Prime Minister, Shinzo Abe, and his personality. Hae-in and DeDominicis describe Abe as a charismatic person (2017, pp. 1–6). In spite of the hiatus between his first and second term of his political career, which was mainly due to the failure of achieving public trust and a lack of leadership, Abe managed to turn the tides and change his general approach in doing politics. Burrett says that Abe's successful career is owed to changes in his environment, such as weaker opposing parties as well as a rising tension between China and Japan (Lee & Dedominicis, 2017, pp. 11–23). Other reasons were his improvement in leadership skills such as charisma and better decision-making skills. Not to mention, his Abenomics policy to improve the declining economy of Japan was another driving factor. To sum up, he took advantage of the international and domestic situations going on at the time to strengthen his position as a politician.

Moving on to the general negotiation culture of the country. It is worth noting that Japan is a collective country rather than an individualistic one, hence its culture differs substantially from western countries. Naturally, a person who grows up in a certain culture will adopt its practices or will be greatly influenced by them. According to Brett and Okumura, the Americans see power in a negotiation as having a best alternative to a negotiated agreement (BATNA), while the Japanese do not share this view (1998, pp. 503–507). In retrospect, one can see that the Japanese gained less from intercultural negotiations precisely for to this reason. Joint gains proved to be lacking in that sense.

This phenomenon can be further explained by taking a look at the self-interest of parties. Americans have been known for their strong individualistic goals, i.e. self-interested gains. On the other hand, the Japanese have had a rather altruistic position when it comes to fierce negotiations. A mismatch between these two leads to one party reaching their goals early on while leaving the other party unsatisfied or with barely any gains which is the exact opposite of an integrative approach. Oikawa and Tanner Jr. shed more light on this analysis by explaining that the Japanese have rigid ways of thinking when it comes to the hierarchical power structure and social status (1992, pp. 67–72). To them, a high status is the definition of power. However, most of the time they have trouble recognizing this structure when dealing with foreign people. They would rather say yes than no when it comes to discussion with foreigners as it leads to less conflict between the parties. Negotiations for the Japanese are an opportunity to build a long-term relationship of mutual benefit.

To fully comprehend the negotiation behavior of Shinzo Abe, one cannot neglect the negotiation situation by first assessing the nature of the negotiation. The nature can be split into two concepts, either integrativity or distributivity. While the latter describes a situation of who gets the larger piece of cake, the former seeks to find a footing where everyone is better off. In our case study, the TPP represents an unequivocal example of integrativity. Second, the significance of the negotiation result and the relationship of the parties. The importance of the TPP for Japan was to give a chance to small–medium-sized enterprises to grow internationally so as to secure a stronger position as an exporter and boost the Japanese economy. Davis on the other hand firmly believes that the TPP serves as a golden standard agreement since trade negotiations are usually a cumulative process in which agreements lay the foundations for future agreements (2017, pp. 91–92). This is why the Japanese held the TPP in high regard. However, another motive was to set up an alliance in the Pacific countries to shield itself against the growing threat posed by China. Katada describes this as a geo-economic strategy (2017, p. 151). For these reasons, it becomes apparent that Japan attached a great deal of importance to the outcome of the negotiation and relationship between the TPP members.

The last element worth considering that might appear as trivia are the negotiation partners Japan had. Since most of the TPP members are westernized, the cultures between the members varied quite a bit. Voeth and Herbst construe this as a reason for a better success in a negotiation (2015, slide 127). Cultures that are thought to be similar but end up being different in some areas, tend to inhibit a fluent process. On the other hand, when parties are aware of their stark differences, they will have a smoother negotiation development. In this case study, as already mentioned, Japan's culture is by no means similar to the other members of the TPP, which is why the process of the negotiation was effortless.

Verification of authenticity

Having scrutinized all essential elements of the case at hand, this chapter would like to verify whether Japan's actions and its individual negotiation style were coherent. Voeth and Herbst define this trait as authenticity (2015, slide 129). This attribute is important in negotiations as it proves to be a crucial component in achieving a successful long-term relationship with the other parties. In part three, this chapter mentioned that, on one hand, Japan had taken the leadership after the United States decided to withdraw from the TPP. Ping accurately described Japan as a proactive pusher after years of a being a passive responder, ultimately, depicting Japan as a shaper of decision-making processes (2017, p. 128). Not to mention, its adamant takes on the tariffs not being completely removed showed Japan's resolve of not giving in so as to achieve better gains in the TPP negotiations. Conversely, the concession of two thirds abolishment of the tariffs and the increase in quota for rice was a clear sign of cooperation from their side. By taking a closer look at how Japan acted, it can safely be assumed that Japan behaved authentically through determination, as well as by making concessions.

On the other hand, Japan's society is notorious for being an altruistic and collective one, adopting a passive role during negotiations has been the norm. Shinzo Abe however refused to adopt this particular trait. One could argue that this was due to his charisma, which tends to be uncommon for Japanese Prime Ministers generally. An undeniable fact is that Japan has rather been uninvolved in international affairs in recent years, thus making this Abe's leadership style noticeably uncommon. Moreover, Japanese self-interest is rather pronounced. This is not necessarily a bad sign since ambitious objectives tend to give one party more gains (Voeth & Herbst, 2015, slide 101). Nevertheless, this does not properly align with the standard norm in the Japanese society.

In spite of Abe's unhabitual leadership style, Japan's commitment to integrativity appeared to be in line with their practice. Referencing Yoshimura's quote at the beginning of this part, the Japanese view negotiations as a process to find an area of agreement that is beneficial for both parties. It is not an egotistic competition where ripping-off the other party is the goal. Instead, to them it is an opportunity to build a long-lasting and favorable relationship. This was depicted by the abolishment of tariffs as a form of willingness to cooperate.

In the end, the results appear to be interwoven as there is no distinct dichotomy. However, one point tends to push the verdict more toward an authentic behavior. Taking the aforementioned measures in order to materialize the TPP was a critical point for Japan as it had been in an economic downturn for the years preceding the TPP. In addition, China's surging trading power posed a threat to Japan's economy. Which is why it was only plausible for Japan to have taken this route in solving this problem, ultimately making it authentic as it played with open cards.

Top learnings

- *The five main difficulties in this negotiation were the object, the partner, the history, the local circumstances as well as the different cultural backgrounds of the negotiating parties.*
  - *Japan's extreme lowering of tariffs helped to advance the negotiation object.*
  - *The usage of interdependent ties amongst partners propelled an open-door policy through the agreement.*
  - *Previous agreements such as NAFTA or the OECD laid the foundations for positive and mutually beneficial historical relationships amongst members.*
  - *Japan's local pressure with strong opposition against the agreement, as well as political expediency were important circumstantial drivers, which eventually were overcome.*
  - *The negotiation behavior was characterized by coming to terms with parties of different cultures with stark differences.*

- *Japan's motives for joining the TPP were a desire to revitalize its own economy as well as creating a framework for a win-win situation where all members would flourish through economic growth and a fair, relationship-oriented collaboration.*
- *Japan's Prime Minister must be seen as a lead figure in the negotiation process as he was a charismatic and compelling negotiator who catapulted the TPP to success during its formative days.*
- *Japan's position benefited as well by taking over the agreement since it was able to infuse themes of fairness as well as authentic cooperation throughout the entire operation.*
- *The integrative potential lifted can be classified as high, since the TPP put all of the participants in a better position geopolitically and economically. Hence, the TPP can be viewed as an outstanding agreement in spite of antagonistic mentalities between the western and the eastern countries. It is realistic to assume that the TPP looms large on the horizon of mega FTAs for there are few other agreements that adjusted their expectations quite as pragmatically and beneficially as the TPP did.*

References

Amari, A. (2016). The Trans-Pacific Partnership (TPP) agreement. *Asia-Pacific Review, 23*(1), 11–20. doi: 10.1080/13439006.2016.1195948

Backer, L. C. (2014). The Trans-Pacific Partnership: Japan, China, the U.S., and the emerging shape of a new world trade regulatory order. *Washington University Global Studies Law Review, 13*(1), 49–81.

Brett, J. M., & Okumura, T. (1998). Inter- and intracultural negotiation: U.S. and Japanese negotiators. *Academy of Management Journal, 41*(5), 495–510. doi: 10.2307/256938^

Burrett, T. (2016). Abe Road: Comparing Japanese Prime Minister Shinzo Abe's leadership of his first and second Governments. *Parliamentary Affairs, 70*, 400–429. doi: 10.1093/pa/gsw015

Davis, C. L. (2017). Foreign policy and trade law: Japans unexpected leadership in TPP negotiations. *Proceedings of the ASIL Annual Meeting, 111*, 90–92. doi: 10.1017/amp.2017.68

Ishiguro, K. (2016). TPP negotiations and political economy reforms in Japan's executive policy making: A two-level game analysis. *International Relations of the Asia-Pacific, 17*, 171–201. doi: 10.1093/irap/lcw010

Kagitani, K., & Harimaya, K. (2017). Electoral motives, constituency systems, ideologies and a free trade agreement: The case of Japan joining the Trans-Pacific Partnership negotiations. *Journal of the Japanese and International Economies, 45*, 51–66. doi: 10.1023/a:1025316911337

Katada, S. N. (2017). The true dynamics of Japan's participation in the TPP negotiation: Analysis of its policymaking process. *Social Science Japan Journal*, 150–153. doi: 10.1093/ssjj/jyw053

Latz, G., & Notehelfer, F. G. (2019, December 12). Encyclopedia Britannica: International relations. Retrieved from https://www.britannica.com/place/Japan/International-relations. Accessed December 14, 2019.

Lee, H.-I., & Dedominicis, B. (2017). The results of a "Fighting Politician"?: Prime Minister Shinzo Abe's strengthened political leadership and changes in Japanese National Security Policy. *Organizational Cultures: An International Journal, 17*(3), 1–25. doi: 10.18848/2327-8013/cgp/v17i03/1-25

Lewicki, R. J., Hiam, A., & Olander, K. W. (1998). Verhandeln mit Strategie-Das Grosse Handbuch der Verhandlungstechniken, St. Gallen/Zürich 1998.

Loewenstein, G. F., Thompson, L. L., & Bazermann, M. H. (1989). Social utility and decision-making in interpersonal contexts. *Journal of Personality and Social Psychology*, 57, (3), 426–441.

McLean, J., & Lewis, R. D. (2010). Communicating across cultures. *Management Matters*, 30–31. doi: 10.1017/9781316651032.006

Mukhopadhyay, K., & Thomassin, P. J. (2018). The impact of Trans-Pacific Partnership agreement on the Canadian economy. *Journal of Economic Structures*, 7(1), 2–29. doi: 10.1186/s40008-017-0102-y

Office of the United States Trade Representative: Executive Office of the President. The Trans-Pacific Partnership: Preamble. (2016). TPP full text. Retrieved from https://ustr.gov/trade-agreements/free trade-agreements/trans-pacific-partnership/tpp-full-text. Accessed December 11, 2019.

Oikawa, N., & Tanner, J. F. (1992). The influence of Japanese culture on business relationships and negotiations. *Journal of Services Marketing*, 6(3), 67–74. doi: 10.1108/08876049210035962

Ping, H. (2019). New developments in Japan's free trade strategy and their implications. *China International Study*, 20, 121–137. doi: 10.1057/9780230288560

Radcliffe, B. (2019, November 21). The basics of tariffs and trade barriers. Retrieved from https://www.investopedia.com/articles/economics/08/tariff-trade-barrier-basics.asp. Accessed December 14, 2019.

Ross, D. (2019, March 8). Stanford encyclopedia of philosophy: Game theory. Retrieved from https://plato.stanford.edu/entries/game-theory/. Accessed December 14, 2019.

Rüegg-Stürm, J. & Grand, S. (2019). *Managing in a complex world: The St. Gallen management-model*. utb GmbH.

Stanojević, N., & Masadeh, M. (2017). The advantages and challenges of Japanese membership in the Trans-Pacific Partnership. *The Review of International Affairs*, 68(1168), 7–22.

Sutter, P. (2017, February 6). China's global trade impact. Retrieved from https://www.livingstonintl.com/chinas-global-trade-impact/. Accessed December 14, 2019.

TPP. (2016). Online Source: https://ustr.gov/trade-agreements/free-trade-agreements/trans-pacific-partnership/tpp-full-text

Voeth, M., & Herbst, U. (2015). *Verhandlungsmanagement: Planung, Steuerung und Analyse*. Stuttgart: Schäffer-Poeschel.

9
CLOSING REMARKS ON THE CASEBOOK

As seen in the cases earlier, integrativity is a powerful tool as well as a mind-set to not only achieve superior outcomes for the negotiator but also the opposing party as well as the future relationship between the two. We have seen this across industries, across professional fields as well as in bilateral and multilateral negotiations. To us, this is a powerful and empirically backed statement for the world at large. As briefly touched upon in the introduction, the world we live in gets more complex, volatile and uncertain by the second. The times, where easy answers provided viable solutions are long gone – if they ever existed in the first place.

Especially today, however, where we are now well in the first quarter of the 21st century, we must look these insights be a reminder on what kind of negotiating behavior succeeds and which only brings about disruption. If leaders – no matter from politics or business – stick to outdated ideas on what makes successful negotiations all over the world, this global society is in jeopardy. The decisions, which must be taken in the decades to come, require the ability to put oneself in our opposite's shoes; whether we talk about the global climate crisis, refugee crises, armed conflict, traditional or trade wars.

To the unsuspecting reader, this might seem like a bit of a stretch, but the fate of the world is sealed in relatively countless small negotiations every day all over the world between people, states or supranational entities. Having the conviction that integrativity is the best outcome to strive for, is only one part of the equation, the other one being the ability to strive for it. Understanding how to manage negotiations for integrativity, hence plays an integral part for a world worth living.

INDEX

Note: Page numbers in *Italic* refer to figures.

Abe, S. 46, 147
Abenomics 154
adjustment strategy 37
Agenda Kabine, agreement 97
AirBerlin 94, 95
Air France: founded in 1933 53; fragile economic situation 54; market deregulation, impact on 53; merger with, Dutch carrier KLM 54; salary negotiations 2018 51 (*see also* Air France strikes, and negotiations); situation prior to 2018 54
Air France strikes, and negotiations 51; analysis of negotiation 51, 55; BATNA analysis, complex 60–61; concession offered 61; costs of, and final agreement proposal 62, 64; employee mobilization 65; employees, participation rate of 65; Evain's SNLP, role in 61, 63; evaluation of 64–65; fairness and equality arguments 56; graphical representation, situation 59; higher stakes 56–57; important items on agenda 55; initial proposal, to increase pay 61; Janaillac's involvement, and leadership 57–58, 61–62, 65; lessons learned 65–66; mediatized, charismatic figures in 64; motive, objective and strategy in 58–59; negotiation circumstances 56; negotiation partner, the unions involved 55–56, 57; new leadership 63; object of negotiation 55; preparation for negotiations 58; public opinion 56; short-term tactics 60; Smith's leadership, and resolution 58, 61, 63–64; SNPC role 57; time pressure 56

AirItalia 95
Amazon.com, Inc. 6–7
Amazon Go store 6
Amazon Prime 71
Amazon-Whole Foods merger 3–4, 7; announcement of 20; battle plan, of negotiations 14–16; dominant power-based style 17–19; Evercore hiring 11, 18, 21; involvement intensity, of top people in 14, *15*; lessons learned 23–24; non-disclosure agreement signing 13; preparation period 14; reaching agreement 18–19; start of negotiations 13–14; Sullivan & Cromwell in 19; time line, negotiations 8–9; transaction finalisation 19–20; Wachtell Lipton, hiring and engagement 10, 15, 17, 21; *see also* Whole Foods Market, Inc.
American airline industry, deregulation 52
Ashton, C. 41
aspiration level strategy 102–103
Aspirin 122
atomic bombs 28
atoms 27
AT&T Inc. 71, 74–75
aviation industry 52–53; airlines, categorized into profiles 95; average airline profitability 94; Brexit impact 94; capital-intensive business 52; digitalization in 99; disputes, between employers and employees 92; disruptions, and changes in 52–53; divergence of pay 99; European aviation space, unification 94–95; European markets and 94–95; external factors,

Index

exposure to 54; Hub and Spoke, network structures 53; new players entry in 95; oil price impacts on 52; pressure for tackling emissions 94; reduce costs, efforts to 54
avoidance strategy 37
avoiding negotiation style 102
Azur 95

bargaining zone 82
Baublies, N. 98, 99, 103, 106
Baumann, W. 127, 133, 137, 138, 141–142
Bayer (German company) 121; Aspirin invention 122; founded, by Bayer/Weskott 122; four divisions of 123; globalization of 123; history, and foundation of 122; merged into I.G. Farbenindustrie AG 123; pharmaceuticals, new market for 122–123; reasons to merge with Monsanto 126–127; reconstruction/reestablishment of 123; World War impact 122–123
Bayer, F. 122
Bayer CropScience Ltd. 137
Bayer-Monsanto merger negotiations 121; analysis of process 128–130; antitrust law, issues with 135; characteristics of 128; company's personnel, impact on 139; competition strategy in 135; cultural factor, role in 134; cultural merge in 140; differences between, two companies 132; economic perspectives of 136; final deal, Bayer official owner 136–138; future expectations 137; governmental authorities rules 130; initial deal, and offers 127–128; issues concerning 134–136; major criticism of deal 137; new crop science executive leadership team *139*; objectives of deal 137–138; object of 129; organization of strategy 130–131; outcomes, bad for Bayer 138–139, *140*, 141–143; phases of 131; points of convergence for 131–133; process, steps in 122, 125–126; Pro forma sales-2017 *138*; reasons to merge 126–127, 135; side deals 130; synergies/benefits expected after 121–122; top learnings 143
Best Alternative to a Negotiation Agreement (BATNA) 8, 33–34, 155
Bezos, Jeff 6, 14
Bic Box format 4

Blockbuster 71
Brett, J. M. 155
Business Insider 18

Carney, Jay 13
Centre for Aviation (CAPA) 57
Chicago Pile-1 28
civil aviation workers 57
Cobalt 95
competition strategy 37
compliant negotiation style 102
compromise strategy 38
concession management strategies 102
concessions management 39–40
Condon, L. 137
Connelly, M. 133
cooperation strategy (Lewicki's) 37, 154
cooperative games 134
Couderc, A.-M. 63
cross-negotiation analysis 10, 55, 147–149

Davis, C. L. 149, 156
Dedominicis, B. 155
Denter, P. 53
Deutsche Bahn and the GDL dispute 98, 110
"direct-to-consumer" strategy 71–72
Disney-21CF merger negotiations 70–71, 88–89; 21st CF's intentions to sell 73; analysis of process 73, 77; bargaining zone in 83; BATNA analysis, 21CF/Disney 83–84; Comcast biggest competitor 73–76; concessions offered 85; cross negotiation analysis 77–78; deal approved by DOJ 75, 81; Disney's competitive disadvantage 72; first offer by Disney 84–85; Iger-Murdoch's, impact on negotiation style 86; key assets acquired 76; major events 73–75; media reports of 74; motives, and objectives of 81–83; negotiation controlling 88; negotiation-related analysis 78–79; organization of 79–80; outcomes of merger 76–77; package offer, advantages 85–86; preparation of 81; principle leaders role in 80–81; rapid disclosure 81; relation-oriented approach 84, 86; reverse breakup fee 74; Sky and Hulu, side deals around 71, 74–76, 79; Sky auction 74–75; style, and behavior of 86; success indicator, stock performance 87; tactics used, use of promises 87; tasks division 80; top learnings 88

Disney's: content delivery in Asia and India 72; direct-to-consumer strategy 71–72; family-oriented service Disney+ 72; Hulu, adult-oriented service 72; sports network ESPN 72
Dow Chemical's-DuPont Co. merger 137
DreamWorks 71

EasyJet 96, 98
e-commerce 5
Einstein, A. 28
Endemol Shine Group 76
entertainment industry, and digitalization 71
ESPN, sports network 72
European Airline Industry 94
European aviation space, unification 94–95
European Transport Workers' Federation 57
European Union 32
Eurowings 95
Evan, P. 57, 61, 64
Eylea 142

Fat Man 28
Financial Times 16
Fischer, R. 93, 108–110, 113
fission process 27–28
France: unionization and strike culture in 51–52; unions affiliated with ETF 57
free trade agreement (FTA) 145
French organized labor unions and strikes 51
French Republic 32–33

Gagey, F. 63
game theory 146–147; model variant of 134
Gelfand, M. 20
General Agreement on Tariffs and Trade 148
Germanwings 95
Germany 32; Bayer and Monsanto merger in 121; IGL 98; role of labor unions in 97; UFO, and Ver.di, largest labor-union in 97–98, 101; *see also* Bayer-Monsanto merger negotiations; Lufthansa strike, and negotiations
Goldman Sachs 17–19
Grant, H. 127
grocery industry 4–5; importance of technology/innovation in 4–5; reforms in 5

Harvard negotiation concept 93, 107; focus on interests 108–109; generating options 109–110; objective criteria-based agreement 110–111; separate problems from people 107–108
HBO 71
Heavy Water Production Plan 44
Henning, E. 135
Herbst, U. 37, 55, 82, 84, 85, 93, 102, 105, 128, 147, 149, 152–154, 156
Hormuz channel 42
Hub and Spoke, network structures 53
Hulu 71–74, 76, 81, 82, 86
hybrid negotiation approach 102

Iger, B. 70, 72, 77–78, 80, 82
IGL 97, 98
integrativity 2, 149, 156, 157, 160
interim agreement; *see* Joint Plan of Action (JPOA)
International Atomic Energy Agency (IAEA) in Vienna 28–30
Iran nuclear deal negotiations: alternative actions 34–35; Ashton, C. role in 41; attitude towards, negotiation 43; BATNA analysis for 33–34; competition strategy, by Iran 39; concessions, management and scope for 39–40; conducting 40–42; economic sanctions on Iran 30, 32, 34–36, 38; EU3 role, peaceful negotiator 38; IAEA, as nuclear watchdog 43; interim JPOA, implementation 41; Iran's objective in 31–32; Joint Plan of Action (JPOA) 29–30; lack of transparency 30–31; lessons learned 47; negotiation leading to JCPOA 28–29, 31, 40–42; as nonnuclear-weapon power state 28; Non-Proliferation Treaty (NPT) 29; Obama administration stance and role in 32, 36, 38, 41–42, 45; P5+1 nations strategies 38–39; parties involved 31; prelim/framework 30; preparations for 33; president Abe, role in 46; reaching JCPOA, final agreement 42–44; Russia and China interests in 36–37; sanctions on Iran 41, 46; strategies employed 37–38; Trump administration's announced retreat from JCPOA 37; Trump's criticism of 45–46; US as primary antagonist 34–36
Iran's nuclear program, and U.S 34–36

164 Index

Janaillac, J.-M 57–58, 61–62
Japan: atomic bombs in 28; interest in middle east 46; key player in TPP 146–152, 154–157; motives/objectives behind, involvement in TPP 152–153; Shinzo Abe, PM 46, 147, 149, 154–157; *see also* Trans-Pacific Partnership (TPP) negotiations
Jerry Maguire 50
Joint Comprehensive Plan of Action (JCPOA) 28; diplomatic engagement 41; final agreement 42–44; historical background 28; intention of 31; Iran's slow withdrawal from 46; Mogherini's role in negotiation of 33; negotiation leading to 28–29; Obama's speech about 42; positive results of 44–45; restrictions, on Iran 44; Trump's opinion about 45
Joint Plan of Action (JPOA) 29–30

Katada, S. N. 151, 156
Kolmar, M. 53
Krawiec, P. 13

labor disputes 97–99
Lee, H.-I. 155
legal rules 130
Le Maire, B. 62
Lewicki, R. J. 154
Lewis, R. D. 151
Liberal Democratic Party 149
Little Boy 28
Littleton, C. 87
Loewenstein, G. F. 153
loyalty programs 5
Lucasfilm 70, 72
Lufthansa group 95–96; bargaining dispute with UFO 99; business model, pillars of 95; expansion, and network strategies 95–96; lean program for 96; low-budget airlines inclusion 95, 96; negotiations between Ver.di and 105; strategy of 95; UFO employee representative body 96–97
Lufthansa strike, and negotiations 92–93; Baublies dismissal 99, 103, 108; behavioral-based perspective 93; behavior during negotiations 102; during Christmas holidays 106; communication process, flaws in 112; concessions offered 101–102, 104, 106; derived power, negotiation tactic 107; EBIT, impact on 105, 109; emotional involvement 105, 107–108, 110, 114; Harvard negotiation concept, application of 93, 107–111; human needs understanding 112; interests, focus on 108–109, 112; issue of mixing interests, personal/substantial 111; lessons learned 115; Lufthansa and UFO, phases of 103–104; options generation, barriers for 109–110; parties, Lufthansa and UFO 93, 95; people problems 107–108; personal/ miscommunication issues in 107–108; Platzeck's role in negotiation 98–99, 108; "power-based negotiating" 101; premature judgment problem 109; pressure applying 110–111; steps, in inventing options *113*–114; styles of negotiation 102–104; tactics used, in negotiation 105–107; third parties, IGL/Ver.di to negotiations 97–98; threats tactics 106–107, 111; time games to leverage 105–106; timeline of events 99, *100*, 101; UFO's superior negotiation position in 101, 104; zero-sum game, situation as 110

Mackey, John 9–12, 14
Macron, E. 52
Manhattan project 28
Marvel 70, 72
Masadeh, M. 153
MasterClass (2019) 84
McLean, J. 151
Means-End-concept 152–153
Meyer, R. 20
Miller, D. 86
Moffett Nathanson 73
Mogherini, F. 33, 43
Monarch 95
Monsanto (U.S. American chemical corporation) 121; agent-orange creation 124, 125; Bayer's to buy 125–126; commercialized Aspartame 124; ethical stance of 124–125; in field of agriculture 124; PCBs invention 123, 125; pursuit of Syngenta 141; Queeny, J. F. founded 123; Roundup line product (herbicide/seeds) 124, 125; saccharin production 123; uranium research, with U.S. military 124, 125
Monsanto India Ltd. 137
Moskow 36
Murdoch, J. 77, 82, 87
Murdoch, L. 79
Murdoch, R. 73–75, 77, 79–80, 82, 86
mutually agreed rules 130

Nash, J. 146, 147
National Geographic 72, 76
natural products, demand for 5
NBCUniversal 71
negotiation management: case studies, from perspective of (*see* specific entries); constructs of, literature 2; cross-negotiation analysis 10, 55; defined as 7; education structure, lacking in regard of 1; emphasis on "integrativity" or "win-win" 2; importance for companies 21–24; improves, negotiation skills 1; model, in-depth analysis 77–87; negotiation controlling 8, 44–46, 64–65, 87; non-management related approaches to 1; process of, subtasks 8; real-world cases, lack of 2; students of 2; two factors, importance of 128–129
negotiation management theory 58
negotiations: aim, and issues of 134; analysis, and organization 8, 130; approaches to conduct 101; behavior of 8, 22, 37, 58, 87, 102, 105, 154; conducting 8, 61, 154; controlling 8, 44–46, 64–65; defined 3, 133; difficulties in, reasons for 147; example of 3; focus on interests 108–109; Harvard approach to 93, 107; local newspaper articles on 2; long-term (personal) relationship(s) impact on 111; merger and acquisition, complex 9; miscommunication issues 107; model variant of game theory, options of 134; objective criteria for 110–111; part of daily lives 1, 3, 87; people problems during 108; personal and emotional involvement, impact on 107; power-based 17–18; preparation 8; problems, regarding aspects of 107–111; relationship building and 2; rules that apply to 130; styles, types 102; two-sided affairs 8
negotiation tactics 87; defined as 105; of threat 106–107; time games as 105–106
Netanyahu, B. 45–46
Netflix 71, 72, 76
Nielsen TDLinx 4
Non-cooperative Game 134
Non-Proliferation Treaty (NPT) 29
North American Free Trade Agreement (NAFTA) 148
North Korea 35
nuclear bomb/weapon possession 28; China 33; France 32–33; Russia 32; United Kingdom 32; United States 32

Obama, B. 45
objective criteria-based agreement 110–111
Oikawa, N. 155
Okumura, T. 155
O'Leary, M. 94
one-sided rules 130
Organization for Economic Cooperation and Development (OECD) 148

package offer 85
pay negotiations, and disputes 50
Perrella, C. 142
Philippe, É. 62
Ping, H. 149, 156
Pixar 70, 72
Platzeck, M. 97, 98
power, defined 17
power-based negotiating approach 101
premature judgment 109
Primera 95
PrivatAir 95
Professional Air Traffic Controllers Organization (PATCO) 60
Progressive Grocer 4

Queeny, J. F. 123

Radcliffe, B. 147
Reagan, R. 60
reciprocity strategy 102, 153
relation-oriented approach 82, 84, 86, 154
Render, R. 140
Republic of China 33, 36–37
reservation price 83
Rouhani, H. 40, 41, 43, 46
Russia 32, 36–37
Rutherford, E. 27
RyanAir 94, 96, 98

saturation, in retailing 4
Sebenius, J. 86
self-service model 4
The Shape of Strikes in France, 1839–1960 (Tilly and Shorter's) 52
Shorter, E. 52
Sky 71–76, 79
Small Planet 95
SMART-formula 82
Smith, B. 58, 61
Spohr, C. 96, 98, 104
Stanojević, N. 153
Steinberg, L. 50
strikes, and demonstrations 50; in France 51–52

structure–conduct–behavior paradigm 4
supermarket industry, in U.S. 4
Swissair 53
Syngenta acquisition 137

Tanner, J. F. 155
Teheran 35
Texas Monthly 10
ThomasCook 95
Thompson, L. 81
Tilly, C. 52
Time Warner 74
traffic-related strikes 52
Trans-Pacific Partnership (TPP) negotiations 145–146; Abe's role in, negotiation behavior of 147, 149, 154–157; analysis of 146–149; analytical-prescriptive approach 146; China's, aggressive trading power 148–149, 152–153, 155–157; circumstances of 149; cooperation strategy use 154; cross-negotiation analysis 147–149; cultural differences, impact 150–151, 156; globalization, bridges cultures 150–151; history of 148; issue linkage, and foreign pressure 151; Japan as key player in 146–157; Japan's way of conducting 154–157; laid in 2011 145; negotiating partners, and economic difficulties 148; object of 147; organization of 149–151; preparation of, by Japan 151–154; psychographic factors 150; reciprocity strategy 153; relation-oriented approach for 154; starting point of, FTA 145; styles, factors influencing 154–155; tariffs lowering under 147–148, 153, 156; top learnings of 157–158; U.S. signature withdrawal 146
transportation sector strikes 56
Trat, J. 52
Treaty for Non-Proliferation of Nuclear Weapons 28
Trump, D. 45–46, 137
Tryhorn, C. 86
21st Century Fox [21CF] 70; *see also* Disney-21CF merger negotiations

UFO (Unabhängige Flugbegleiter Organisation) 96–97; 48-hour strike 101; beginning of 96; labor union status, Lufthansa court filing to withdraw 99; largest labor-union, in Germany 97, 101; role in Lufthansa strikes (*see* Lufthansa strike, and negotiations); Ver.di and IGL, competition with 97–98
United Kingdom 32
United Nations (UN) 148
United States of America 32; European Union and 36; nuclear bomb possession 32; stance on Iran's nuclear program 34–36
Universal Pictures 71
Uranium-235 28
Ury, W. 93, 108–110, 113
U.S. food industry 5
U.S negotiation style 134

value-based negotiating approach 101
Ver.di 97–99, 105
VLM 95
Voeth, M. 37, 55, 82, 84, 85, 93, 102, 105, 128, 147, 149, 152–154, 156
Volkens, B. 108

The Wall Street Journal 140, 142
Walmart 4
Walt Disney Company 70; *see also* Disney-21CF merger negotiations
Weise, Frank-Jürgen 108
Wenning, W. 141–142
Weskott, J. F. 122
Whole Foods Market, Inc. 5–7; Albertsons offer/interest in 11–12, 16; Amazon's acquisition of 9, 20–21; Amazon's offer 17, 22–23; BATNA, securing of 16; company culture 12; culture conflict with Amazon 20–21; exploring integrative potential with Amazon 12–14, 18, 20; JANA acquisition 10–11, 22; JANA partners demands 13; need for change 9–10; negotiation management of 23; official negotiations, timeline 9; post-sale 20–21; private equity firms, business offers from 11–12, 22; Wachtell Lipton hiring 10, 14, 15, 19–21
win–lose/win–win, negotiation style 102
World Cup in France, 1995 56
worst alternative to a negotiated agreement (WATNA) 60
Wowereit, K. 97, 98

Xarelto 142

YouTube 71

Zarif, M. J. 43